The Great U-Turn

THE GREAT U-TURN

*Corporate Restructuring and
the Polarizing of America*

BENNETT HARRISON
&
BARRY BLUESTONE

Basic Books, Inc., Publishers *New York*

Library of Congress Cataloging-in-Publication Data

Harrison, Bennett.
  The great u-turn.

  Includes index.
  1. United States—Economic conditions—1981–
  2. United States—Economic policy—1981–
  3. Corporate reorganizations—United States.
  4. Industrial relations—United States.   5. Income
  distribution—United States.   I. Bluestone, Barry.
  II. Title.
  HC106.8.H364   1988   338.973   88–47675
  ISBN   0–465–02719–9

CONTENTS

Contents

PREFACE

IN OUR FIRST BOOK TOGETHER, *The Deindustrialization of America*, our principal focus was on the loss of jobs, especially as it related to the closing down of plants or the relocation of industry out of the United States altogether. But even as we were completing that project in 1982, we were already aware that life in America was no longer so secure even for those who *did* retain their jobs.

More and more, wages were being cut, the pace of work speeded up, and full-time jobs replaced by part-time work schedules. It was already becoming apparent that the decline of manufacturing and the growth of services were shifting the economy's center of gravity in the direction of lower and more unequally distributed pay. Moreover, American companies were doing much more than simply closing factories or moving to Mexico. Merger mania was again in the air. The much talked about new wave of urban "revitalization" was refashioning the look of one big city's downtown after another, even as poor and working class neighborhoods situated within a stone's throw of the new office towers were already beginning to undergo the process known as "gentrification"—a polite term for forced dislocation.

Since the completion of *Deindustrialization*, it has taken us six years to write the story of what is happening in America to those who *do* have jobs. To explain *why* work and wages have changed so drastically—mostly, we think, for the worse—we have had to learn a lot of things about which we really did not know very much when we started. This new book embodies a good deal of theorizing about the changing organization of business, how government deregulation works (or does not work), and the various ways in which debt functions in a modern capitalist economy.

The central argument is straightforward. For U.S.–based corporations, a quarter-century of unparalleled postwar growth gave way, by the late 1960s, to unprecedented global competition. As a consequence, profits were severely squeezed. Companies might have responded by going "back to basics": improving product quality, investing in new technology, and fashioning more constructive relationships with their workers. Instead, they abandoned core businesses, invested offshore, shifted capital into overtly speculative ventures, subcontracted work to low-wage contractors here and abroad, demanded wage concessions from their employees, and substituted part-time and other forms of contingent labor for full-time workers—all in the name of "restructuring." Government supported these corporate strategies through deregulation, the engineered recessions of 1980 and 1981–82, cutbacks in social programs, and direct attacks on organized labor.

Profits rebounded indeed, but the costs to American society have been—and continue to be—enormous. These public and private policies have led to a great U-turn in the American standard of living. After improving steadily for a generation, average wages have fallen, family incomes have stagnated, and wages, incomes, and wealth have become increasingly polarized.

Conservatives hoped that such sacrifice would at least produce a new era of sustained economic growth. It has not happened. What growth we have experienced has been driven purely by a combination of unprecedented debt and military spending. Restoring the basis for stable long-run growth and rising incomes, more equally shared, is going to require a radical shift in policy and attitude away from the romance with laissez-faire of the last fifteen years.

ACKNOWLEDGMENTS

AS HAS ALWAYS BEEN our good fortune, literally dozens of friends, critics, and correspondents helped us along the way. The individual names would be far too numerous to mention (except that Ann Markusen and Richard Rothstein deserve special thanks for reading everything). But four categories of helpers really must be identified.

First, we are grateful to those who helped pay our research bills, during a period when this sort of iconoclastic investigation was generally out of fashion. In Washington, the U.S. Congressional Joint Economic Committee and the Economic Policy Institute were there when we needed them. In Geneva, the International Labour Office published some preliminary findings. Closer to home, Boston College's Social Welfare Research Institute provided computer time and the space necessary to spread out thousands of pages of printout that we waded through for months.

Second—and we are not being coy here—a number of mainstream and conservative economists, journalists, and public officials relentlessly challenged us to reexamine our methods and strengthen our arguments. They may not be entirely happy with what has emerged from the debates in which they engaged us, but there is no question in our minds that the book is far better—perhaps even more persuasive—because of those debates.

Then there are our students. They really lived through every step in the research and writing that led up to publication of *The Great U-Turn*. In classrooms, office meetings, coffee shops, and walks to the parking lot, they listened, questioned, laughed, and generally egged us on through what in retrospect has been the single longest project either of us has ever undertaken. To Chris Tilly and Lucy Gorham, especially, our deepest appreciation.

Male authors often thank their wives for "helping." In our case, Maryellen Kelley and Mary Ellen Colten have doctorates at least as prestigious as our own, and the "help," as often as not, came in the form of their saying, "What exactly do you mean here?" "You're wrong about that" or "Here's how you might make that point better." Fortunately for us and our readers, we usually took their advice.

The Great U-Turn

1

The Great U-Turn

THE STANDARD OF LIVING of American workers—and a grow-ing number of their families—is in serious trouble. For every affluent "yuppie" in an expensive big-city condominium, working as a white-collar professional for a high-flying high-technology concern or a mul-tibillion dollar insurance company, there are many more people whose wages have been falling and whose families are finding it more and more difficult to make ends meet.

For more than a decade, the United States has been evolving as an increasingly unequal society. This development has been hidden by the ability of consumers, government, and businesses to maintain their accustomed spending by accumulating more and more debt. Now, on the eve of the 1990s, the underlying weaknesses of the economy are finally becoming apparent, while the assurance of a new era of stable economic growth and vitality is being challenged by debt and global competition. The time has come for a serious reappraisal of just how poorly the economy has performed under the conservative business and government policies of the last decade, and how the prospects for average American workers and their families have actually worsened.

The story is one of a series of changes in direction—reversals in course, great U-turns if you will—in the strategic policies of both business and the government, and as a consequence, a great U-turn in our material well-being. Between the end of World War II and a watershed that dates to a time between the late 1960s and the mid-1970s, the standard of living of the average American worker rose steadily. Adjusted for inflation, average family incomes were on the rise. Hourly, weekly, and annual wages and salaries were trending upward. The share of the work force whose wages were at or below the poverty level fell sharply. The numbers earning high wages rose rapidly. More and more workers could count on such basic benefits as unemployment and health insurance, paid vacations, and sick leave. This was especially true in the goods-producing industries, but even in the burgeoning service sector, the trend was toward a higher standard of living.

Perhaps no one has captured the spirit of that age better than David Halberstam in his epic work, *The Reckoning*. The symbol for the Ford Motor Company and for the nation during those days was the sporty Mustang.

> It came out in 1964, at what would prove to be the highwater mark of the American century, when the country was rich, the dollar strong, and inflation low. It was almost twenty years since the end of World War II, and it was more than a decade since the end of the Korean War. The Vietnam War was still a guerrilla action involving relatively small numbers of American advisers. The bitter and costly part of that war, which was to take more than fifty-one thousand lives, divide the country, start a runaway inflation, and completely divert the nation's attention, was still ahead. The economy was expanding. Though many of the forces that would afflict American industry were already beginning to form, they were not yet visible, and the domestic economy had never seemed so strong. . . . There was enough for everyone; the country was enjoying unparalleled prosperity, and the pie was bigger than ever. The pie would turn out to have its limits after all, but at the halcyon moment, the future seemed unbounded.[1]

Not only was the pie growing, but especially during the 1960s, the shares were becoming more equally distributed among working people and their families. At the same time, greater income equality itself contributed to the more rapid economic growth out of which public expenditures (and even further redistribution, for example, through the War on Poverty) could be financed. Most important of all, more and more parents could realistically expect that their children would eventually be better off financially and less insecure than they had been.

That belief in the future in turn brought about a greater commitment to work, saving, and investment in the present.*

After about 1973, the direction changed. Wages, adjusted for inflation, began a long downward trend (fig. 1.1). Median annual family income stopped growing, even though more family members were working than ever before (fig. 1.2).[2] And, by the latter half of the decade, even the most stable "core" workers in the economy—the roughly three-fifths of the labor force working year round and full time (YRFT)—were becoming more and more likely to earn low wages. In particular, between 1973 and 1979 one out of every five net additional YRFT workers earned less than $11,000 a year (in 1986 prices). But since 1979, fully 36 percent of such employees have earned wages and salaries below that threshold. After 1980, at the other extreme of the job distribution, the number of elite earning high wages rose as well, leaving a declining proportion of employees receiving middle-level incomes. Inequality was again rising, in the labor market and at the level of family income (fig. 1.3). The distribution of wealth—income from property, such as stocks, bonds, and real estate—was also becoming increasingly unequal. Worst of all, no longer could parents assume that their children would do better than they had at the same stage of their own careers.[3]

What caused this dramatic reversal in the fortunes and expectations of American workers and their families—this great U-turn in the structure of economic opportunity in the United States?

The explanation lies not in bad luck or in something out of our control. It cannot be blamed on the Japanese or the Europeans, or on unions, or on the "social welfare state." The real explanation, we believe, lies in a more fundamental set of dramatic shifts in direction, taken first by the leaders of American business in the early 1970s and then ratified by policies of the government, beginning in the latter half

*We know all too well that these gains were never equally shared. Men of color and women of all races were systematically crowded into the least attractive jobs. They faced the greatest difficulties in obtaining government services to which they were entitled by law. And, too often, they were excluded altogether from the "social contract" between business and labor that implicitly governed a growing proportion of American workplaces in the prosperous years after World War II. Nevertheless, the promise was there, the basic economic possibilities for more widespread participation were present, and in fact, as we shall demonstrate, the economic conditions of the "minorities" improved greatly during the last years of the great postwar expansion, and continued to do so through most of the 1970s.

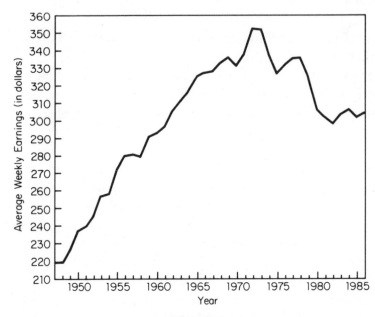

FIGURE 1.1

Real Average Weekly Earnings, 1947–86
(in 1986 dollars)

SOURCE Council of Economic Advisers, *Economic Report of the President, 1987* (Washington, D.C.: Government Printing Office, 1987).

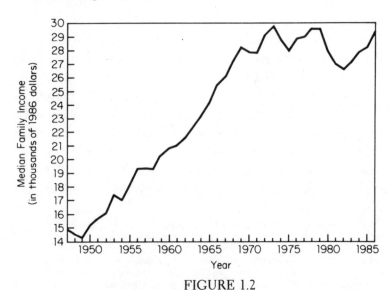

FIGURE 1.2

Real Median Family Income, 1947–86
(in 1986 dollars)

SOURCE Council of Economic Advisers, *Economic Report of the President, 1987* (Washington, D.C.: Government Printing Office, 1987).

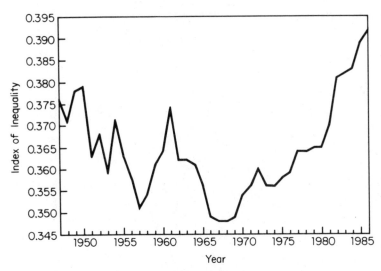

FIGURE 1.3

Family Income Inequality, 1947–86
(GINI index)

Source U.S. Department of Commerce, Bureau of the Census, "Money Income of Households, Families, and Persons in the United States: 1984 (Washington, D.C.: Government Printing Office, 1986) and unpublished tabulations provided by the U.S. Census Bureau.

of that decade, even before the election of Ronald Reagan. What ultimately motivated these shifts, which add up to an across-the-board U-turn in managerial, economic, and social policy, was what happened to corporate profits—private enterprise's bottom line. While wages and family incomes continued to grow for another eight years after the midpoint of the decade of the '60s, corporate profits did not.

The Profit Squeeze

Whether measured as business owners' share of the total national income or by the conventional rate of return on investment, profits peaked in the mid-1960s and continued to fall or stagnate for the next fifteen years. From a peak of nearly 10 percent in 1965, the average net after tax profit rate of domestic nonfinancial corporations plunged to less than 6 percent during the second half of the 1970s—a decline of more than a third (fig. 1.4).

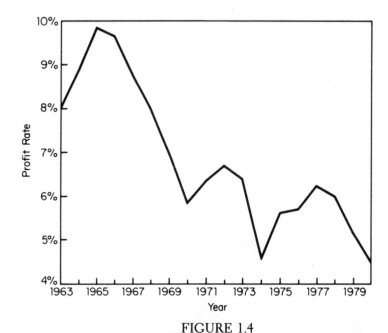

FIGURE 1.4

U.S. Corporate Profitability, 1963–80 Net After-Tax Rate of Return

SOURCE Samuel Bowles, David Gordon, and Thomas Weisskopf, "Power and Profits: The Social Structure of Accumulation and the Profitability of the Postwar U.S. Economy," *Review of Radical Political Economics* 18, nos. 1, 2, (Spring–Summer 1986), as revised and reported to the authors by Weisskopf in December 1987 to reflect new government capital stock series.[4]

What caused the profit squeeze was mainly the sudden emergence of heightened international economic competition—a competition to which U.S. business leaders were initially blind. At the beginning, one could perhaps forgive the corporations their myopia. For the longest time, foreign competition was hardly a concern. Indeed, even as late as 1969, imports were no greater a share of gross national product (GNP) than before the Great Depression in 1929. Forty years had passed and U.S. industry was no more burdened by imports than before jet transports crisscrossed the globe or geosynchronous orbiting satellites provided instantaneous worldwide communications.

But in the course of the single decade between 1969 and 1979, the value of imports practically doubled. In the manufacturing sector, a trickle of imports turned into a torrent. The value of manufactured imports relative to domestic production skyrocketed—from less than 14 percent in 1969 to nearly triple that, 38 percent, only ten years later. By 1986, for every $100 spent on goods produced in the United States,

TABLE 1.1

The Import Surge into the United States

	Total Imports as a Percentage of GNP	Imported Merchandise as a Percentage of GNP Originating in the U.S. Manufacturing Sector
1929	5.7	—
1939	3.7	—
1949	3.8	9.5
1959	4.7	10.8
1969	5.7	13.9
1979	10.9	37.8
1986	11.4	44.7

SOURCES: Council of Economic Advisers, *Economic Report of the President, 1986* (Washington, D.C.: Government Printing Office, 1986); Council of Economic Advisers, "Economic Indicators" (September 1986); and U.S. Department of Commerce, Bureau of Economic Analysis, *Survey of Current Business* 67, no. 4 (April 1987).

families and businesses were buying $45 worth of imports (table 1.1). In one industry after another—shoes, textiles, apparel, autos, steel, machine tools, consumer electronics, and eventually even computers and semiconductors—imports from Germany, Japan, Scandinavia, Italy, and the newly industrialized countries (the so-called NICs) such as South Korea, Taiwan, and Brazil made major inroads into the domestic markets of U.S. corporations.[5]

For the first time in modern economic history, all of the major industrialized countries (as well as the NICs) were producing very much the same collection of products and were engaged in "intra-industry trade"—the trading back and forth of essentially the same products. The United States now both buys steel from *and* sells it to the United Kingdom, while Mexico both imports and exports auto parts. Along with the two-way movement of commodities came two-way investment in factories and equipment, and the composition of both inward and outward foreign direct investments became increasingly similar.[6] The United States once built auto plants in Germany, France, England, and Mexico; now the Koreans and Japanese build them here. This complementarity led to the emergence on a global scale of chronic excess capacity in one mass-production industry after another.[7] With every country attempting to supply its neighbors with computers, let alone shoes, each country found its corporations operating their own plants at well below full capacity.* This necessarily eroded productivity and raised the unit cost of production. Nowhere was this more true than in the United States. And to make matters worse, while foreign competition raised unit costs, it simultaneously made it more difficult for firms in any one country to pass these higher costs onto their own citizens in the form of inflated prices. As a result, profits were squeezed—on the one side by rising costs; on the other by constrained prices.

Charles Sabel, a political scientist at M.I.T., summarizes the U-Turn in international economic development this way:

> A fundamental cause of the slowdown of the 1970s was the saturation of domestic markets for consumer durables and hence exhaustion of new investment opportunities in the business lines that had been the mainstay of the post-war expansion. In the United States, for example, there was one car for every two residents in 1979, as against a ratio of one to four in the early 1950s. By 1970, 99 percent of American homes had refrigerators, electric irons, and radios; more than 90 percent had automatic clothes washers, vacuum cleaners, and toasters. Statistics from other advanced capitalist countries tell a similar story.
>
> Saturation in one market led to saturation in others as producers looked abroad when the possibilities for domestic expansion were exhausted. The results were simultaneous export drives by companies in all the advanced countries, with similar, technologically sophisticated products going into one another's markets. . . . Increasing exports . . . from developing countries such as Taiwan, Korea, Mexico, and Brazil further increased the congestion of mass markets in the advanced economies.[8]

In the short run, the squeezing of profit margins may have been exacerbated by continued popular demands for a higher and more widely shared standard of living, especially through an expansion of the welfare state.[9] Larger tax contributions from businesses and expanded wage-and-benefit packages for hitherto excluded groups added to the cost of doing business and reduced short-term profits still further. In

---

*This does not mean, of course, that there is literally too much productive capacity in the world. Obviously even more capacity is needed in a world where so many still go ill, hungry, and homeless. The point is that, given the uses to which profit-seeking private business is prepared to direct its investments, by the 1970s there were more suppliers of those "profitable" goods and services than there were paying customers.

America, these demands reached a crescendo during the late 1960s when, under the twin engines of accelerating consumer spending and burgeoning expenditures for the war in Vietnam, unemployment rates fell to levels not seen since 1945. With the supply of labor that tight, wages had to be bid up, and the bargaining power of labor as a whole improved. Broader unemployment insurance, as well as larger payments, also appreciably reduced what Harvard economist Juliet Schor has named "the cost of job loss," further contributing to the willingness of workers to stand up to their bosses.[10] All of these developments contributed to the reduction of corporate profits.[11]

As always, when the distribution of income between capital and labor arouses political and economic conflict, and both sides try to protect their share of national income, the result is growing inflation. Together with other unexpected market shocks, such as increases in the price of oil by OPEC and increases in wage, tax, and governmental regulatory pressures, the inflation of the 1970s made the squeeze on profits intolerable. Corporate managers ultimately felt impelled to develop new long-run plans.[12] Stockholders would tolerate a dip in profits for a year or two perhaps, but the red ink that began to spill from corporate balance sheets in the late 1960s screamed out for remedy.

The Response of Business to the Crisis

And what were the new strategies? How did American business respond to these new competitive pressures? At least a few industry leaders undertook a variety of experiments in the organization of work and in labor-management relations, designed to increase productivity and thus allow their firms to cope with higher costs.[13] Others, facing greater increases in costs and greater uncertainties in their markets, searched for more "flexible" arrangements with employees, subcontractors, customers, and governments. Some scholars believe that these corporate experiments will eventually culminate in the emergence of entirely new forms of business enterprise. In this scenario, "flexibly specialized," small-scale enterprises will continually prowl the marketplace for new niches. Already, entrepreneurs pursuing this strategy are said to be clustering together into tightly knit regional complexes or "industrial districts." Ironically, using state-of-the-art, microelectronics-based technologies, they are actually reintegrating work in a way that invokes images of the most old-fashioned, traditional, craftlike forms of production.[14]

There is no doubt that such creative experiments in the reorganization of work are occurring in some companies and in some locations. Evidence of the vitality of at least a small number of industrial districts organized according to the flexible specialization model seems compelling.[15] But the much more prevalent response to the crisis in profitability, particularly in the United States, has been to change little in the nature of the product or even the production process, and instead to launch what former United Auto Workers President Douglas Fraser has termed a "one-sided class war." In the words of a recent pamphlet printed jointly by the Service Employees International Union and 9 to 5, the organization of office workers:

> With the widespread image of a more "hostile" environment, U.S.–based corporations were confronted by two very different choices: (1) Improve product quality and productivity by investment and innovation while looking to public policy to "manage" trade; or (2) turn back the clock on U.S. job standards to attempt to make U.S. products "cheaper" rather than better. In the 1970s and 1980s, U.S. corporate and government leaders chose the second route—to lower job standards in order "to compete."[16]

Specifically, the vast majority of American businesses have undertaken a series of experiments in what can best be described as *corporate restructuring.*

In this book, we tell the story of this restructuring in terms of three broad movements: qualitative changes amounting almost to a 180-degree U-Turn in the prevailing relationship between business and its workforce; financial restructuring, both within and among companies; and a profound alteration in the posture of the federal government, which moved to support the short-term interests of private business in direct opposition to the needs of working people and their families.

Consider the restructuring of the organization of work and of the deployment of finances. Managers have increasingly reallocated the capital at their disposal, directing it into different industries, different regions of the country, and different nations. In doing so, corporate leaders have introduced new technologies—especially in transportation and communications—to facilitate the coordination and control of the far-flung activities of their home offices.[17] At the same time, corporations began a dramatic restructuring of their internal hierarchies. They moved toward "vertical disintegration" of their large, highly centralized industrial organizations, with their characteristic "internal labor markets." In doing so, they removed many of the career ladders that had provided well-defined paths of upward mobility for a significant fraction of the work force.

While such changes in work organization may provide "flexibility" for management, they tend to bring with them increased instability and insecurity for employees. In the course of this restructuring, managers have pared employment and increased their use of "contingent" labor, leasing more of their employees from agencies that supply temporary employees and putting more of their own workers on part-time schedules—increasingly, against their wishes. Much more blatantly, more and more managers have simply "frozen" wages, imposed outright reductions in pay, or unilaterally introduced two tiered pay systems to reduce the cost of labor by paying different wages for essentially the same work. With the threat of layoffs and plant closings all around them, labor unions found it difficult, if not impossible, to contest these actions. Lee Iacocco's famous remark during the Chrysler crisis—"It's freeze time, boys. I've got plenty of jobs at seventeen dollars an hour; I don't have any at twenty"—haunted labor in virtually every industry.[18]

In the financial sphere, investors—especially those responsible for managing pension funds and other large pools of finance capital—accelerated the shift from productive investment to investment, often overtly speculative, primarily for short-term financial gain, while freewheeling and well-heeled "entrepreneurs" pursued "hostile takeovers" and "forced mergers." In the colorful language of British political economist Susan Strange, language later popularized by *Business Week*, America became a "casino society."[19] One indicator of this trend—the volume of futures trading in stocks and bonds—rose ninefold between 1973 and 1985 in contrast to only a threefold increase in the nation's total output.[20]

Government to the Rescue

For a short period between the mid-1970s and the early 1980s, there was intense debate about whether the government should play a more constructive role in mediating the relationship between business and labor. Various corporate, labor, and academic circles called for the federal government to adopt a domestic industrial policy and intervene more actively in foreign trade. Guaranteed federal loans that saved both Lockheed and Chrysler from bankruptcy were the two best-known instances of an industrial policy in actual practice.

But beginning in 1978, and increasingly after the election of President Ronald Reagan, the administration and the Congress intervened in a very different way. Washington began to adopt policies that effectively forced workers to accept wage concessions, discredited the trade-union movement, and reduced the cost to business of complying with government regulations. Social programs were either restricted to their present levels or, like publicly assisted housing, actually cut back. A restrictive monetary regime introduced in 1979 by Paul Volcker, chair of the Federal Reserve Board, was indeed successful in curtailing inflation, but only by creating the worst recession since the 1930s. With more than one out of ten Americans unemployed by 1982, the government supported management's demand for a docile work force that would swallow wage concessions without a major fight.

The deep recessions of 1980 and 1981–82 were, by their nature, two-edged swords for the corporate sector. The drastic drop in consumer demand obviously cut into short-term profits. But at the same time, the recessions established the foundation for greater long-term returns by undercutting organized labor and by forcing workers to choose between a modicum of job security and higher wages. In the end, the recessions contributed handsomely to the corporations' bottom line.

The federal government's curtailment of its regulation of business also promoted corporate restructuring. Responding to deregulation, leaders in the airlines, trucking, and telecommunications industries were forced to devise strategies for responding to more intense competition. Virtually all of them turned to their work forces to bail them out. Management demanded wholesale wage concessions from their employees and increased pressure on the job to squeeze out more productivity from them. In some industries, especially the airlines, the quality of the deregulated service seems to have deteriorated, often dangerously, in the face of heightened competition.[21] At the same time, government entered into more contracts with ununionized outside companies—so-called "privatization"—eroding civil-service wage standards. The growing inclination of the government to sell off what had previously been publicly owned and operated services (Conrail, for example) had the same effect.

For the first time since the 1920s, direct attacks on labor emanated from the White House. The assault began with the disbanding of the air traffic controllers' union and the appointment of conservative members to the National Labor Relations Board (NLRB). These highly publicized acts of the president contributed to shifting the balance of power between labor and management toward business, implicitly legitimating "union avoidance" as a socially acceptable posture for even the most "liberal" of managements.[22] Unions were deliberately made the scapegoat of an economy that increasingly seemed unable to perform acceptably at home or abroad.

Lurking not far below the surface of all of these particular policies was the growing dominance of a conservative ideology that pinned the blame for the profit squeeze on "big government" itself. It followed that the most appropriate public policy for the 1980s was, to quote Reagan's campaign rhetoric, to "get the government off the backs of the people." Translated into budgetary terms, this meant cuts in social legislation, but not in the size or influence of government per se. In fact, after eight years of "Reaganomics," the public sector's influence on the economy on the eve of the 1990s is greater than ever, as evidenced by the explosive growth of military spending and the stubbornly mushrooming budget deficit. The federal government takes a larger share of the gross national product (GNP) today than when Reagan took office in 1981. Nevertheless, even middle-of-the-road Democrats and Republicans have accepted the new conventional wisdom that government spending, regulation, and redistribution of income are somehow "bad for business."[23] What could not be sold at any price to the voters by presidential candidate Barry Goldwater in the go-go days of 1964 became the coin of the realm a mere twenty years later.

These public policies of government-induced deflation, deregulation, regressive tax reform, privatization, and out-right union-bashing have contributed directly to corporate strategies that single-mindedly concentrate on cost containment, especially the cost of labor, as the principal basis for meeting the global economic challenge. They have created a new civil war among firms and among regions of the country competing for job-creating investments, and they have pitted worker against worker. This, we believe, is what is mainly responsible for reducing both the standard of living and the economic security of the average family. It is the main reason for the great U-turn in the distribution of income since the 1970s—what Lester Thurow has aptly called the "surge in inequality"[24]—and what we see as the growing polarization of our society.

The Failed Promise of the New Economic Era

There are those who argue that the wage cuts and inequality that we have experienced have been absolutely necessary for U.S. industry to regain its competitive edge. "No pain, no gain," they say. After all, profits rebounded smartly after the recession of 1982. Moreover, sheer job-creation between the mid-1970s and the late 1980s was substantial enough to earn the United States the sobriquet of "the great jobs machine," especially among European planners and policy makers who seemed totally incapable of stimulating any new growth in employment whatsoever during these years. But as we now know, these gains benefited a few at the expense of a great many. And in the end, it is unclear whether the high price we paid bought us much of lasting value.

To be sure, some social scientists think they see a brave new postindustrial world already emerging from the wreckage of the old. Perhaps they will turn out to be right.[25] But on the eve of the final decade of the twentieth century, after the longest "peacetime" economic recovery on record, a new round of stable economic growth has demonstrably *not* yet emerged. The rate of personal savings has actually fallen to less than before Reagan's election. The production of non-military capital goods—business plant and equipment—has been lethargic since the end of 1984. The long-run growth in productivity remains just under 1 percent, where it has been since the late 1960s.[26] And the overall ability of the economy to produce goods and services—the GNP—continues to grow at a pace far slower than in the two decades following World War II, and generally less than in the countries with which we are engaged in the most intense economic competition.

Worse still, what growth we *have* been able to muster—at the cost of declining average living standards and growing inequality—has been achieved almost entirely by two manifestly undesirable means. One is a boom in military spending which has aggravated the federal deficit and distorted the long-term development of civilian research and development. The other is the piling up of incredible levels of debt. In the face of falling incomes, consumers have attempted to maintain their living standards by borrowing unprecedented amounts of revolving credit. In 1986, the average family was carrying more than $11,000 worth of outstanding consumer credit, and was spending a fifth of its monthly disposable income to pay it off.[27] At the same time, the federal government had amassed more than $1.5 trillion of new debt. In the short span of four years, the United States had transformed itself from the world's leading creditor to the nation most in hock to the rest of the world. The consolidated burden of the debts of households, government, and Third World countries could bring the entire world trading system down in a crisis unprecedented since the Great Depression of the 1930s.

Reversing the Great U-Turn

Given the increasingly competitive—and, as we shall see, fragile—international environment, and in light of such domestic constraints as the daunting federal debt, is there room for a progressive restructuring of the economy, aimed toward achieving stable economic growth, more equitably shared? We believe there is.

Essentially, the nation must move forward in at least seven areas: (1) industrial (and related educational) policy; (2) democracy in the workplace; (3) renewed public support for the right of unorganized workers to be represented by unions of their choosing; (4) managed international trade; (5) the reconstruction of the nation's physical infrastructure; (6) reregulation of specific private market activities, especially in the runaway financial sector; and (7) public fulfillment of the promise of universal social benefits, including health insurance, child care, and care of the aging. It is at least possible to imagine political and economic conditions under which a combination of programs in these areas might reverse the calamitous U-turn that America has taken since the 1970s.

The specific elements needed for a more equitable industrial policy are by this time well known, having been much debated over the past decade. More research and development, more attention to technical and lifelong (recurrent) education, and greater involvement of the community or government in productive enterprises must certainly be on the list. All three might be expected to increase average incomes and narrow the disparities among workers and their families. What needs to be stressed is the need for *balance* in the planning of these activities. If we are going to produce a more educated work force, then we had better be sure that jobs are being created (or upgraded) so as to fully utilize and reward the skill and ability of that work force. One policy without the other simply will not do. We need both re-planned education *and* better-planned job creation.

Analogously, we are unlikely to bring about a maximum contribution to national economic growth, or correct the tendency toward the increasing inequality of income, if government subsidizes or otherwise promotes research and development in the private sector without simultaneously enforcing a quid pro quo by stipulating *where* the actual manufacture of the new products is located. Market and geopolitical forces are driving multinational corporations to forge more and more partnerships with foreign firms, partnerships designed to divide up markets, share technology, and rationalize use of the labor forces of different countries. These arrangements would be impossible without a host of licenses, subsidies, and exercises of military power by governments. If we are to regain popular control over the development of the domestic economy, we must employ the still considerable influence of the American government to at least constrain these corporate transactions to fit the social objectives of equitable domestic growth.

It is by now abundantly clear that the casino society must be tamed.

The long-run goal should be the rechanneling of capital into productive investment. We must find ways to separate the useful purposes of such mechanisms as futures markets from their purely speculative aspects. Even the editors of *Business Week* now recognize that major reform is required:

> Stiffer capital requirements for dealers and stricter margin rules for their customers would put more real money under all those mountains of IOUs . . . the system's bias toward debt [should be] corrected by limiting the tax deductibility of interest. And instead of being so quick to defer to the invisible hand, Washington now must apply itself to the long-neglected task of creating a tough, comprehensive system for regulating all the markets.[28]

One turn in the right direction would be a revival of the pursuit of universal social security, broadly defined. The shift of both business and government toward no-holds-barred laissez-faire has torn dangerous and morally unacceptable holes in the social safety net. We need national health insurance, universal portable pensions, a higher minimum wage, laws mandating hourly pay for part-time workers equal to that of full-time employees doing comparable work, more child care, and more adequate welfare payments for those who cannot work. Why? For one thing, because so many of the countries with whose companies ours are now in competition already have such public—and universal—support systems. In contrast, companies in this country are forced to build these "benefits" into their wage and salary scales, making the cost of labor less competitive. By socializing more of these costs, we not only gain the advantages inherent in any kind of insurance—pooling of risks, economies of scale, and the like—but we also make our companies more competitive in world trade. And secondly, if more and more work *is* going to become part-time, temporary, or subcontracted, then we need a set of institutional arrangements that puts a floor under individual and family incomes, in order to sustain the growth of consumer spending without which economic expansion is impossible in a mature capitalist economy.

To deal with the trade deficit in the short run, and the promotion of U.S. exports in the long run, we must fashion a combination of strategies. Again, balance is needed; narrowly focussed approaches will fall short. Clearly the United States needs to take the lead in the creation of a new international regime of managed exchange rates. But we must also use our influence—and controlled access to our domestic markets—to help increase wages (and thereby spending) in the countries that buy goods and services from us, especially in the Third World. Such a policy might well include forgiveness of existing Third World debt and restrictions on imports from countries that employ the powers of a police state to suppress labor organizations.

If global reflation is ever to happen at all, it is going to require these sorts of accommodations. Essentially, the United States must turn back toward greater planning and away from the treacherous path of laissez-faire. Do we believe this will occur? Absolutely. The world of laissez-faire is too unstable and its presumed benefits too inequitable. Sooner or later, the pendulum will swing back toward a better balance between unfettered free enterprise and democratic planning. Otherwise, there is no chance at all of reversing the great U-turn that has undermined both our standard of living and our progress toward a more just society.

2

"Zapping Labor"

"BUSINESS IS WAR," blared the full-color, three-page advertisement for the communications giant, GTE, as it introduced a new satellite communications system to its corporate customers in mid-1987.[1] Hearkening back to the messenger Phidippedes, who raced from Marathon to Athens in 490 B.C. with news of the Greek victory over Persia, GTE reminded its audience of the critical importance of fast, accurate communications from the front lines to headquarters in "the battlefields of Intercorporate War." In ominous tones, GTE warned:

> If, by 3 PM, you do not know how many beefburgers, round-trip tickets, designer turtlenecks, or 3-year CDs you sold nationwide this morning, you cannot truly know if you are beating the Persians. Or if the Persians are beating you.

Such advertising hype may seem ludicrous to those who do not spend the better part of their lives in the corporate boardroom "commanding a thousand battle stations," but there is no denying the fact that during the 1970s open corporate warfare broke out in America. The complacency of the 1960s, built during two decades of unparalleled economic prosperity, was shattered by the sudden awakening to international competition and sharply falling profit rates. Tried-and-true methods of production and pricing, and of customer and labor relations, no longer functioned to maintain market share or traditional rates of return on capital. Corporate managers were forced to don their combat garb and develop new economic weaponry. They are still at it.

The process by which business leaders have been attempting to boost their profits has not been smooth or without major setbacks. It often appears to be anarchic rather than planned. It involves a great deal of experiment and trial and error. No single approach has proven fail-safe. Nevertheless, by the mid-1980s, the strategies that had been adopted were already helping to rebuild corporate profits.

Unfortunately, as we shall see, the war has resulted in many casualties. It has changed the economic landscape of America and it has shaken the very foundations of the economic security of millions of families. What has emerged may be a "post-industrial society." But if so, it appears to be a terrain much bleaker than that first described by Daniel Bell more than a decade ago.[2] It is a society in which firms have been merged and acquired, downsized, deindustrialized, multinationalized, automated, streamlined, and restructured. In the process, the rich have gotten richer, the poor poorer, and life for the middle class more and more precarious.

Strategic Planning in the Corporate World

Between the end of World War II and the invasion of foreign business in the 1970s, U.S. managers generally kept their stockholders content by concentrating on boosting their companies' sales and revenues. In one industry after another, profits could be raised simply by raising prices. Every year, for example, General Motors would raise the price of its new models and Ford, Chrysler, and now-defunct American Motors would follow suit. Consumers would pay the new, higher prices, for there was little choice. When the cost of labor rose or the price of raw material inched up, managers simply raised their prices to maintain their profits. Economists term this practice "mark-up pricing." It was a neat system and it worked reasonably well as long as increased productivity helped firms to keep their total costs down and as long as consumers had little choice but to "buy American" at whatever prices the managers chose to charge. In the words of Lester Thurow, America enjoyed "effortless economic superiority" during this extraordinary period of relative economic isolation.[3]

Unfortunately, once competitive imports appeared, the old pricing strategy no longer worked. As the availability and quality of European and Japanese goods rose, U.S. managers found that they no longer had the luxury of boosting their revenues by the simple expedient of altering their price tags. Increased prices drove consumers into the waiting arms of foreign competitors. The loss in market share more than offset the increased price per unit. Revenue fell and, along with it, profits. As a consequence, by the early 1970s, frustrated corporate leaders began to shift their attention to cutting costs rather than raising prices.[4]

In certain industries there was a concerted attempt to reduce the cost of raw materials. Auto producers downsized their cars and began to substitute cheaper plastics for expensive steel. This strategy increased the efficiency with which the American car used fuel by reducing its total weight, but world events ultimately undermined the value of this plan as a cost-cutting measure. Beginning after the Egyptian-Israeli war in 1973, OPEC negated the advantage of this tactic by driving up the price of petroleum, the basic ingredient of virtually all of the new synthetic materials. Plastic products doubled in price between 1973 and 1980, along with rubber, chemicals, and allied products.[5] The U.S. automakers' gambit was defeated by decisions made in Saudi Arabia, Iran, and Abu Dhabi.[6]

Still another way to reduce costs was to use less or cheaper capital. But this introduced a dilemma. By cutting back on new capital investment, corporate managers could certainly increase profits in the short run. But this was inherently an end-game strategy. By not replacing aging plant and equipment and failing to install capital equipment that embodied new technology, managers would almost surely doom their firms to extinction. This was especially true because foreign competitors were adopting the latest technology in one industry after another.

Lowering the price of capital by paying lower rates of interest for investment capital would have helped in this regard. Yet this strategy also disappeared after 1965 as the prime rate of interest charged by banks began to climb steeply. The prime rate had stood firmly at 4.5

percent during the first half of the decade. However, as the Federal Reserve Board began to boost the discount rate—the interest rate the FED charges its member banks—the prime rate shot up. By the end of the decade, the prime rate was close to 8 percent, and it rose to nearly 11 percent by 1974.[7] The cost of capital was accelerating and the corporate executive could do little about it. By early 1981, even the most favored corporate customer was being charged interest rates in excess of 18 percent.

This left a limited set of feasible strategies for American managers. They could, of course, go back to traditional methods. Offering the consumer new or improved products was the "old-fashioned" way for firms to make a profit. Innovation, both in products and processes, was the key. Yet here, by all accounts, American companies in the 1970s failed miserably. The captains of industry could not figure out how to produce fresh products, improve the quality of old ones, or even market the ones they had. In such key industries as automobiles, they were all but oblivious to changing consumer tastes. That the typical, newly minted chief executive officers (CEO) in the mid-1970s were financial wizards or lawyers rather than production specialists is now widely believed to have contributed to their ineptness in the marketplace.

No one has expressed this better than Robert Hayes and William Abernathy, in what has become one of the most important contributions ever to appear in the *Harvard Business Review*.[8] In "Managing Our Way to Economic Decline," the two business school professors argued that a modern management orthodoxy had taken hold in the United States, one which made maximum short-term financial return the most important criterion of corporate performance. Instead of making new investments in innovative products and processes which could assure them a secure share of their market in the future, modern American managers—in contrast to their European and Asian colleagues—were being trained to expand their companies through mergers and acquisitions, and by imitation rather than by invention.[9] Drawing on years of careful observation, the two scholars wrote:

> Our experience suggests that, to an unprecedented degree, success in most industries today requires an organizational commitment to compete in the marketplace on technological grounds—that is, to compete over the long run by offering superior products. Yet guided by what they took to be the

newest and best principles of management, American managers have increasingly directed their attention elsewhere. These new principles, despite their sophistication and widespread usefulness, encourage a preference for (1) analytic detachment rather than the insight that comes from "hands on" experience and (2) short-term cost reduction rather than long-term development of technological competitiveness. *It is this new managerial gospel, we feel, that has played a major role in undermining the vigor of American industry.* [10] [emphasis added.]

As a result, in one industry after another, U.S. companies lost out to foreign producers. The Japanese bested U.S. auto producers by introducing small, fuel-efficient cars and took over the lead in consumer electronics, completely freezing out U.S. manufacturers of video tape recorders and overcoming their lead in the manufacture of semiconductors. They took major shares of the sales of farm implements, steel, and even in peripheral accessories for computers. The Swedes and the Germans entered the high-technology machine-tool industry and literally captured the computerized numerical control machine-tool market. The Italians, perennial leaders in high-style clothing and footwear, learned new techniques of production, sales, and distribution and succeeded in making brand names like Benetton world famous.

Unable to raise prices at will, having lost control over the cost of resources and capital, and unskilled at designing or producing quality goods, American corporations were left with a limited number of ways to regain their lost profits. They could get out of the producing end of business altogether and find alternative ways of making a paper profit. They could, in the words of Arnold Weber, assistant secretary of labor under President Nixon, "zap labor." [11] Or they could make a new bid to control government so as to reduce their taxes and the cost of meeting government regulations. In the end, under the banner of "restructuring," they did all three. They abandoned major parts of their basic operations in traditional businesses in favor of what Robert Reich has named "paper entrepreneurialism." [12] They found ways to cut the cost of labor drastically. And they cajoled government—both Democratic and Republican administrations—into coming to their rescue. Along the way, some of America's most fundamental values and institutions were challenged and transformed, notably the nation's long-standing commitment to a rising and more equally shared standard of living.

The Globalization Gambit

The strategy that became the most intriguing to U.S. managers involved "going global." Following the old maxim "If you can't beat 'em, join 'em," thousands of U.S. firms set up operations abroad, substituted foreign-made components for ones that they had originally made for themselves at home, cultivated agreements whereby they would share trade secrets and new technology with foreign firms in order to gain access to foreign markets, or simply turned themselves from producers into importers of foreign companies' products. No matter how or why they pursued this behavior, however, at least one result is common to them all. Firms benefit from substituting cheaper foreign labor for U.S. workers and cheaper foreign parts for those with a U.S. label.*

One of the key tactics in the new globalization strategy is not new at all. For most of this century, the largest U.S. firms had been pursuing direct investments in foreign countries—setting up operations abroad primarily to serve the foreign market. As early as 1911, Henry Ford had placed assembly lines in Europe, while Singer Sewing Machine had, by the turn of the century, captured the British market through its wholly owned foreign subsidiary.[13] Still, the great boom in direct foreign investment in foreign countries occurred only after 1970, as table 2.1 demonstrates.

In 1965, total direct U.S. investment abroad—investment in factories, office buildings, machine tools, and office equipment—was less than $50 billion. It took only ten years to reach $124 billion. And in just the next five, it surpassed $213 billion. The profits that came back to U.S. corporations from their subsidiaries grew even faster, from $5.2 billion in 1965 to more than $424 billion in 1980, clearly justifying these investments on the basis of standard accounting principles.

---

*To be sure, there are discernible tendencies in the contemporary world economy that operate in the direction of greater geographic *recentralization,* or "reconcentration in the core." Examples include the threat of domestic protectionist legislation, the development of technology that reduces the share of labor in total production, cost, and such organizational innovations as Japanese-style "just-in-time" inventory management, which puts a premium on the geographic clustering of subcontractors around their large customers. Nevertheless, we strongly believe that the balance of forces still greatly favors continued spatial decentralization.[14]

TABLE 2.1

The Growth of U.S. Private
Investment Abroad, 1950–1980
(in billions of dollars)

Year	Value of Physical Assets	Repatriated Profits
1950	11.8	1.5
1955	19.4	2.1
1960	31.9	2.9
1965	49.5	5.2
1970	75.5	7.9
1975	124.1	18.4
1980	213.5	42.5

SOURCES: Compiled and reported by Berch Berberoglu, *The Internationalization of Capital* (New York: Praeger, 1987).

Indeed, unlike their purely domestic counterparts, the multinational corporations of the United States have consistently performed well in overall world commerce. From the detailed research of economists Robert E. Lipsey and Irving B. Kravis, we know that the U.S. share of total world exports plummeted from more than 21 percent in 1957 to 13.9 percent in 1983. Yet, at the same time, the export share of foreign affiliates of U.S. companies actually *grew*—and grew swiftly at that, from 5.8 percent to 10.0 percent of the total world market.[15] The major part of the revenues of a large number of U.S. multinational companies, and the bulk of their operating profits, now come from sales made by their offshore affiliates. This is by no means limited to oil companies or U.S.-based international airlines like Pan Am. Dow Chemical, American Brands, Colgate-Palmolive, Parker Pen, Hoover, and American Family Products (despite its name) all received half or more of their total revenue in 1983 from the global sales of their foreign-based affiliates.[16] A survey conducted by *Business Week* of the overseas operations of two hundred leading U.S. nonfinancial companies revealed that, on average, sales made through offshore operations accounted for a third of their worldwide revenues in 1984 and more than a third of their pretax operating profits.[17] During the recessions of 1980 and 1981–82, the profits generated abroad became absolutely crucial. They saved the day for many a company like Ford, whose overseas profits were needed to offset multibillion-dollar losses at home.

The Hollowing of America

At first, the increased globalization of U.S. firms could easily be interpreted as a sign of political power and economic strength. This certainly was so when the French journalist, Jean-Jacques Servan-Schreiber published his European call-to-arms, *The American Challenge,* in 1968.[18] Servan-Schreiber described a Europe dominated by U.S. multinational corporations which threatened, at least from a European's perspective, to overshadow the Continent's own producers. The implications of U.S. hegemony were frightening enough to the average West German or Italian. One can only imagine the terror they struck into the hearts of the fiercely independent French!

In 1968, there *was* reason for concern in Europe. The American economy was in its eighth consecutive year of expansion; American firms were on the prowl, intent on maintaining or increasing their share of the world market, and the surplus profits being generated inside the United States provided a large investment pool for the acquisition of foreign enterprises. The dollar was strong and the United States, although bogged down in Vietnam, looked materially, if not militarily, invincible. Little did Servan-Schreiber—or for that matter, most anyone else—suspect that economic fortunes would change so profoundly or so rapidly. By 1971, only three years after *The American Challenge* appeared in the bookstores, the United States was mired in recession, the balance of merchandise trade had become negative for the first time this century, and the era of stagflation was beginning.

The U.S. drive toward globalization did not cease. But as time went on, it became increasingly clear that this trend did not signify growing strength but, in many ways, growing domestic weakness. Globalization of production was no longer supplementing domestic manufacture, but replacing it. As one measure of this phenomenon, domestic employment attributable to manufacturing fell from 27 percent in 1970 to 19 percent in 1986. In the same period, the share of the gross national product (GNP) contributed by manufacturing, measured in current dollars, tumbled from nearly 25 percent to less than 20 percent.[19] Even in dollars adjusted for inflation, in every manufacturing industry except computers the contribution to GNP declined.[20]

Of course, not all of this loss can be traced to U.S. firms moving abroad, substituting foreign for domestic components, or re-importing subassemblies from offshore "export platforms" and "free trade zones." But such behavior was certainly a major reason the United States lost a significant fraction of its manufacturing base. In the new U.S. and Western European lexicon, the country was becoming "deindustrialized."[21]

Akio Morita, the chair and co-founder of the highly successful Sony Corporation, has his own interpretation of what was happening in the United States and has coined a graphic term for it:

> American companies have either shifted output to low-wage countries or come to buy parts and assembled products from countries like Japan that can make quality products at low prices. The result is a *hollowing* of American industry. The U.S. is abandoning its status as an industrial power.[22] [emphasis added.]

Mr. Morita is hardly alone in his criticism of U.S. industry's abandonment of domestic production. A growing chorus of economists, business publications, and corporate leaders themselves has been raising storm signals about the long-term consequences of the hollowing strategy adopted by U.S. firms to reap short-term profits. Greater reliance on foreign assembly, the "outsourcing" (subcontracting) of components to foreign manufacturers, the introduction of coproduction arrangements between U.S. and foreign firms, and the licensing of technology to foreign competitors have all come under fire.

Until recently, no one had much idea of the extent of offshore assembly and production of components by U.S. companies. This has been remedied by the work of Joseph Grunwald of the University of California and Kenneth Flamm of The Brookings Institution, who have conducted an in-depth investigation of what they term the "global factory." They conclude from their research that "while firms in all industrial countries have engaged in foreign assembly, U.S. firms have done by far the most."[23] Under various government tariff regulations, U.S. companies are permitted to re-import, without payment of duty, goods that originate in the United States, but which are fabricated or assembled offshore. The U.S. Tariff Commission has kept track of the value of such subsidized imports for nearly two decades. What Grunwald and Flamm found is that the total value of such imports escalated from $1.8 billion in 1969 to almost $22 billion in 1983. Of these duty-free goods, about half involved assembly in Japan, West Germany, or Canada. The assembly of the other half was accomplished in developing countries. Mexico, Malaysia, Singapore, the Philippines, Korea, Taiwan, Hong Kong, and Haiti have been the favorites (in that order) of U.S. firms seeking locations for assembly operations. Checking the cartons at any local department store will confirm the validity of this list.

By no means are these global factories restricted to producing relatively unsophisticated goods like apparel, footwear, pottery, or simple metal products. Increasingly, they are being used by U.S. companies to manufacture textile machinery, radio and television receivers, semiconductors, automobile and motorcycle parts, and watches and clocks. For example, by 1982, more than $8.3 billion worth of motor vehicle parts and $3.1 billion worth of semiconductors containing duty-free parts assembled offshore were coming into the United States. The Hermosillo Ford auto plant in Mexico, opened in late 1987, is indicative of the growing technological sophistication of offshore production. It is

> the only Ford North American facility to combine stamping, manufacturing and assembly in what has been called a "state of the art" plant. When operations are at full capacity at Hermosillo, it is expected that 90 percent of the auto parts will be imported from around the Pacific while 90 percent of the output will be shipped to the U.S. Mazda Motor Corp., which is [already] 25 percent owned by Ford, will provide the basic design and major components. When all the cars are coming off the line, 3,000 workers will be employed making 100,000 cars annually.[24]

The Hermosillo plant, the most sophisticated auto plant in Mexico, is only one of many. By the end of 1987, General Motors had twenty-three plants operating south of the U.S. border, the majority of them *maquiladoras*—U.S. owned factories built in Mexico along the Rio Grande to take advantage of the special provisions of U.S. tariff law.[25]

Color TVs are another example of offshore production. Between 1971 and 1976, the proportion of the value of color television subassemblies and parts produced in the overseas operations of U.S. firms for re-import rose from 23 percent to more than 90 percent—and these figures do not include the value of parts purchased by these offshore plants from foreign suppliers![26] What is ironic about this particular episode of abandonment of U.S. workers by U.S. firms is that, at the very same time, the Japanese were setting up shop inside the United States to produce color TVs for the U.S. market. The average U.S. consumer could therefore buy a Sony made in the United States or settle for a Magnavox assembled in Mexico, Taiwan, or Hong Kong. The same is true of that quintessential high-technology product, the IBM Personal Computer. Nearly everything inside the chassis of this marvelous machine is manufactured outside the United States.

Outsourcing is no longer restricted to hard goods such as automobile engine blocks and television chassis. Even services are being located offshore for "processing" and re-export to the United States. Consider, by way of example, American Airlines' establishment of a sweatshop in Barbados for entering computerized data. The service center is connected to the company's Tulsa, Oklahoma accounting hub by computers and satellite telecommunications. It is staffed almost entirely by women who are paid wages that fall near the bottom of even Barbados's meager pay scale.[27]

Keeping labor costs from rising is not the only reason that U.S. firms have gone abroad to set up assembly or service operations. Some firms have established foreign subsidiaries to improve their chances of selling their merchandise in foreign markets or to take advantage of special tax incentives offered by foreign governments eager to attract employment-producing investment.[28] In others, they have set up foreign operations because they are forced to by "local content" laws (or so-called "performance criteria") which require that an investment provide a quid pro quo for access to a foreign sales market. Twenty-five developing nations, for example, have requirements covering the domestic content of automobiles produced there. These include Argentina, Brazil, Greece, Mexico, Portugal, South Korea, Spain, and Taiwan.[29]

Still, one of the most powerful motives for doing business globally is the search for ever-cheaper labor. The figures in table 2.2 compare the average hourly cost of labor (including fringe benefits, bonuses, medical coverage, and employer contributions to social welfare) in the United States with those in the various "newly industrialized countries," the so-called NICs. The differentials are so great—the *smallest* is five to one—that even if productivity in the NICs were substantially less than in the United States, it would still appear profitable to produce abroad. In fact, technology has been diffused so rapidly, and the skills of the foreign workforce have been improved so quickly, that unit labor costs—

TABLE 2.2

Wages Around the World
Total Hourly Compensation for Production
Workers in Manufacturing in Various Years
Between 1979 and 1982

United States	$11.79
Brazil	2.43
Mexico	1.97
Singapore	1.77
Taiwan	1.57
Hong Kong	1.55
South Korea	1.22
Sri Lanka	0.21

SOURCE: Unpublished U.S. Bureau of Labor Statistics data, prepared by Tom Ashbrook. See "US Workers in Worldwide Job Scramble," *Boston Globe*, 26 September 1983.

the real cost of labor per unit of output—continue to decline in many of the NICs. Thus, doing business in these countries seems almost irresistible to many U.S. producers. This is particularly true in the Far East. The unit cost of labor in Hong Kong fell from 82 percent of U.S. levels in 1978 to 69 percent in 1985. Similarly, in South Korea, the cost fell from 93 percent to 64 percent vis-à-vis the United States.[30] Since these two nations peg their own currencies to the U.S. dollar, the weakening of the dollar since 1985 has not appreciably affected these ratios.

Such continuing differentials in the cost of labor have played a major role in bringing into existence what has been termed the "new international division of labor."* Firms disperse their various operations across the globe, keeping their central administrative personnel in the United

*The original—and rather one-dimensional—statement of the thesis was by a group of German Marxist theorists.[31] Some scholars, notably David Gordon, Arthur MacEwan, and Andrew Sayer, are critical of the theory.[32] Gordon, especially, thinks that we and others have exaggerated the importance of geographic labor cost differentials in shaping the locational pattern of direct foreign investment (DFI), and indeed that such investments are themselves of declining significance in the global system of the 1980s.

We think that a focus on DFI is too narrow. The "multinationalization" of capital operates through many other, more indirect forms of linkage (co-production, licensing, outsourcing, invisible partnerships to avoid arousing local anti-U.S. sentiments and so forth). Moreover, while one should not focus exclusively on variations in nominal wages per se (as do the orthodox economists for whom price differentials make the world go 'round), so long as the cost of labor (which depends very much on political as well as narrowly "economic" conditions) is unequal across the globe, there are always new opportunities for destabilizing shifts of capital. Indeed, that is what political economists mean by "uneven development." Such a perspective leaves plenty of room for nonmechanistic theories of the role of governments in shaping observed outcomes. While our position implies great difficulties for the labor movement of any particular region or country, as Gordon suggests, one should by no means conclude that all is hopeless. Presumably, the old saw still holds that to be forewarned is to be forearmed.[33]

States, a growing portion of their production workers in low-cost nations, and a sales staff stationed in every country in which they can market their products. The trend is strong enough that a fair-sized consulting industry has blossomed to assist U.S. companies with the intricacies of language barriers, local customs, and government red tape. Even the U.S. Department of Commerce has joined in, sponsoring conferences (EXPO trade fairs) where government experts provide tips to U.S. business representatives on how to start up foreign assembly operations successfully.[34]

The foreign subsidiary is not the only manifestation of hollowing. An increasing number of once powerful manufacturing concerns have stopped producing altogether and are simply buying the finished product from a foreign manufacturer, slapping on their own label, and merchandising it. Everything about the product but its wholesale distribution is foreign: its design, engineering, production, and packaging. The tiny "Made in Japan" or "Made in Korea" label under the bold U.S. name hardly tells the full story of just how far the hollowing process has proceeded. Instead of outsourcing particular components, the firms engaged in this practice are importing the entire product, even the carton!

Examples abound. In 1985, General Electric spent $1.4 billion to import products sold in the United States with GE labels. Eastman Kodak buys its video cameras and videotapes from Japanese suppliers. General Motors is marketing South Korean Daewoo cars through its Pontiac dealerships, under the venerable GM namesake LeMans, while Chrysler markets Mitsubishi Colts. The 3M Company markets plain-paper copiers wholly designed and manufactured by Toshiba.[35]

To be sure, the United States continues to be a major innovator in a number of key fields—including aerospace, computer, and medical technology, and genetic engineering. However, by outsourcing production, U.S. firms are increasingly yielding fundamental technology, manufacturing management experience, and design and engineering skills to what, in another era, would have been considered the competition. By entering into licensing agreements and joint ventures, U.S. firms are literally selling off U.S. technology.* Clyde V. Prestowitz,

---

*A *licensing agreement* permits one firm to manufacture and sell a product which has been designed by another. The designing firm is paid royalties for this privilege. A *joint venture* involves the creation of an enterprise which is jointly owned by two parent firms. In many cases, one of these firms provides the technology while the other supplies the manufacturing expertise.

foreign trade counselor to the Secretary of Commerce and from 1981 to mid-1986 one of the nation's top trade negotiators with Japan, argues "There is hardly an industry where we haven't transferred technology to Japan."[36] The problem with joint ventures and licensing agreements is that they often come back to haunt the innovator.

The aircraft industry is just one example. Under a recent joint-venture agreement signed between a consortium of Japanese aircraft-parts companies and Boeing, the consortium will advance 25 percent of the $4 billion or more it will cost to develop a new generation of fuel-efficient propjet aircraft. In return, the consortium will receive a corresponding share of future profits from the endeavor.[37] In reality, however, they will get much more, because Japanese engineers and technicians, already proficient in other fields, will be given specialized training in the design and manufacture of aircraft. The first contingent of Japanese engineers has already moved to Seattle to begin a course of study at what is equivalent to "Boeing University." These engineers will ultimately be able to fulfill their own government's vision of building a Japanese aerospace industry that can compete directly with the United States'. As Robert Reich has written:

> It will not be the first time an American technological leader entered into such a Faustian bargain. In 1953, Western Electric licensed its newly invented solid-state transistor to Sony for $25,000, and the rest is history. A few years later, RCA sold its color television technology to the Japanese, and that was the beginning of the end of video electronics in America. In 1968 Unimation licensed Kawasaki Heavy Industries to make industrial robots. The list goes on.[38]

Pointing to a study of more than one hundred recent joint ventures between U.S. and Japanese companies, Reich notes a consistent pattern: the Japanese partner gets knowledge of and experience with the technology that the U.S. partner invented; the U.S. firm gets a cheap source of financing. Eventually, the Japanese partner takes over the advanced manufacturing, leaving the U.S. partner with (at most) the sales and distribution rights to the U.S. territory. So it goes. Executives at Boeing pooh-pooh the idea that a transfer of technology will ultimately make Japan competitive with the U.S. aerospace industry. But not everyone agrees with Boeing. Richard Drobnick, a specialist in international business at the University of Southern California who has studied the matter, told the *Wall Street Journal,* "If that's a real strong belief [at Boeing], these guys are lunatics."[39]

Finally, we now know that the forms of hollowing or deindustrialization that in one way or another move production entirely out of the country often take design and service jobs along with them. As Steven S. Cohen and John Zysman of the Berkeley Roundtable on the International Economy (BRIE) project have estimated, "some 25 percent of G.N.P. consists of services purchased by American manufacturers. Lose manufacturing and we would lose not just millions of direct production jobs but also a good hunk of those service jobs."[40]

Corporate Hollowing and Loss of Domestic Jobs

By no means does everyone place the importing of components, the outsourcing of entire products, joint ventures, and the licensing of technology in the same unfavorable light as Akio Morita or Richard Drobnick. On the contrary, many view these business strategies as signs of the successful adaptation of U.S. firms to the exigencies of global competition. They represent not hollowing or deindustrialization, but "cost-effective restructuring" that takes advantage of lower wages and flourishing technology abroad. After all, multimillionaires have been created virtually overnight through shrewd investment in these restructured manufacturing firms.

To be sure, the national debate about the ultimate impact of the United States' deindustrialization has not been completely resolved. Nonetheless, there is probably a greater consensus today than at any time in the past. Economist Robert E. Lipsey of the City University of New York sums up the dilemma well. Restructured firms, he notes, "prove that American business can compete on a firm-by-firm basis," but the resultant job losses and other macroeconomic effects "may not be beneficial for the economy in the aggregate."[41]

For workers, the hollowing strategy is not merely a potential threat. It is a reality. In key sectors throughout the economy, workers have lost jobs numbering in the millions, and those fortunate enough to hold on to theirs have often had to submit to substantial reductions of wages and benefits.

The U.S. Bureau of Labor Statistics (BLS) has reviewed the results of deindustrialization and the rise of the service economy. The Bureau concludes that in "about 20 manufacturing industries, including steel, leather, and tires, the past 15 years have seen steady declines in both output and employment."[42] Moreover, the BLS notes, there have been negative output and employment trends in "recent problem industries." These include the crucial machine-tool sector and those industries that produce construction machinery, electrical transmission equipment, and engines and turbines. In all of these, production levels in the boom year of 1984 were below those that existed before the 1980 recession. In our own research, conducted with Alan Clayton-Matthews, we came to a similar conclusion. In studying 92 manufacturing industries that account for 97 percent of total manufacturing employment in the nation, we found that employment in one-third of the industries either entered a long-term decline after 1968 or saw previous growth totally arrested. These troubled industries had accounted for more than seven million jobs in 1969.[43]

General Electric provides an unhappy example of what is happening to premier U.S. manufacturers. When Jack Welch took over the reins of GE in 1981, the company was as traditional as any large manufacturing firm in the country. Welch set out almost immediately to build GE into a massive diversified firm "that is constantly renewing itself, shedding the past, adapting to change."[44] To Welch that meant concentrating on business in the service and high-technology sectors, and retaining only those traditional businesses that could turn a respectable profit by dominating their respective markets. Welch spent $6.5 billion to acquire RCA and its largest subsidiary, the broadcasting firm, NBC. He used another $1.7 billion to purchase Kidder Peabody and Employers Reinsurance, investment banking and financial services firms. At the same time, he eliminated the entire housewares division of GE— the group that produced products ranging from toaster ovens to steam irons. In the first five years of his tenure, Welch sold off 190 subsidiaries worth nearly $6 billion. During the same period, his acquisition spree cost the company nearly $10 billion.

What has been the end result? GE's profit margins have increased sharply and productivity has boomed. Total sales per employee have increased from $62,000 to $93,000 in just five years. But this has come at the expense of more than a hundred thousand jobs, more than a quarter of the company's work force when Welch took over in 1981. Some of these were lost at the new RCA subsidiary that used to produce TV sets domestically. When GE bought RCA out, it closed down this operation and subcontracted the production work to suppliers in the Far East.

There is an enlightening twist to this story. In February 1987, when new, automated production processes were developed that drastically reduced the need for labor, GE brought its color-television production back to U.S. shores. The combination of automation and a falling dollar had made it once again profitable to produce at home. Yet it was obviously not profitable enough. Only five months later, GE called this experiment a failure and in late July announced the sale of its *entire* consumer electronics division—a $3-billion-a-year business—to the French concern, Thomson S.A.[45]

Since 1980, company after company has imitated Jack Welch's strategy, although not always with such flair. By the end of 1986, this meant a 17 percent decline in employment in the textile industry, 30 percent in primary metals, and 40 percent in steel.[46] Even during the booming recovery period of 1983–84, the U.S. General Accounting Office (GAO) working with the Congressional Office of Technology Assessment (OTA) estimates that 7,800 establishments with a hundred or more employees either closed down altogether or laid off workers. The consequence: the displacement of more than a million workers.[47] This came on top of much larger dislocations in the years just before this period. According to Candee Harris, a former research analyst at the Brookings Institution, large manufacturing firms eliminated more than 900,000 jobs a year beginning in the mid-1970s, simply in the course of closing domestic branch plants. She estimates a total loss of 3.5 to 4 million jobs between 1978 and 1982, or one out of every four jobs in large manufacturing facilities.[48]

The sharp declines in employment are no longer restricted to old-line manufacturing firms or blue-collar workers. Plant closings, layoffs, and pay cuts have swept the high-technology industries as well. In just the first six months of 1985, for example, employment in the computer and semiconductor industries—the core of the new technology—shed more than twenty thousand jobs.[49] Japanese suppliers of semiconductors and Asian suppliers of disk drives and computer printers are overtaking these markets, too.

Ironically, middle management has become the latest casualty in the restructuring of U.S. business. As one executive recruiter put it, "the list of walking wounded from management is now long enough to fill a war memorial."[50] *Business Week* called managers "sitting ducks".[51] The BLS reported that, between 1981 and 1986, more than 780,000 managers and professionals lost their jobs as the result of plant closings and permanent layoffs.[52] And the pace has apparently increased, even as the economy entered its fourth year of recovery. In the drive to make the ranks of management "leaner and meaner," nearly 600,000 middle and upper-level executives lost their jobs between 1984 and 1986.[53] Such companies as AT&T, United Technologies, Union Carbide, and Ford are leading the "management massacre."

The Assault on the Wages of Domestic Labor

Side by side with their efforts to reduce their dependence on domestic labor by shifting capital abroad and by turning themselves into importers and distributors of foreign-made goods, American corporations have been experimenting since the late 1970s with new policies for curtailing domestic wages and benefits. So much of this has been going on that in recent years the enumeration of these experiments has become something of a booming industry among students of labor.[54]

What is labor cost to the firm, of course, is the principal source of income for the vast majority of the population. It is primarily out of wages (or money borrowed against future wages) that families finance their consumption of everything from food and new clothes for the children to payments for summer vacations and the monthly mortgage or rent. Long ago, at the dawn of the twentieth century, no less passionate a capitalist than Henry Ford understood that unless he paid his workers a high-enough wage, the question would arise: "who would buy my cars?" In an era of heightened international competition, when the ability of American firms to sell their goods to foreigners has been seriously eroded, the significance of Ford's insight into this fundamentally contradictory aspect of capitalism—that labor is both a cost of production and the ultimate consumer who needs income with which to play this role—is as relevant as ever. Hence, all of the new attempts to reduce wages and cut benefits have an eerie ring to them.

Nevertheless, cutting wages and what professionals in the field term "union avoidance" have been hallmarks of corporate restructuring policy. The practices by which companies have cut the cost of labor in response to the profit squeeze fall roughly into four categories, all of which business leaders describe euphemistically as ways to increase labor "flexibility." A growing number of managers in an increasingly diverse set of industries have succeeded in extracting concessions (or "givebacks") from their employees—that is, reversals of previously won arrangements about wages, benefits, or work rules. There has also been a diffusion of two-tiered wage systems, allowing for workers performing the same duties to be paid substantially different wages depending on how recently they were hired. There appears to have been an increase in companies' use of "contingent" or "temporary" labor, both inside large firms and outside, in the shops of subcontractors or in the homes of the peripheral workers themselves. Finally, managers have been pursuing more or less explicit anti-union policies, attempting to avoid unionization by building new nonunion plants rather than expanding their older ones, or by "busting" the unions already present in their workplaces.[55]

Concessions

Wage freezes and outright pay cuts were practically nonexistent in at least the unionized sector of the American economy between 1964 and 1980. Wages rose more or less continuously, in step with increases in productivity and rises in the cost of living. Then, during the recession of 1981–82, concessions exploded onto the labor scene. In the latter year, the trough of the recession, 44 percent of the unionized work force bargaining for new contracts took wage cuts or forewent increases for at least the first year of the new contract. In 1980, that proportion had been zero![56]

The concessions fever did not abate during the economic recovery. Three years later, in 1985, a third of all workers covered by new collective-bargaining agreements submitted to a total freeze or cut in wages. The same proportion received lump-sum payments in lieu of raises in that year. But since these are not averaged into the hourly wage rate, they afford employers a smaller base from which to bargain for the next contract. Moreover, 40 percent of those workers who previously had cost-of-living-adjustment (COLA) clauses in their contracts lost them in 1985. In fact, "only one-third of the workers with new contracts in 1985 were covered by COLA, down from 50 percent in 1983 and 40 percent in 1984. In the contracts negotiated during the first three months of 1986, only 15 percent of the workers had COLA."[57]

The steel industry has been an especially fertile site for corporate experiments with concessions. For example, in November of 1986 the United Steelworkers of America (USW) was forced by ARMCO, the nation's fifth-largest steel company, to agree to a contract according to which the company and the union negotiate different wage rates (for the same work) at four different mills. Thus, ARMCO employees were thrown into direct competition with one another—something the labor movements of all democratic countries have sought to eliminate for the past half-century.[58] Moreover, in their January 1987 agreement with USX (formerly the United States Steel Corporation), following a six-month lockout of 22,000 employees, the USW was forced to give up jobs, wages, a portion of employer-paid health insurance premiums, and certain overtime pay, paid holidays, and vacation time. These terms were codified for a four-year term.[59] At ailing LTV Steel, the USW was put in the uncomfortable position of having to ratify a new contract in 1986 that included, among other concessions, a cut of $3.15 an hour in wages and benefits.[60]

By mid-decade, the concessions were no longer concentrated in a few highly unionized sectors. Nor were they restricted to manufacturing. Table 2.3 illustrates how rapidly the practice has spread. What began as arguably a short-term response to recession has turned into something far more lasting. To Daniel P. Mitchell, a labor economist at the University of California, there is a "demonstration effect," as even

TABLE 2.3

The Spread of Concessions, by Industry January 1981–June 1985

Industry	1981	1982	1983	January 1984–June 1985
Metals	X[a]	X	X	X
Motor vehicles[b]	X	X	X	X
Retail food stores[c]	X	X	X	X
Machinery	X	X	X	X
Meatpacking	X	X	X	X
Airlines	X	X	X	X
Printing and publishing	X	X	X	X
Health care	X	X	X	X
Lumber and paper	X	X	X	X
Ordnance	X			X
Construction		X	X	X
Transit and bus lines		X	X	X
Rubber		X		X
Trucking		X	X	X
Aerospace		X	X	X
Textiles		X	X	X
Food manufacturing except meatpacking		X	X	X
Instruments		X	X	X
Chemicals		X	X	X
Furniture		X	X	X
Hotels and restaurants		X	X	X
Shipping		X	X	X
Other transportation equipment[d]		X	X	X
Brick, clay, stone		X	X	X
Finance, insurance		X		X
Communications		X		X
Apparel		X		X
Business services			X	X
Railroads			X	
Unions[e]			X	X
Cement			X	X
Entertainment			X	X
Mining			X	X
Warehousing			X	X
Glass			X	
Education			X	X
Retail except food stores				X
Leather				X
Petroleum				X
Tobacco				X
Utilities				X

a. An "X" indicates the presence of at least one contract involving a concession in the industry and period indicated. Concessions are first-year wage freezes and cuts.

b. Includes motor vehicle parts.

c. Includes related wholesale operations.

d. Transportation equipment excluding motor vehicles and parts and aerospace.

e. Unions in their role as employers of their own staffs.

Reprinted from David J.B. Mitchell, "Shifting Norms in Wage Determination," *Brookings Papers on Economic Activity*, 2, 1985, table 5, p. 585. It is based on a biweekly survey conducted by the Bureau of National Affairs, Inc., covering union settlements involving fifty or more employees.

companies which are not in any immediate difficulty observe their competitors' success in gaining concessions and demand their own. The table shows that in recent years, even workers in such robust industries as printing and publishing, aerospace, finance, business services, and hotels and restaurants have had to make concessions to their employers.

Two-Tiered Wages

Concessions take many forms, and employers have been experimenting with new ones. One of these is the two-tier wage structure. Under a two-tier collective bargaining agreement, newly hired workers are paid less than more senior workers to do essentially the same job. While this has been traditional during short probationary periods, the two-tier systems now being put in place often prolong the wage differential for ten years or more, by establishing two schedules for pay raises, the one for recently hired employees being well below that offered those already on the payroll. The practice seems to have originated in the retail food industry.

In some cases, "catch-up" does occur more quickly. For example, according to a recent contract between General Motors Corporation and the United Auto Workers, newly hired workers are paid only 85 percent of the old base wage, but they achieve full parity in 545 days. By contrast, according to the contract between the International Union of Electrical Workers and GM's Packard Electric Division, new workers making auto parts are paid only 55 percent of the old base rate and must work for ten years before reaching parity. Line mechanics at American Airlines take twelve years to catch up.[61]

Professor Mitchell's own survey of employers, coupled with his analysis of data on concessions from the Bureau of National Affairs (BNA), have led him to conclude that the use of two-tiered wage arrangements is on the rise. By 1984, some 10 percent of all agreements containing concessions included language about the new dual system. The proportion rose again in 1985. New contracts containing two-tier provisions now cover more than a third of the unionized work force. They are especially common in the supermarket, aerospace, airline, and construction industries.[62] In 1984, President Reagan bestowed his official imprimatur on the practice by imposing on the U.S. Postal Service a second tier of wages 25 percent below the previous standard wage.[63]

It is clear why companies find such arrangements attractive—at least in the short run. In those with high rates of turnover, such as the fast-food and supermarket industries, where new employees are unlikely to remain for a long time, or in those whose most skilled workers will soon be retiring (as in machining), two-tier systems offer a quick payoff because entry-level (and therefore low-paid) workers tend to make up the bulk of the payroll. In firms with little or no growth in employment, unions have often gone along with the two-tier systems in order to protect their senior members' wages and benefits. But this has had the effect of alienating their newest members, on whose shoulders the future of the union must rest.

For all these reasons, Jane Seabury, an economics reporter for the *Washington Post*, observed that the advent of two-tiered of wage systems "may be dividing union leadership from their members, damaging productivity, and permanently lowering the wage structure of many industries."[64] Employers are also becoming cautious as they watch the "B-scalers" (those in the lower tier) increase in political force as their numbers increase. Some managers with a background in the humanities might recall from Gibbon's *Rise and Fall of the Roman Empire* that the Emperor Macrinus cut military spending by instituting a lower tier of wages for new recruits in 217 A.D. A year later, Gibbon tells us, dissension in the new ranks was so great that the army revolted and killed the emperor.

Part-Time Contingent Work Schedules

Whether or not firms introduce two tiers, they have still another way to reduce the cost of labor dramatically. They can place part-time employees in what were once full-time jobs. This is in sharp contrast to earlier practice. From World War II through the early 1970s, a growing proportion of American companies organized the division of work and the management of employees within their firms around the key institution of a full-time work force and an "internal labor market." Ordered hierarchies, promotion from within rather than from outside the company whenever possible, the erection of promotion ladders with relatively explicit rules and flexible procedures by which workers would be judged worthy of upgrading—these were the dominant characteristics of this form of corporate bureaucracy. Companies valued such arrangements both because they contributed to on-the-job training (on the principle that only reasonably secure senior workers would be prepared to teach what they knew to younger people, who would otherwise be seen as dangerous competitors) and because such procedures were less expensive than the unscheduled strikes, sit-ins, slowdowns and even sabotage that had been so widespread during the 1930s.[65]

One of the more dramatic aspects of restructuring has been what Thierry Noyelle has termed the "devolution" of these internal labor markets. In the place of job ladders are new arrangements for contingent labor.[66] These fall into two broad categories. The first includes less than regular, full-time status (part-time, temporary, and leased) employees, usually *within* large firms. The second type of contingent work occurs *outside* the primary firm, either under the company's own direction (when, for example, work is done at home by the employee) or within an ostensibly independent business which holds a subcontract to deliver some product to, or perform some task for the primary firm. Work which has been outsourced often entails part-time or part-year work schedules.

Within this realm, the use of such services as Manpower, Inc. and Kelly Services has mushroomed during the past decade. Short-term workers are usually referred to in the trade as "temps"; large companies seem especially likely to employ them. By contrast, "leased" workers are often hired by smaller firms, in larger numbers and for longer periods.[67] Roughly half of all temporary and leased employees are hired to perform clerical functions; others are drafters and assemblers (especially in the electronics industry), computer programmers, chemical engineers, drivers, gardeners, or lifeguards. Between 1970 and 1984, the payrolls of agencies providing temporary help grew twice as fast as the nation's GNP.[68]

All researchers agree that the extent of these developments is difficult to measure. However, one estimate, assembled by *Business Week,* is that contingent labor—leased and temporary workers, involuntary part-timers, employees of subcontractors, and home workers—grew from 8 million in 1980 to 18 million by 1985. That number is nearly 17 percent of the total work force. If those whom the BLS considers to be "voluntary" part-time workers are added to the count, fully a quarter of the 1985 labor force could be considered contingent employees.[69] In particular industries, the growth has been phenomenal, especially in the service sector, in such industries as retail groceries and fast foods, in colleges and universities, and in hospitals and health-care services. The United Food and Commercial Workers' Union estimates that perhaps *half* its members are now part-timers.[70] Nurses in Minneapolis who decided in 1984 to strike for full-time work schedules certainly seemed to have a legitimate concern. As recently as 1977, 70 percent of the registered nurses employed in the Minneapolis–St. Paul area worked full time. By 1984, only 30 percent did![71]

What has happened, to induce more and more companies to tinker with well-worn methods of hiring, managing, and differentiating among their employees? With respect to the various forms of contingent labor, what corporations seem to be doing is "insulat[ing] a set of relatively permanent 'core' employees from a set of peripheral workers who are used to buffer or absorb fluctuations and environmental changes."[72] But why *now?* Eileen Appelbaum, an economist at Temple University, offers an answer which places the phenomenon squarely into the mold of crisis-driven restructuring. "Internal labor markets," she argues, "play a special role in meeting the needs of companies that are poised for expansion. . . . Today, however, companies are poised for contraction."[73] In slack periods, employers are less concerned with developing promotional ladders to keep their most prized employees and more interested in finding cheap and efficient ways of reducing the number of workers at the first sign of a downturn in sales. The use of contingent labor provides them with just such a mechanism.

But the corporate benefits of substituting temporary, leased, and part-time workers for regular, full-time employees are not restricted to bad economic times. Apart from its capacity to help shelter the firm from unstable market conditions in a period of intense competition, the increased use of contingent labor can greatly reduce the everyday cost per employee, and managers are well aware of this advantage. Not only direct wages, but fringe benefits as well are often less when an employer uses contingent labor. After all, as Appelbaum notes, full-time employees in many medium and large firms have won substantial benefits, including health insurance and pensions. Firms can often avoid making these benefits available to those in the pool of contingent workers. The savings to these companies can be substantial.

Appelbaum's suspicion that at least part of the enthusiasm of managers for short work schedules is related to the opportunity to reduce the cost of fringe benefits is given strong support by statistics from the Employee Benefits Research Institute in Washington. The Institute reports that, in 1986, 70 percent of all part-time employees had no company-provided retirement plan, and 42 percent had no company-provided health insurance.[74] Further confirmation comes from a recent econometric analysis conducted by Ronald Ehrenberg, a labor economist at Cornell University, and his colleagues. They found that, in March 1984, in the majority of forty-four different manufacturing and service industries studied, part-time workers were systematically paid lower hourly wages than full-time employees and were less likely to be covered by health insurance and pension plans, even after accounting for individual differences in schooling, work experience, gender, race, marital status, family size, residential location, and military service.[75]

If the *goals* driving the revival of the use of contingent labor are flexibility and cost reduction, what seems to be making it *possible* for managers to re-fragment work and disperse their labor force is a combination of factors that include demographic changes, the changing nature of work, and new technology. The most important of these has been the tremendous increase in the number of working women. Some of these women desire "mothers' hours," but many more are forced to take part-time jobs because these are the only ones available. In addition, many of the skills needed in the burgeoning service economy are taught in school rather than on the job, as are construction and manufacturing skills. As a result, there is less need for a stable work force to pass specific skills on to a new generation of workers. Finally, there is what sociologists Jeffrey Pfeffer and James Baron, of Stanford University, term the "meterability" of much contingent work, which facilitates the supervision of a geographically and organizationally dispersed labor force.[76] We would add that the stagnation of real wages since the early 1970s also means that more and more families *need* whatever work their members can find, however "contingent."

In recent years, business lobbyists have often argued that part-time jobs, usually in the service sector, are exactly what most people (especially women) desire. Yet the official data on part-time work make it clear that practically 100 percent of the net additional part-time jobs created in the United States since the late 1970s are held by people who would have preferred full-time jobs but could not find any.[77]

Ronald Ehrenberg confirms this trend:

> Our analyses of the aggregate time-series data for the United States suggests that there has been a tendency towards increased employment of part-time workers in recent years, a trend that is observed *after* one controls for cyclical factors. Moreover, this trend has come from an increase in "involuntary" part-time employment, not from an increase in voluntary part-time employment. Searches for explanations for the recent growth of part-time employment in the U.S. should therefore focus on the demand side of the labor market.

That is, we should look to the behavior of employers and not employees to explain the growth in part-time jobs. Moreover, other Census data tell us that, since 1979, this rising trend in involuntary part-time work can be observed in every state in the Union.[78]

Finally, if there is any remaining doubt about the involuntary nature of this kind of work schedule, the results of a survey undertaken by a women's magazine in 1985 should put these to rest:

> Contrary to the myth that women [invariably] want to work at home so that they can also mind their children, a 1985 *Family Circle* survey of over 7,000 homeworkers revealed that the vast majority do not even try to work when their children are awake and active. . . . Most women squeeze frantic periods of work in between family responsibilities. One insurance processor brings to mind stories from the turn of the century as she describes her schedule: "When I get the claims at night, I try to put in an hour while the kids are watching TV. Then I get up at 4:30 A.M. to work before the kids get up . . . I work between 5:50 and 7:30 A.M. . . . During the day, I turn on the TV and tell my preschooler to watch. When she takes a nap, I can work some more."[79]

Most women would apparently prefer adequate day care and the opportunity for regular, full-time work.

Union Avoidance

Finally, a growing number of corporate managers have sought, with great success, to cut the cost of labor by pursuing what is referred to in business circles as "union avoidance."[80] Part of this strategy is tied to the outsourcing of parts and services that we discussed earlier in this chapter. The other involves a direct attack on unions in already unionized firms.

One example of the results of outsourcing is a former pipe fitter employed at U.S. Steel. As an employee at the huge Gary Works, he earned $13 an hour plus benefits. After he was laid off, he located a job with a small local subcontractor at $5 an hour and no benefits and found himself making parts for his old employer. According to a study conducted by Paine Webber, such subcontractors now employ as many as 8 percent of the entire steel industry work force, up from only 3 percent in the mid-1970s.[81]

Outsourcing has also become a major issue in the auto industry. Data on General Motors and Ford are not available, but Chrysler is known to procure fully 70 percent of the value of its final products from outside suppliers.[82] Given that the United Auto Workers have been able to organize only a portion of the independent suppliers of parts, the major auto producers constantly search for these cheaper, nonunion sources of parts.

The other emerging problem for U.S. auto workers lies in the outsourcing practiced by of the growing number of foreign companies who are building assembly plants inside the United States. These "transplants," which soon will include Toyota, Suzuki, Mitsubishi, Mazda, Hyundai, and other smaller firms, import as much as 75 percent of their parts from their home countries. As a result, the average transplant creates only about 27 percent as many jobs at U.S. suppliers as are created by a U.S. assembly plant using domestically produced parts. As the transplants' share of total productive capacity within U.S. borders continues to grow, the loss of jobs and wages in the United States is likely to become even greater.[83]

Thus, outsourcing is becoming an increasing problem for American workers who are trying to maintain their standard of living. Moreover,

Noyelle's case studies of large insurance, banking, and retail firms show that outsourcing is at least as common in the service sector.[84]

When outsourcing is not available or not sufficient, unionized firms are searching out loopholes in the labor laws to circumvent their unions. Legal scholars, including Paul Weiler of Harvard, have documented the rising incidence of abuses of poorly enforced labor laws which were originally put in place under the Wagner Act to protect labor's right to organize. Weiler himself has discovered a *fivefold* increase since the 1950s in the volume of unfair labor practices by management.[85] With the help of a bevy of consulting firms who advise companies on how to avoid unions (or to rid themselves of the ones they already have), managers have been able to produce a climate in which union election victories are down, decertifications of unions are up, and a declining share of the work force is even given the chance to vote on whether to be represented by a union.[86] In the quest for a "union-free environment," older plant managers experienced in, and often sympathetic to orderly collective bargaining, are often pushed aside by their companies' senior executives and replaced with new "human resources" officers or line managers who have little or no prior history of "hanging out" with union representatives.[87] At the present rate of decline, by 1990 only about one in every six American workers will be represented by an independent union—down from one in three at the peak of union strength in the postwar era.

The decline of unionism in the United States has been attributed to a range of factors. The relative growth of the labor force in the largely ununionized South and shifts in the number of workers away from well-unionized manufacturing industries toward the less-organized service sector are often placed at the top of the list.[88] However, according to research by economist Philip Doyle of the BLS, only about one-third of the reduction in the number of production workers covered by collective bargaining is due to regional and industrial shifts. The remaining losses of union membership took place *within* existing industries and regions.[89]

These findings provide at least some circumstantial evidence that the current explicit opposition to unions by more and more corporate managers is responsible for much of the overall decline in union strength. We believe that Thomas Kochan, Harry Katz, and Robert McKersie have captured and articulated better than any other mainstream labor theorists of our time the underlying shift in managerial strategy.

> During the 1950s and 1960s, the prevailing view in the industrial relations literature was that American managers had accommodated to collective bargaining and accepted unions as legitimate and lasting parties to the employment relationship. Many were convinced that management hostility toward unions was a thing of the past. But the accommodation was only temporary in character and . . . usually involved only industrial relations specialists and not the key members of management who formulated business strategies and plans. Thus the conclusion that management had adopted and accepted unions as legitimate partners misinterpreted as a change in managerial *preferences* or *ideology* what was actually a *pragmatic* or *strategic* adaptation to the high costs of avoiding or dislodging established unions. Instead, the following statement of Douglas Brown and Charles Myers probably better captured the prevailing ideologies of American managers [even] in the 1950s and 1960s: "It may well be true that if American management, upon retiring one night, were assured that by the next morning the union . . . would have disappeared, more management people than not would experience the happiest sleep of their lives."[90]

When it appeared to management that the cost of accepting unions was accelerating as a consequence of growing international competition, management changed its strategy but not its ideology. It dreamt up new tactics to combat the organization of labor. Closing plants and moving shops were doubly effective. They eliminated union labor directly and made other workers think twice before challenging corporate authority or forming new unions. When the union could not be dislodged, management pled its perceived precarious economic position to weaken the unions and demand concessions. Still other companies, including Continental Airlines and LTV Steel, sought government protection under Chapter 11 of the bankruptcy law in order to abrogate their union contracts.

None of this negates the fact that management was itself under growing pressure because of mounting competition. But it suggests that, when the chips were down, the typical response was not to find ways to co-operate with organized labor to solve mutual problems, but to work independently to solve its own problem—falling profits—by challenging labor directly.

The Common Denominator: "Zapping Labor"

This brings us back to where we began: the profit squeeze and the strategies that management began to put in place in the 1970s to counter it. Essentially, the restructuring process involved more than anything else the abrogation of the social contract that labor, management, and government had slowly but surely constructed in the course of nearly fifty years of union struggle, collective bargaining, and government regulation of the age-old battle over the disposition of the nation's total output. The common denominator of many, if not all, of management's "innovations" was an assault on the cost of labor. By the middle of the 1980s, the broad outlines as well as many of the details of these experiments could be summarized in the globalization of production, the hollowing of the firm, outright union busting, and revised labor-management relations that included demands for the lowering of wages, the proliferation of part-time work schedules (in opposition to the workers' expressed preference for full-time employment), and the increased subcontracting of work. Together, these developments added up to a realization of the objective—publicly enunciated by a conservative government back at the very beginning of the 1970s—of "zapping labor." While some employers may not have relished sending out thousands of pink slips to trusted employees, or closing down entire plants, the consequences were the same. Average wages declined, employment at low wages grew, and the overall long-term trend toward equality of wages and income underwent a great U-turn—in the wrong direction.

Labor cost containment was not the only strategy adopted by management seeking renewed profits, for even cutting the cost of labor to the bone was not nearly sufficient to meet the new global competition. For an entire platoon of corporate managers, attention was drawn not so much to the labor market as to the financial market. Faced with shrinking opportunities for making competitive rates of profit at home through direct investment in productive plant and equipment, the new financial wizards of the business world accelerated the shift of their capital into financial assets of every imaginable sort. The resulting financial explosion—a special case is the boom in urban real estate and the "revitalization" of downtown business areas—contributed to the polarizing of American society into rich and poor. The emergence of the "casino society" has not only altered the nature of the American corporation internally, but contributed to the development of a postindustrial society with a highly unequal service sector. Let us examine these developments in more detail.

3

Restructuring and the World of High Finance

IN THE EARLY AUTUMN OF 1985, *Business Week*'s editors published a special report on the growing magnitude and dangers of the "casino society." Taking a warning from John Maynard Keynes that had been issued in the middle of the Great Depression of the 1930s, the popular business magazine bemoaned the emergence of "a nation obsessively devoted to high stakes financial maneuvering as a shortcut to wealth."[1]

As indicators of the frenetic pace of financial activity in the 1980s, by mid-decade some 108 million shares of stock were changing hands daily on the New York Stock Exchange, up from 49 million only five years earlier. In the same period, turnover in the market for government securities had quadrupled. In 1984, a single Wall Street investment bank, the First Boston Corporation, handled trades worth more than $4 *trillion* dollars—more than the nation's entire gross national product (GNP). Meanwhile, investors took even riskier positions in commodity markets. The volume of trading in these markets based on the future prices of such commodities as pork bellies and oil reserves, probably the most speculative investments in our system, began to skyrocket in 1973. It has hardly paused for breath since.* By 1985, the volume of trade in such commodities was nearly four times its level in 1977. Futures trading in general was growing at ten times the rate of industrial production (fig. 3.1). No less impeccable a conservative than Paul Volcker, former chair of the Federal Reserve Board, was openly worried about this trend toward speculation in securities, commercial real estate, and commodities, as well as the proliferation of mergers and acquisitions. "A strong case can be made," he argued, "that the spread of financial gamesmanship is diverting resources from truly productive enterprise."[2]

What brought about this U-turn from productive to financial ventures is at root the same profits squeeze that propelled corporate leaders to adopt cost-cutting strategies in their production and service operations. By the early 1970s, the return on nonfinancial assets had fallen so low in the "mature" industrial sectors—such as steel, auto, machine tool, apparel, and textiles—that the financial officers who came to dominate the firms in these industries chose to divert their available cash to activities other than manufacturing. Hence, the financial boom reflected corporate management's response to the shortage of profitable "real" investment opportunities within the United States as much as to the lure of making a killing on Wall Street in highly speculative activity.

In this turn toward financial speculation and away from productive investment, the federal government, perhaps unwittingly, played an important role. Our tax laws actually permit corporations to make money in the process of dismantling productive enterprise. They can "write off" the estimated value of the plants they shut down against profits made elsewhere in the corporation's empire. During 1985 alone,

---

*Professor John Parsons of M.I.T.'s Sloan School of Management points out that such markets have a function. They put capital into the hands of producers who need ready cash in advance of their ability to bring their goods to market. Pledging that ability as the basis for a good short-term investment seems perfectly reasonable. Parsons suggests that in a complex economy, in the absence of such arrangements, many useful goods and services would never get produced at all.[3]

This is true enough, up to a point. The problem is one of balance. What writers across the ideological spectrum from *Monthly Review* editors Paul Sweezy and Harry Magdoff[4] to the editors of *Business Week* have argued is that the wholesale redirection of corporate effort from the process of making goods and services into that of buying or selling them implies a breakdown in the process of economic growth itself. Futures markets are necessary, but they become counterproductive when they become a substitute for, rather than a complement to, the production of tangible goods and services.[5]

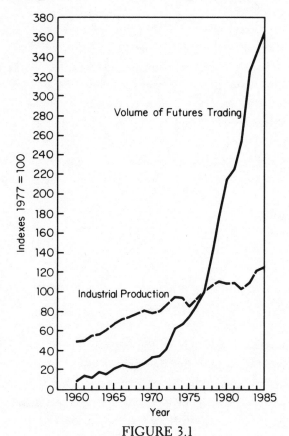

FIGURE 3.1
Speculation vs. Production
Source "Review of the Month," *Monthly Review*, October 1986, 16.

Union Carbide, for example, received an after-tax payment from the government of $620 million for closing chemical plants; United Technologies earned $424 million for shuttering Mostek, its computer-equipment subsidiary; TRW wrote off $142 million in tax liability for discontinuing the domestic manufacture of a line of aircraft components, and Crown Zellerbach was rewarded with a tax break of $106 million for closing a sawmill and tissue paper plant.[6]

The future consequences of diverting resources from production to speculation are potentially serious enough. Yet such shifts in investment not only affect capital markets, but are partially responsible for the great U-turn we are witnessing in the labor market today. Jobs in the financial capitals of America tend to be highly polarized. The financial sector, as well as the other service activities which surround it, is structured very differently than manufacturing. It tends to be staffed by well-paid, white-collar professional and technical workers at one end, and poorly paid, semiskilled and unskilled workers (whose collars may be blue, white, or pink) at the other. The general rule, with a few exceptions, is: men at the top, women at the bottom; whites at the center, workers of color and immigrants at the margin. In sum, not only is the explosive growth of high finance a symptom of a breakdown in America's global competitive position, but it is also a force toward increasing inequality—a trend toward polarization—within the American work force.

The Casino Society and the Precarious World of Speculation

Financing investment through debt became crucial in the 1970s. With the rate of return on productive investment squeezed both by international competition and domestic pressure for higher wages, corporate managers adopted the strategy of borrowing enormous sums in order to finance mergers and acquisitions that promised a better short-term payoff than investments in plant and equipment. The depressed prices of stocks made many of these acquisitions bargain-basement specials. It was often cheaper to acquire another company and its entire capital stock than to invest in new plant and equipment. Firms went deeply into debt to finance such mergers, a practice that contrasts sharply with the conventional method used in earlier periods: the straightforward exchange of shares of stock between the partners to a merger.

To bankroll the casino society, banks and securities firms created a magnificent array of new financial instruments. Over-the-counter equities, floated on behalf of tiny companies with absolutely no track record, became commonplace. Drexel-Burnham extended the process to the fixed-income segment of the market with its invention during the early 1980s of so-called junk bonds: instruments of such low investment grade that no respectable bankers would have been caught dead ten years earlier with them in their portfolios. The war among the big banks, insurance companies, and securities dealers for customers, both domestic and foreign, produced a bewildering array of investment "funds" and escalated the charging of brokerage fees into a major industry. The number of mutual funds has grown so dramatically that it takes a full page of the business section of the typical newspaper to list their opening and closing prices on the previous day. Fidelity Investments alone offers seventy-seven different mutual funds to its customers.

On the surface, these funds seem to represent a new source of capital for productive investments. The "Fund for Tomorrow," the "High Yield Fund," and the famous "Magellan Fund" were all established after the repeal of Regulation Q, a repeal which took the cap off interest rates that banks could pay their depositors. Supposedly these funds are invested in new entrepreneurial activities, and indeed some are. But much of the money has also been used to finance mergers and acquisitions rather than productive new investment.

These funds were created precisely to attract money away from traditional banks by promising high interest rates and dividends. Virtually all of the money raised this way is merely shifted from one type of "savings account" to another—usually a more risky one for the depositor. Economists term this "disintermediation." In the best-case scenario, disintermediation moves money from, say, housing construction financed by a savings or mutual bank to a smart young entrepreneur with a hot new high-technology product. But disintermediation can work in just the opposite way as well. It can mean that deposits that would have been loaned out to a Fortune–500 firm to build a new plant or expand an existing one end up being used to finance a corporate merger of dubious value. Merger and acquisition activity, because it provided securities managers with a way to make millions in commissions, produced a bias *against* "old-fashioned" loans for drill presses and lathes, forklifts, and welding equipment. These tried-and-true investments had once turned a respectable profit for the established banker. The young securities analyst found the real "action," not to mention the real profit, in the merger and acquisition game or in the commodities market.

All of this speculative activity created a new generation of millionaires, but along the way it also inflated stock prices and discouraged responsible assessment of risk. In addition, it pushed real interest rates upward, since the vast majority of transactions in the casino society are financed by borrowing, not by bellying up to the table, stakes in hand.

What is surprising is that so *few* big lenders went bankrupt in the midst of the financial feeding frenzy, Continental Illinois Bank being the most prominent exception. Between 1977 and 1981, Continental Illinois expanded its foreign and domestic loans by 22 percent *per year,* in apparent imitation of the high-stakes games being played by securities firms. As a result, by 1981, outstanding loans made up 79 percent of its total assets. When foreign bankers became anxious about Continental's balance sheet in May 1984, they began withdrawing millions of dollars they had on deposit. Over a period of several days, panic spread among other money managers, leading to a massive run on the bank. When Continental had to absorb losses stemming from $1 billion in energy-related loans it had acquired from the Penn Square Bank in Oklahoma, it found itself unable to honor its deposits. To stem the outflow, it borrowed $3.5 billion from the Federal Reserve System and arranged a $4.5 billion line of credit from several big commercial banks. Even that was not enough. In the end, the Federal Deposit Insurance Corporation (FDIC) paid Continental $2 billion in exchange for $3 billion of the bank's bad debts and assumed the $3.5 billion Federal Reserve loan. Thus one of the nation's top banks, with more than $28 billion in deposits, ran itself into bankruptcy and finally had to be saved by the federal government when the casino society got out of hand.[7]

That more banks have not followed Continental into bankruptcy is due only to the fact that the Federal Reserve Board has made it clear that it would come to the rescue of any large bank in trouble in order to avoid widespread financial panic. State governments—Maryland and Ohio were the first—have had to use their legislative powers to stabilize precariously leveraged private savings-and-loan associations.

The computerization of the financial sector, begun during the 1970s, has made finance capital increasingly "hypermobile." Fluctuations in stock and bond prices are now signalled instantly across the globe, putting further pressure on brokers and managers to act quickly. And the quicker they act, the quicker their actions lead to counteractions by competitors. Computers have thus greatly exacerbated the tendency which Hayes and Abernathy identified as central to America's economic decline: the shortening of American business planning horizons. The chickens came home to roost in the stock market crash of October 1987, which most experts think was exacerbated (if not actually caused) by a combination of huge sell-offs by a few major players such as

Fidelity Investments, the automatic triggering of computerized "sell" orders in one Wall Street and Chicago brokerage house after another, and the nearly instantaneous follow-the-leader behavior of the markets in Tokyo, Hong Kong, and London. This is one case where modern technology and high-speed information processing may have actually proven harmful.

As one economics newsletter put it:

> The casino society has an increasingly evident Achilles heel: the collective ability to execute financial transactions has far outpaced the ability to analyze creditworthiness. [Moreover,] the face-to-face relationship that traditionally bound borrower to lender is breaking down as local credit markets are subsumed into national ones. Credit standards inevitably are relaxed [at the point of sale] when lenders know they can easily transform loans into securities and pass them on to far-away investors.[8]

Merger Mania and Hostile Takeovers[9]

To comprehend just how explosive the growth in corporate mergers and acquisitions has been, it is necessary to put it in historical context. There were two great waves of merger in the twentieth century before the late 1970s: one around the year 1900 and another in the late 1960s. As mammoth as they were, they pale by comparison with either the number of mergers or the value of the acquisitions (adjusted for inflation) that occurred in the 1980s. Figure 3.2 shows that the value of mergers in 1985 alone was more than five times as great as in 1955 or, for that matter, in 1965 or 1975.

In fact, figure 3.2 actually *understates* the extent of the explosion, limited as it is to the acquisition of manufacturing and mining companies. Between 1983 and 1986 alone, some 12,200 companies and corporate divisions, worth almost a half-trillion dollars, changed hands. The merger-acquisition-takeover business amounted to nearly a fifth of the 1986 market value of all traded stocks.[10] Wall Street firms, led by Merrill Lynch, Drexel Burnham, Goldman Sachs, First Boston, and Salomon Brothers, earned hundreds of millions in commissions engi-

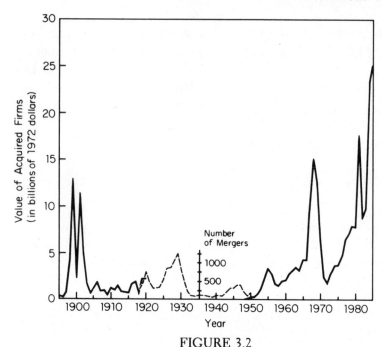

FIGURE 3.2

Constant-Dollar Volume of Manufacturing and Mineral Firm Acquisitions,
1895–1985

Sources F. M. Scherer, *Industrial Market Structure and Economic Performance,* 2d ed. (Houghton-Mifflin, 1980), p. 120; extended using data from the U.S. Federal Trade Commission and W. T. Grimm & Co. Data on the value of manufacturing and mineral company acquisitions are not available for the years 1921–47. The broken line reflects the number of acquisitions in those years. *From* David J. Ravenscraft and F.M. Scherer, *Mergers, Sell-Offs, and Economic Efficiency* (Washington, D.C.: Brookings Institution, 1987), 21.

neering these huge deals, and law firms earned profits of 33 to 73 percent for making sure that all of the i's were dotted and the t's crossed.

By no means are all takeovers hostile. But a large number do involve outright raids, with threats to reorganize production and shut down operations if the raiders are not paid "greenmail" to induce them to withdraw their bids. For this reason, the corporate raid exemplifies the interaction between the "merely financial" transactions in the casino society and the destruction of real productive capacity and jobs. Reorganizing to be more productive—to make one's business "more lean and mean"—is one thing. But what we have been witnessing since early 1983 is a radical shrinking (the experts call it "downsizing") of American manufacturing, often required in order to pay the cost of hostile takeovers.

The people at the Goodyear Tire and Rubber Co. understand this phenomenon only too well.[11] Early in November of 1986, British corporate raider Sir James Goldsmith bought nearly 12 percent of Goodyear's stock in one fell swoop. He then made an offer of $4.7 *billion* to Goodyear's other shareholders. If they had sold, Goldsmith would have become the controlling owner of the company. To prevent that from happening, Goodyear's managers raised $2.6 billion to buy back 41 percent of its outstanding stock (including the shares already owned by Goldsmith), as well as to pay all of the raider's legal and accounting expenses—another $37 million. Goldsmith ended up with a net profit of $90 million for a deal that never went through.

And where did Goodyear find the cash to pay such a huge bill within two weeks? By borrowing. And what did it have to promise its creditors in its restructuring plan? It put three subsidiaries up for sale; eliminated nearly four thousand jobs; reduced the budget for research and development, advertising, and promotion by $170 million each year; and reduced capital expenditures in plant and equipment by $275 million annually—all in order to provide enough cash to service the enormous debt forced upon it by the raider from London and by the laws of casino economics.

Nor does the fate that befell Goodyear (and its employees) even depend any longer on whether the takeover is officially hostile. According to Jim Mahoney, editor of the National Review of Corporate Acquisitions, "the idea that white knights are friendly rescuers is often wrong. . . . Many . . . are not only no better than the feared hostile raider, but sometimes worse." The problem, encountered in the last several years by the managers of such major acquisitions as CBS–TV, Safeway Stores, and John Blair & Co., is that the skyrocketing cost of financing a takeover forces even "friendly" acquirers to resort, sooner or later, to the same tactics as the corporate raider: selling off assets, cutting research and development, and laying off large numbers of employees.[12]

The managers of capital have become tremendously inventive, using ever more ingenious ways to move assets from owner to owner like chess pieces or checkers around a game board. Yet all too often, they still cannot find the *patience* to permit a fledgling company with a useful product to survive long enough in the stormy early days after incorporation to become stable. Thus, in 1987, Shearson Lehman's managing director, Roger Altman, added credence to Hayes' and Abernathy's original concern about the short-term planning of the typical U.S. venture capitalist. The current rule of thumb seems to be that any new investment should be "liquified"—what a marvelous term!—by offering shares in the company to the public or by finding an acquirer within three to five years.

The all-too-frequent consequence of such premature, impatient treatment is the sort of fate that befell Unimation, Inc., once the leading young manufacturer of robotics in America. In 1982, the company needed $30 to $40 million to expand, retool, and upgrade its line. When neither banks nor sources of venture capital were willing to become involved (remember that this is high-technology *robotics*, not basic steel or work shirts), Unimation sold out to Westinghouse to gain access to the desperately needed cash. The new parent was never very generous or patient with its new acquisition. As a result, in spite of the economic recovery of the 1980s, Unimation has quietly gone down the high-technology tubes.[13]

No one has written more eloquently of the costs of "merger mania" than Walter Adams, an economics professor at Michigan State University and perhaps the nation's most distinguished expert on industrial economics. He and James Brock, a professor of economics at Miami University of Ohio, concluded:

> Amidst the claims and counterclaims, we tend to lose sight of perhaps the most crucial aspect of merger mania—namely the "opportunity cost" of this dubious activity.
>
> Two decades of managerial energies devoted to playing the merger game are, at the same time, two decades during which management has been diverted from the critically important job of building new plants, bringing out new products, investing in new production techniques and creating jobs. The billions spent on shuffling paper ownership shares are, at the same time, billions not spent on productivity-enhancing investments.[14]

What is perhaps most ironic is that by commonly accepted accounting standards, a large fraction of big-time mergers simply do not work—not for the work force, the community, *or* the stockholder. One out of three acquisitions is later undone. And according to a recent report from the management-consulting firm of McKinsey & Co., twenty-eight of the fifty-eight mergers it studied failed to produce a return on the investment exceeding the actual cost of capital nor did they help the parent firm out-perform the competition in the stock market. An additional six mergers failed one of these tests. According to Frederick Scherer of Swarthmore College, the tendency by parent companies to treat acquired businesses as "cash cows" almost guarantees that the subsidiary "will at some point become a shadow of its former self."[15]

The casino society has certainly been responsible for producing billions of dollars in short-term profits. A whisper on Wall Street about an impending corporate raid is often sufficient to double a stock's price overnight (and, in a few cases, put inside traders behind bars). But in the long run, the bubble often bursts after the grandiose acquisition is made, leaving stockholders in the lurch. Meanwhile, in the pitched battle to fend off a hostile raid—or even in the aftermath of a successful one—corporate divisions are shut down and thousands of workers lose their jobs.

The substitution of speculation and merger activity for old-fashioned investment in real plant and equipment and in research and development has contributed to the creation of an entire new class of "industrial skidders"—mostly blue-collar workers who have seen their middle-class life-styles threatened by the continued erosion of basic manufacturing industries. After long periods of unemployment, these workers have often been forced to take jobs in the new service economy that pay substantially less than their old jobs and offer only limited fringe benefits. The government's own survey of displaced workers, carried out in January 1984, concluded that 11.5 million workers had lost their jobs because of plant closings or permanent employment cutbacks at their places of work between 1979 and 1984.[16] Those who had worked at least three years at their former jobs—those officially dubbed "displaced"—numbered 5.1 million.

Of course, not all of these lost their jobs because of mergers and acquisitions, and not all were in the production sector. But fully *half* of these workers lost manufacturing jobs, despite the fact that the total manufacturing labor force comprises less than 20 percent of the nation's work force. Of these, more than two-fifths were still unemployed in January 1984 or had left the labor force altogether. Another 11 percent had to settle for part-time jobs. Even those who found new full-time jobs lost out; 45 percent found that their new jobs paid less than their old ones.[17] Altogether, almost four out of five workers displaced from manufacturing jobs found themselves skidding into unemployment, skidding completely out of the labor force, or skidding down the wage scale. For these workers to hold on to a middle-class life style required that there be two or more workers in the family.

Pulling It All Together: The Greyhound Story

So far, from the discussion in this chapter and the last, it might still appear to some that corporate restructuring of a firm's labor force and financial restructuring of its balance sheet are two totally different developments in contemporary political economy. They are not. They are the two sides of the same coin.

Containing or reducing the cost of labor, union avoidance, and financial restructuring—all in the interest of gaining increased flexibility for management—come together in the fascinating story of one of the best-known names in American business: Greyhound.[18] This world-famous bus and passenger service company, founded in 1926, carried people from one place to another across the continent for more than sixty years, connecting the smallest towns with the largest metropolitan areas. Since 1937, its drivers, mechanics, and most of those working in its bus stations have been represented by what eventually became the Amalgamated Transit Union (ATU).

After a long strike in 1983, the drivers were forced to give back 15 percent of their wages and benefits as the price of re-employment by the company. Airline deregulation had brought into existence a bevy of small airlines, and these were forcing the company to become more cost-conscious than at any time in its history. Indeed, along with the concessions from its drivers, Greyhound announced that it was eliminating a number of routes serving many small towns on the ground that they had become unprofitable.

The original concessions were apparently not enough. In the fall of 1985, Greyhound's management demanded a re-opening of the contract, which still had more than a year to run. This time the concessions demanded by management included virtually every cost-cutting measure reported in chapter 2. Greyhound wanted to abolish, completely and permanently, cost-of-living-allowances for all employees. It demanded a freeze in the pay of everyone except the highly prized (and scarce) diesel-engine mechanics. Management argued for a free hand in hiring part-timers for jobs formerly filled by full-time workers, and the right to subcontract parts of its business from charters to outside firms. Its most dramatic proposal was to convert its terminals to commission agencies, to be operated by independent entrepreneurs who would work for sales commissions. Union members could continue to work in those terminals, but they would work for the wages, benefits, and under the work rules established by the new owners. They would no longer be members of the old ATU bargaining unit. Faced with a management seemingly able and willing to replace strikers with nonunion workers across the country, the ATU reluctantly agreed to almost all of these concessions.

And *still* there was more to come. On March 19, 1987, Greyhound announced that it was selling the company to Fred Currey, a Dallas-based entrepreneur who had been the former president of what was by then the moribund Trailways Bus Company, Greyhound's only national competitor on the highways. To circumvent the Federal Trade Commission's objections to the creation of such a near-monopoly in transportation, Currey used a legal loophole which allowed him to say that he was purchasing the *assets* of Greyhound but not the company itself. In fact, the new owner would pay a royalty to continue to use the famous Greyhound logo, whose ownership therefore legally remained in the hands of the sellers. The old employees were hired back by the "new" Greyhound, at wages which averaged only 50 to 60 percent of what they had originally been. This latest tactic for avoiding the legal rules of successorship—which otherwise would force the new owners to honor existing contracts—enabled Currey to demand an additional round of concessions from the weary transit workers union.[19]

Finally, in the middle of 1987, the current wave of merger mania entered the picture in a most unexpected and remarkable way. The "new" Greyhound corporation announced that it was acquiring what was left of Trailways! There would now be only *one* national passenger carrier on the nation's highways—a total monopoly. Bus drivers could now work for this company or for none at all. In less than four years, an entire industry was reorganized through financial dealings on the one hand and internal cost-cutting on the other. During this entire period, Greyhound was also following the precedent set by many other leading corporations, from U.S. Steel to General Electric, by shifting more and more of its assets into unrelated ventures. Thus, during the 1980s, the nation's premier bus company became the owner of Dial soap, Ellio's frozen pizza, Brillo pads, hotels in Montana's Glacier National Park, a money-order business, and a cruise line.[20]

Urban Revitalization: Refurbishing a Home for High Finance

The Greyhound story enables us to see the connection between the seemingly disparate "real" and "financial" business activity in the post-industrial era. Yet another development brings this interconnection into still sharper focus, enriching our understanding of the revolutionary consequences of the corporate restructuring now under way. It is the phenomenon of urban "revitalization."

Surely one of the most dramatic developments of the last decade has been the wave of downtown redevelopment projects, typically characterized as signifying the revitalization of the nation's cities. Signs of prosperity seem to be popping up in one urban area after another. Just as conservatives point with pride to the record number of new jobs in the United States since the early 1970s as a sign of the economy's basic health, so planners, policymakers and the mass media celebrate the new generation of downtown office buildings, hotels, and convention centers as indicators of economic vitality.

At its core, however, much of the urban revitalization phenomenon is really only one more aspect of the casino society—with all the associated problems of inflated values, the proliferation of risk, and the substitution of short-run "deal making" for productive long-term investment. Moreover, the mix of jobs and working conditions being created in the process of urban revitalization only exacerbates the tendency toward social and economic polarization in the United States.

The boom and then collapse of commercial real-estate values in cities like Denver and Houston are striking evidence of speculative frenzy at its worst. Taking advantage of the tax advantages of investment in real estate, developers transformed the skylines of these cities by erecting new high-rise office towers one after another, on every downtown street corner. As oil prices rose and high-technology firms expanded, rents spiraled from $10 per square foot to $15 and then to $20 and more. Like all speculative bubbles, this one burst. When oil became over-abundant in 1986 and petroleum prices plummeted, vacancy rates soared. In an unusual auction of office space held in Denver, space in a brand-new office was leased at fire-sale prices—as low, at least in one case, as fifty cents a square foot.

The first theorist to realize how the activities associated with speculation and the financial community would alter the urban landscape was Stephen Hymer, a young economist trained at M.I.T. who was teaching at the New School for Social Research in New York City and who died tragically in 1974. Hymer was original and inventive in making sense of a paradox in contemporary capitalism: the simultaneous tendencies toward *decentralization* of production (globalization) combined with *recentralization* of control and co-ordination. It is these two functions—co-ordination and control—that best describe the principal day-to-day activities taking place in the office towers of the new global capitalist system.

In a series of sketchy but brilliantly imaginative books and papers, Hymer set forth a view that today is almost taken for granted.[21] The internationalization of production, he predicted, would encourage multinational corporations to separate their various functions and locate them in different places. Thus, assembly would increasingly occur within the low-wage labor markets of the Third World. Distribution would be handled regionally, as would some aspects of finance. At the pinnacle of this new hierarchical system would be the huge home offices of the corporations. These would tend to be concentrated in the very largest central cities of their home countries. Thus, a new spatial restructuring of labor *within* the multinational company was coming into existence.[22] Hymer saw that this would be one of the driving

TABLE 3.1

*Rate of Growth of Investment in Nonresidential
Structures: 1979–84 (1979 = 100)*

Type of Construction	1979	1984
Hotels, motels	100	160.6
Commercial buildings	100	153.0
Oil and gas distribution plants	100	138.3
Health, education, and nonprofit buildings	100	135.5
Public utilities	100	96.3
Industrial buildings	100	73.8
Agricultural buildings	100	43.3
Total private nonresidential construction	100	115.7

SOURCE: "Review of the Month," *Monthly Review,* October 1985, 7.

forces behind a restructuring of the entire international division of labor.*

In the cities housing these corporate headquarters, Hymer expected that the office buildings of the multinational corporations themselves would come to be surrounded by a dense pattern of other high-rise buildings to house their most important suppliers of services—legal, advertising, foreign relations, accounting, and computer programming. Even though manufacturing per se would be on the decline in these large cities, the same principle of "agglomeration" that had character-ized the great production centers of the past would become the main organizing principle underlying the spatial structure of the new world cities.[23]

One simple indication of how the landscape is changing is provided by data on new investment in buildings across the country. Table 3.1 shows the dramatic shift from agriculture, industry, and public utilities to the structures required to house offices and the hotels and motels that serve the business community.[24] In the boom year of 1984, the value of new industrial buildings being constructed was less than three-

---

*Many of Hymer's critics point out that in fact the majority of transnational corporate assembly jobs are still located within the *developed* capitalist countries. To a great extent, it is the relatively lower-wage (but still built-up) peripheral regions within Europe, Canada, and Australia that are gaining much of the new work. Much low-wage "informal" production is also to be found in the alleys and tenements of the largest "world cities." In a moment, we will examine Saskia Sassen's attempt to reconcile these seemingly contradictory aspects of modern urban growth. For now, suffice it to say that we believe these developments to be broadly consistent with Hymer's original hypothesis, after taking into account such factors (admittedly ignored by him) as tariff barriers, local-content requirements, laws and practices concerning immigration, and other public policies.

fourths of that in 1979. Instead, there was more than half again as much investment in commercial buildings in 1984 as in 1979. The rate of increase in hotels was even greater. One merely had to travel downtown to marvel at what appeared to be a new and more vibrant America literally rising from the ground.

Jobs in the New Urban Service Economy

The revitalization of downtown did create millions of new jobs nationwide. The high-profile jobs being created within the revitalized urban centers are overwhelmingly connected directly to the restructured economy. These are jobs devoted largely to co-ordination, marketing, and central management—jobs for information brokers, secretaries, computer programmers, and legal and financial specialists. The central headquarters of multinational corporations and international banks, together with their bevy of accounting, legal, and consultant services, fill towering downtown office structures in a growing number of cities. At the same time, inside and around the office towers—in the hotels, restaurants, taverns, and health spas—millions of new workers serve as chambermaids and waiters, bartenders and janitors. Just listing the occupations suggests that a polarized society is being created within the very capitals of high finance.

Among the scholars paying attention to this matter, two have been especially important. Both are associated with Columbia University. Thierry Noyelle has done more than anyone else to measure the magnitude of the growth of urban services, while Saskia Sassen has conducted the richest and most insightful analysis of the emerging dual class structure in the revitalized American city.[25] In their view, the upper tier of the labor market includes the managers, lawyers, accountants, bankers, business consultants, and other technically trained people whose daily duties lie at the heart of the control and co-ordination of the global corporation and the corporate services that are closely linked to them. Professionals in health and education are also part of this new upper tier.

At the bottom of the labor market is the other, less fortunate pool of urban residents whose collective function is to provide services to the workers in the upper tier. They are the ones who wait tables, cook meals, sell everything from office supplies to clothing, change bed and bath linen in the dozens of new hotels, provide custodial service and child care, and find lower-level employment in the city's hospitals, health clinics, schools, and municipal government itself. The high cost of living in cities containing corporate headquarters requires that professional households include more than one wage earner in order to sustain a middle-class life style. This, in turn, forces this new labor aristocracy to consume more and more of the services that workers in an earlier generation would have produced for themselves. The provision of these services to the office workers becomes *the* major economic activity for the rest of the city.

Within this new labor market, there is a continuing racial and gender division as well. The jobs at the top are held disproportionately by white Americans, with men continuing to dominate the top positions. Workers of color, women, and a growing mass of immigrants (especially from Latin America and Southeast Asia) fill the bulk of the positions at the bottom of what some have termed the "hourglass economy"—an economy with a shrinking middle.[26] Thus, cities housing corporate headquarters increasingly resemble New York City, with its desperately poor South Bronx, its gentrified Upper West Side, and—with manufacturing activity continuing to move away—a shrinking middle layer of traditional workers in between.*

For the U.S. economy as a whole, the official statistics confirm the broad outlines of the occupational analysis that lies at the heart of Noyelle and Sassen's arguments about the cities. According to the U.S. Bureau of Labor Statistics (BLS), between 1984 and 1995 the ten

---

*Where urban manufacturing *has* revived, to fill the needs of the service firms in the office towers or to take advantage of the new waves of immigrants who are still available at very low wages, Sassen and others have shown that workers in urban manufacturing, too, tend to be polarized into highly competitive, poorly regulated, low-wage occupations such as garment-making on the one hand, and high-wage craft work such as printing and metalworking on the other.

The construction trades are a continuing anomaly in any such taxonomy. As we demonstrated earlier, the construction industry has received an enormous shot in the arm from the activities of the casino society in general, and especially from the urban revitalization that was necessary to prepare a new environment for the players. Construction workers are the quintessential new American middle class, at least by the measure of average income, suburban life style, and aspirations for their children. Yet once a new environment is substantially built, the long-term unemployment rate of these workers typically rises far above the national average and remains there until another new round of growth occurs.

occupations that will require the largest number of new workers (in order) are:

- cashier
- registered nurse
- janitor
- truck driver
- waiter and waitress
- wholesale trade salesworker
- nurses aides and orderlies
- retail salespersons
- accountants and auditors
- kindergarten and elementary school teachers

Workers in six of the ten categories earned well below the average weekly wage of $344 in 1984, while the second, sixth, and ninth earned well above it.[27] Lawrence Chimerine, formerly the chief economist of Chase Econometrics, is one who worries about these numbers and their implications. "More and more workers are being channeled into low-wage occupations. . . . As the shift is made to services, we can expect it to put pressure on living standards." One might add that the limited income-generating power of the service occupations could in turn constitute a serious drag on the long-term economic growth that ultimately affects everyone.[28]

The BLS's figures report on the *mass* of new jobs being created. Yet we all have images of which kinds of jobs are growing most rapidly, even if there are in fact not that many of them. It is these fastest-*growing* occupations to which critics of Noyelle's and Sassen's thesis point. It is true, as Neal Rosenthal, chief of the Occupational Outlook Division of the BLS, argues, that the fastest-*growing* occupations are computer-service technicians, legal assistants, computer systems analysts and programmers, and electrical engineers.[29] As percentages, the growth looks impressive. But closer inspection of the BLS's data show that these occupations are growing from a small base, and that they will not employ very many people. Between 1986 and the year 2000, the BLS predicts, there will be openings for 64,000 new paralegal personnel, 56,000 data-processing equipment repairers, 24,000 peripheral data-processing equipment operators, and a quarter-of-a-million computer systems analysts. But these numbers pale beside the *absolute* growth in the ranks of waiters and waitresses, chambermaids and doormen, department store clerks and building custodians. By the turn of this century there will be nearly 2.5 million new workers in restaurants, bars, and fast-food outlets, more than half a million new employees in hotels and motels, and almost 400,000 additional workers in department stores. An overwhelming proportion of all of *these* jobs will be part-time and will pay extremely low wages.[30] Thus the reality of the new service economy entails a great many low-paying jobs and a much smaller layer of high-paying ones.

The statistics just presented cover the U.S. economy as a whole. What about urban areas in particular—the places for which these new theories of the polarizing labor market were initially constructed? A recent econometric analysis of the relationship among industrial structure, low wages, and the incidence of year-round versus intermittent employment among the nation's hundred largest metropolitan areas sheds new light on these questions.[31] At Illinois State University, Robert Sheets and his colleagues measured the incidence and causes of low-wage employment in these urban areas. Workers might receive low annual wages mainly because they earned low hourly wages or because they worked only intermittently over the course of the year. Studying data for 1980, Sheets found that in the urban areas with the highest concentration of business services—the "control centers" of Hymer's thesis—underemployment was more likely to take the form of *full-time, year-round, low-wage work* than of low annual earnings attributable to the intermittent nature of the work. In cities where high-level services were less important than retail trade and consumer services, the opposite was found to be more common. Workers earned low annual wages because the personal services jobs they could find offered only part-time or seasonal employment.

The authors also confirmed the existence of pronounced racial and gender inequalities within the service sectors of these hundred largest cities. White men earned considerably more than any other group, *especially* in the advanced corporate and retail services. The racial difference was even more pronounced among *young* men: in 1980, whites earned an average of 12 percent more than black or Hispanic youth of equivalent skill and experience. As for gender divisions, the rapid expansion of service industries has been a double-edged sword for most women:

> Although service industries have provided new employment and earnings opportunities and have contributed substantially to the rapid increase in female labor force participation, they have also channeled most women into low-wage, female-typed jobs leading to substantial labor market hardships, especially for single mothers. . . . [Even] after controlling for a variety of other possible explanatory factors (in particular, human capital characteristics), advanced corporate and retail service industries were found to have a strong effect on total female underemployment.[32]

These trends toward polarization in the job markets of the country's big cities were made dramatically manifest in a set of predictions drawn up for the city of Boston by the local redevelopment agency. In Boston—the city known above all in the country for high technology, its major universities with their sophisticated computer programmers, and its world-famous hospital system—the number-one growth occupation is *building custodian,* which currently pays about $236 a week. Between 1985 and 1990, the city's office employers are expected to create more than 14,000 new jobs for secretaries and clerks, but fewer than 4,500 new jobs for computer programmers and systems analysts. Altogether, of the ten occupations expected to provide the most new employment, workers in five currently earn wages which would leave a person supporting a family of four well below the poverty line, even if he or she worked year-round, full-time. Taken together with the growing demand for managers and technical professionals, we see once again the tendency toward polarization, even in the "Athens of America."[33]

Corporate Restructuring and the Explosion of the Service Sector: A Reassessment

Many observers and researchers have connected the explosive growth of the service sector, including high finance, primarily with demographic and income trends. Thus, for example, we are often reminded of the tremendous increase in the number of working women. The growth in the number of two-earner couples and working single parents has forced many families to buy services that they formerly produced by themselves at home when they had more time. Others attribute the growth of the service industries, led by the financial sector, to increases in discretionary incomes. In other words, mainstream explanations of service sector growth tend to be grounded in stories about *consumption*.

What these observations miss is the fact that *the boom in services has grown organically from the restructuring activities of American corporations*, particularly those which once made up the manufacturing base of the nation. The roots of the casino society are precisely the same as those that led to multinational investment, outsourcing, and hollowing. They are all aspects of the response of corporations to the profit squeeze of the 1970s.

Richard Walker, an economic geographer at the University of California, has written a brilliant paper which delineates this connection between services and the goods-producing sector of the economy.[34] Walker's central argument is that the growth of services constitutes not so much a fundamental transformation of what capitalism produces as much as a manifestation of how it does it. "Indirect labor" is becoming increasingly weighty vis-à-vis "hands-on" labor in the production of commodities. As technology becomes more complex, as actual production is spread across far-flung locations, as businesses need to tend to their relations with more and more governments around the world, and as the labor force of multinational corporations must be co-ordinated and controlled over greater distances, legions of supervisors, machine and building repairers, and paper shufflers become an ever larger part of day-to-day business. The objective of private capital is still the same—to make commodities which can be sold to customers at a profit—but the playing field has grown very much larger, as has the number of players interposed between the producer and the ultimate customer. It is not so much that we are a post-industrial society as that we have become a far more complex industrial society.

To be sure, the new industrial structure has created millions of new opportunities for employment in the burgeoning service economy, in its center in high finance and in its subsidiary industries. Unfortunately, as we have noted, these jobs provide a very different array of opportunities than were offered in the old labor market. The new environment is more polarized, consisting more of high-wage professional jobs at one extreme and low-wage menial employment at the other. And on average the new jobs pay considerably less.

Writing about the growth of contingent workers, one important segment of the new economy, Jeffrey Pfeffer and James Baron hazard a guess at the implications of these developments for the distribution of income:

> The increasing separation of the work-force into primary and secondary workers may increase wage inequality, as workers who are considered to be more essential to the firm will tend to be paid more, while those used as buffers will have less market power and obtain lower wages. . . . We suspect [this] inequality may be based increasingly on hours worked and the stability of employment, the dimensions which [most] distinguish core and buffer employees.[35]

Whether Pfeffer and Baron are right or wrong about the precise mechanisms at work in the new labor market, there is no question that the overall restructuring of corporate America is having a profound effect on the distribution of wages and on family living standards. As we shall show in chapter 5, the restructuring has proceeded far enough that the broad outlines of a sharply more polarized society can already be discerned. What is more, after five years of continuous economic expansion since the recession of 1981–82, the trend toward inequality continues—despite the fact that in the past, buoyant economic times were always associated with less inequality, not more. To put it bluntly, the combined forces of real and financial corporate restructuring have been so powerful as to virtually nullify the traditional "equity dividend" that we had come to expect from economic growth.

4

The Laissez-Faire Affair

THE GREAT U-TURN in corporate strategies, though jury-rigged, was designed with a single purpose in mind: to restore short-term profits by regaining control over an increasingly competitive environment. But these radical "innovations" in the allocation of capital and in the management of workers could not take place in the absence of a supportive public policy. Business leaders needed the help of the government. By the time Jimmy Carter moved into the White House, the federal government was ready to help, but it did not quite know how. Over the next decade, it learned. With deregulation and corporate tax cuts, tight money and military spending, Washington tacitly underwrote—and then increasingly lent active support to—most of the restructuring efforts that took place within American enterprise. In the process, government policy took a great U-turn itself.

As early as 1971, the abrogation of the international Bretton Woods agreement and the half-hearted imposition of wage-and-price controls confirmed what many already believed. The standard liberal approach to managing the economy, based solely on Keynesian "demand-side" policies, was no longer able to cope with the emerging phenomenon of stagflation—unemployment co-existing with inflation. Hence, from at least the mid-point of the Nixon presidency to President Reagan's election in 1980, the answers to how public policy could deal with the crises of heightened global competition, the profit squeeze, and stag-nating productivity were highly contested.

In one camp were advocates of the classical conservative approach which entailed monetarism, suppression of wages through maintenance of a large supply of labor, and constraints on the political power of unions and their social-democratic allies.* In a far-distant camp was an unusual coalition of trade unionists, a small cadre of chief executive officers in the manufacturing sector, assorted academics, and a number of renegade financial consultants who argued for modest planning—this time, under the rubric of "industrial policy." This group sought a formula by which central government, the leading corporations, and the largest unions might somehow negotiate a set of production policies that could contribute to higher productivity and enhanced competi-tiveness. Into the fray came a third force as well. A tiny band of non-monetarist conservatives were advocating a unique brand of "sup-ply-side" economics consisting primarily of deep tax cuts and the pri-vatization of as many public functions and institutions as possible.

By election day 1984, the ideological contest was over. A combina-tion of old- and new-style conservatives had succeeded in capturing the ideological high ground well beyond the wildest dreams of the theoreti-cians who had managed Reagan's electoral victories in 1980 and again in 1984. The long post–World War II expansion of social spending and market regulation—the legacies of the New Deal and its offspring—was arrested, along with any pretense of industrial policy or public planning. Laissez-faire was back in fashion, having lain dormant since the days of Herbert Hoover.

To begin with, the federal government deliberately engineered two deep recessions—in 1980 and then again in 1981–82—through a com-bination of tight monetary policy and cuts in social programs, including

---

*Monetarists argue that the supply and demand for money are the key determinants of national income, output, and prices. When productive capacity exceeds actual output, an increase in the money supply will necessarily increase the GNP. However, if there is anywhere near full employment, any increase in the money supply beyond the normal rate of growth of the economy must necessarily be inflationary. Strict monetarists like Prof. Milton Friedman argue that the monetary authorities—in the United States, the Federal Reserve system—should therefore be required to constrain the rate of the growth of money to the long-term growth rate of the economy, regardless of the level of unemployment. Thus, the money supply would act as an anchor, keeping inflation under control. During periods of slow growth, however, the firmly planted monetary anchor tends to drag the economic ship under water, exacerbating unemploy-ment.

such entitlements as unemployment insurance, Social Security benefits, farm subsidies, food stamps, and welfare assistance. This served to force more people into the labor market and created so much unemployment that workers, both unionized and ununionized, had little leverage with which to demand higher wages or job benefits, and often—in an attempt simply to save their jobs—were forced to agree to major concessions demanded by their employers.

A second way in which government policy supported private restructuring was by widespread deregulation. It was aimed, ostensibly, at reducing or eliminating the wide spectrum of government rules that were said to be responsible for undermining the private incentive to invest. Deregulation was intended to work something like a smallpox vaccination. Forcing business to accept a light dose of domestic rivalry, it was hoped, would protect the entire economy from a more virulent case of global competition. In practice, deregulation worked primarily by forcing firms into a bout of intense competition to lower costs. This in turn induced a frenzy of revisions of wages and work rules, effectively throwing workers in different industries and even in different plants within the same company into direct competition. The Greyhound-Trailways story was a dramatic example of this scenario.

The most extreme form of deregulation consisted of a wave of "privatizations." Services which had formerly been provided directly by public employees—from rail transportation to the dissemination of publicly acquired data on everything from crops to the health of the population—were turned over to private businesses. The managers of the private companies acquiring these public assets then proceeded to follow one or another restructuring strategy, from wage cutting and the increasing use of contingent labor to financial mergers and acquisitions.

Especially after the inauguration of President Ronald Reagan in 1981, the government itself conducted both explicit and implicit attacks on unions—and indeed on the very principle of unionization. The public was increasingly told that unions were responsible for pricing American goods out of world competition and for resisting new technology and new ways of organizing work, even in the government's own offices.

It all came down to a revival of the country's periodic romance with the doctrine of laissez-faire. The theory that leaving commercial markets to function with minimal "interference" from government—in

production, location, environmental, and labor-management decisions—was once again being used ideologically to underpin policies
designed first and foremost to restore the rate of profit. As it turned
out, profits were restored during the 1980s, but not by unleashing
productivity or the capacity to produce useful goods and services.
Instead, the great U-turn toward laissez-faire in public policy ended up
boosting corporate earnings by simply freezing the standard of living
of American workers and their families.

All of these developments have historical antecedents in the long-
term debate over the proper role of government in a capitalist economy. Scholars call this the debate over "planning versus the market."
The recent ideological struggle between the advocates of industrial
policy and the conservative ideologues who crafted the Reagan presidency is merely the latest episode in an age-old controversy—one that
has seen laissez-faire boosted and then rejected time and time again.

The American Experience with Economic Planning [1]

During much of the twentieth century, there have been powerful
advocates for greater governmental involvement in the economy, and
there have been extended periods during which their plans have actually been put into practice. This was especially true during World War
I, the Great Depression, World War II, and again during the late
1960s. Such advocates have hardly been limited to trade union leaders
and socialists. Elders of the business community have often been in the
forefront of the movement. Against this backdrop, the policies in-
stituted since the middle of the Carter presidency and throughout the
Reagan administration were an important reversal of public policy. We
can trace this history back to at least 1914.

At the outset of the American mobilization for World War I, the
administration of President Woodrow Wilson moved quickly to inject
government planning into the economic process. It began by creating
no fewer than five thousand agencies staffed by "dollar-a-year men,"
primarily on paid leave from large corporations.[2] These agencies were
in charge of diverting resources from production for domestic con-

sumption to production for war. After much experimentation, Wilson placed responsibility for production in the War Industries Board (WIB), under the direction of Bernard Baruch, who had amassed a large fortune in stock-market speculation and "creative investment." Baruch, who was also called upon later by President Franklin Delano Roosevelt to help plan the government's response to the Great Depression, viewed his function as a conciliator among powerful organizations, particularly the large corporations. The WIB held ultimate authority over production and had the power to seize and operate plants when industry refused to cooperate. At the height of its power in late 1918, the Board and its associated business organizations directed seventy-three industries with seven thousand plants. With the approval of Congress, Wilson nationalized the railroad industry in December 1917. The following summer, the federal government took over the telephone and telegraph systems and placed them under the direction of the postmaster general. The agricultural sector was also under government mandate during the war. The Food Administration, headed by Herbert Hoover, bought and sold all foodstuffs for the Allies and achieved record wheat, hog, and sugar production by guaranteeing minimum prices to farmers. What we know in retrospect is that, by almost every conceivable standard, planning worked during World War I.[3]

The planning during the war taught some industrialists an enduring lesson, generating within part of the business community a new enthusiasm for similar measures in peacetime. As economic historians Harry Scheiber, Harold Vatter, and Harold Faulkner wrote:

> Many leading industrialists who had been closely associated with the WIB and its coordinating industry committees thus endorsed the idea of continuing government involvement after the armistice, to ensure against a return to "destructive" competition, to set a floor on prices, and to perpetuate the involvement of government in maintaining stability in labor relations.[4]

This continuing enthusiasm for government intervention was not shared by the majority of business leaders, however, and during the 1920s the nation witnessed an almost total withdrawal of the government from interference with the prerogatives of private industry.[5] The new laissez-faire was codified in the policies of presidents Harding,

Coolidge, and Hoover. Until late 1929, the unfettered market seemed a smashing success—at least for those who could afford to speculate in the stock market.

The Great Depression brought planning back. Between 1929 and 1933, the gross national product (GNP) fell from $104 billion to $56 billion; annual per capita income (after taxes) fell nearly in half, from $678 to $360, and unemployment rose from 1.5 million to 12.8 million—25 percent of the labor force.[6] It was not difficult to see that the American economy had become technically and organizationally capable of producing more than its customers were able to buy, but incapable of putting the unemployed back to work to increase total demand. Business only dimly understood that while some small firms could cut wages to reduce costs and therefore prices, *all* small firms could not simultaneously do so without destroying the consumer's ability to buy and so worsen the crisis. Moreover, even a single oligopolist—a Ford Motor Company, a U.S. Steel, a General Electric, or a New Haven Railroad— could not indiscriminately cut wages and employment without eroding its own markets. After four years of falling prices and plummeting profits, the *consequences* of unregulated capitalist competition were everywhere apparent. The backbone of conservative economic thought, Say's Law, had been broken. Supply was not creating its own demand; instead, cuts in wages led to cuts in demand that led to further unemployment and further contraction of the economy. The deflationary spiral was out of control by 1931.

In this setting, it was again the largest companies that took the lead in searching for a solution in a new round of "corporatist" policy. Key business leaders viewed state participation in the economy as good public relations and envisioned the government as a mediator of labor disputes and "a kind of benevolent uncle entrepreneurs could turn to for guidance and material assistance in hard times."[7] The best-known proposal for corporatism as public policy was formulated by Owen D. Young, chair of the board of RCA, and made public, with some modifications, by Gerard Swope, the president of General Electric, in a speech before the National Electrical Manufacturers Association in September 1931.[8] In his speech, Swope advanced the idea that "production and consumption should be coordinated . . . preferably by the joint participation and joint administration of management and employees."[9] In each industry, all companies that employed fifty or more workers should be grouped into trade associations supervised by a federal trade commission. The associations would have the power to regulate output, fix prices, and otherwise organize the activities of the member companies.

The Swope plan included life insurance, pensions, and unemployment insurance for workers, paid for in part by employers. As historian Eric F. Goldman has written, "The depression of 1929, by presenting free enterprise in its most chaotic and inhumane form, brought an onrush of converts to the general idea of national planning of national economic units."[10] Even the U.S. Chamber of Commerce, which represented small business owners and retailers, endorsed what the new president, Franklin Delano Roosevelt, termed "the philosophy of the planned economy." The Chamber's document said that freedom of individual action which might have been justified in the simple life of the past century "cannot be tolerated today," for the unwise action of a single individual might adversely affect the lives of thousands.[11]

The first products of a new round of experimentation with public sector planning were the Agricultural Adjustment Act (AAA) and the National Recovery Act (NRA) codes, developed by business executives and government officials. The "Triple A" and NRA codes, first adopted in the spring of 1933, were attempts to fix wages and prices, and to set out guidelines for both the expansion and contraction of agricultural and industrial capacity. Bernard Baruch's assistant on the WIB during World War I, George Peek, was named by President Roosevelt to head up the Triple A, while another of Baruch's protégés, Hugh Johnson, was made the top official of the NRA.[12]

Ultimately, the detailed pricing and production codes set by the NRA came under attack from liberals and conservatives alike. Trying to produce 546 industrial codes in less than a year's time proved to be an enormous mistake.[13] The NRA codes were ultimately declared unconstitutional by the Supreme Court in May 1935 in the famous Schechter Poultry case. However, much of their spirit survived, to become embedded in newly established regulatory commissions, the Wagner Act, the minimum-wage laws, and other elements of the New Deal. The Federal Communications Commission was created in 1934 along with the Federal Trade Commission and the Securities and Exchange Commission. In the following three years, the National Labor Relations Board, the Federal Maritime Commission, and the

Civil Aeronautics Board were established by Congress.[14] These agencies were all empowered to limit market competition when it was destructive, regulate financial transactions when they threatened economic stability, and provide for the orderly development of industry and labor relations. They represented a continuation of the trend toward a "mixed economy" in which government played a crucial role in national, commercial, and regional policy.

While the New Deal agencies indelibly transformed the regulatory role of the federal government by the end of the 1930s, the involvement of the public sector in the economy was still nothing compared to the planning that occurred after Pearl Harbor. During World War II, the economy was virtually run by Washington.

In the war-planning regime that emerged, the government played a central role in procurement, in setting and monitoring wages and prices, and in establishing cartels and cost-plus contracts for large companies. Behind all of these programs one could spot the central influence of pro-planning corporate leaders, organized into a new interest group called the Business Council. By 1943, all of the various War Production Boards (WPBs) were run entirely by corporate executives affiliated with the Business Council or their appointees. The head of the key WPB was Donald Nelson, a top executive with Sears, Roebuck.[15]

The end of World War II did not automatically evoke a demand that government resume a smaller role in the economy. Even before the end of the war, the leading economists in the country, a large contingent of the business community, senior officials within the administration, and President Roosevelt himself feared that the end of hostilities and a restoration of unregulated market arrangements would bring back the Depression.[16] In his State of the Union message in 1944, the president called for an Economic Bill of Rights, intended to pave the ideological way for a more active postwar government commitment to full employment, which, it was well understood, would require continued planning. Among the rights to be guaranteed were the "right to a useful and remunerative job"; "the right to earn enough to provide adequate food and clothing and recreation"; and the right of every family to a decent home, to adequate medical care, a good education, and protection from the economic fears of old age, sickness, accident, and unemployment.[17] It was a progressive agenda based on the experience of New Deal social programs and World War II economic planning.

The conventional wisdom is that business departed en masse from Roosevelt's agenda when it discovered that the unique international position of the United States after 1945 offered seemingly limitless opportunities for profitable growth, without any sort of government planning. In fact, government activities had played a major role in producing that unique environment. The Bretton Woods agreement, hammered out by top government officials in 1944, established a postwar international economic regime that unabashedly promoted U.S. investment abroad. The Marshall Plan provided $13 billion in loans and grants to our European trading partners, 70 percent of which came back to U.S. firms in the form of payments for exports.[18] And then, the nation embarked on what turned out to be an extremely expensive Cold War that created a "military-industrial complex" beyond anything imaginable before the war.[19]

Domestic legislation also cemented the government's role in the postwar economy. While Roosevelt's Economic Bill of Rights was never codified in the Constitution, the Congress did pass the Employment Act of 1946. This historic Act committed the government to pursue, as a goal, "maximum feasible" employment and created two government agencies to oversee that quest. The Council of Economic Advisers was established to keep the president informed of economic trends and political choices. The Joint Economic Committee was launched within the Congress to advise legislators on these same matters and to review economic initiatives in the executive branch.[20] Essentially, the Act reaffirmed a role for the federal government in *aggregate* (or macroeconomic) policy, although by its conspicuous absence of formal language it failed to institutionalize any of the *sectoral* (or microeconomic) planning mechanisms that had been the mainstay of both New Deal and World War II policy.

With the government more or less committed to a fiscal and monetary policy aimed at balancing employment and inflation, business was now prepared to negotiate a new social contract with labor. The major goals were to forestall the risk of chronic overproduction and to maintain wartime rates of profit. The key ingredient in the system—at least for the most profitable of the manufacturing industries—was what in the auto sector was called the "annual improvement factor," the tying of wage increases to advances in productivity so that profits would be guaranteed and yet workers would have sufficient purchasing power to keep the economy on an even keel. Relations between capital and labor became increasingly bureaucratized and more "orderly." The modern institutions of job ladders for promotion from within, internal labor markets, formal grievance and arbitration procedures, and the other accoutrements of what has been called the "Fordist" system of economic regulation—all of which had been the subject of scattered experiments since the 1920s—were now institutionalized as a *substitute* for more direct forms of planning.[21]

Once more, as in the period following World War I, the subject of planning per se went into hiding, this time until the late 1960s and early 1970s.* By this time, organizations such as the Committee for Economic Development and the Business Roundtable—direct descendents of the pro-planning World War II Business Council—had been captured by business leaders who were deeply opposed to virtually any kind of planning, on purely ideological grounds. The thrust of their laissez-faire approach lasted but briefly, however, broken by the simultaneous rise in unemployment and inflation in 1970–71 and the first trade deficit in merchandise since the end of the nineteenth century. President Richard Nixon, facing re-election in a year, decided on direct across-the-board wage-and-price controls to deal with the specter of an economy unable to avoid stagflation.

While this experiment in government intervention ultimately failed by all accounts, the ideological pendulum did not swing back to pure laissez-faire. As the nature of the emerging global economic crisis became ever more apparent and ominous during the rest of the decade, the Democratic administration of Jimmy Carter did attempt some forms of industrial planning to try to stem the tide of economic disaster. President Carter's White House initiated a classically tripartite effort to negotiate a restructuring program—what the Europeans call a "recession cartel"—for the steel industry. It involved government incentives and protective tariffs in return for some contraction of older

*This is not to say that the Kennedy-Johnson years did not involve public regulation of, and intervention into, private markets. Far from it. But that intervention was of a very different order than what we have been discussing. "Post–New Deal Liberal" economics combined the most modest Keynesian macroeconomic management with a pot-pourri of ad hoc redistributional programs. The planning of investment and productive capacity was never an important part of the "policy mix" of the 1960s.

plant capacity and company pledges to reinvest in more modern facilities. The government also negotiated a textile agreement to protect the domestic industry from surges in imports, and it managed the famous bail-out of the Chrysler Corporation, using government loans to save that company from certain bankruptcy.[22] Labor fought for and won supplements to unemployment compensation for workers whose displacement could reasonably be traced to foreign economic competition.

Unfortunately for those who placed their faith in such an industrial policy, the worsening of the economy—inflation kept growing, along with unemployment—served to strengthen the position of those within the administration who opposed not only planning of investments but even the early idealistic attempts by President Carter to promote social programs of the type advanced by presidents Roosevelt, Kennedy, and Johnson. Another brief experiment with modest planning thus came to an end. In its place, national policy swung back to macroeconomics. The Great U-Turn in public policy was about to commence.[23]

The Democratic Administration's U-Turn

Contrary to conventional wisdom, the reversal in the direction of national economic policy and the new tentative efforts by government to underwrite the private restructuring strategies of American corporations began *before* the election of Ronald Reagan. President Carter, the White House, Congress, and the Federal Reserve Board all shifted policy so as to promote greater austerity in the public sector and to limit the federal role in a range of industries. They were initially motivated by the dread of inflation.

Indeed, by the end of 1978, the rate of inflation was rising into double digits. The proximate causes were the constraints on natural resources (especially OPEC's oil-pricing policies), the efforts of workers to protect their standards of living against higher prices, and continued efforts by corporate managers to pass all increases in costs along to the consumer in the form of higher prices. With a price-wage spiral threatening to break out of bounds, the newly appointed chair of the Federal

Reserve Board (the Fed), Paul Volcker, called for an all-out war on inflation. The Fed took the lead by suddenly and drastically reducing the growth in the nation's money supply. This tight money policy, which continued essentially unchanged for the next five years, submerged the economy in a "cold bath," to use the graphic term of Bowles, Gordon, and Weisskopf.[24]

To augment the forces fighting inflation, President Carter and a Democratic Congress sharply slowed the growth of federal expenditures. In controlling the effect of rising inflation and interest rates on the real size of the federal debt, the Administration actually created the equivalent of budget surpluses in 1978, 1979, and even 1980.[25] Norman Glickman, a political economist at the University of Texas, has shown that, in comparison with the Nixon and Ford budgets, both in real terms and as a percentage of total federal outlays, Carter's actually reduced spending for commercial and housing development; transportation; community and regional development; education, training, employment, and social services; health; family welfare; and general-purpose assistance.[26] The combination of monetary and fiscal restraints did little to curb inflation (at least initially), but it sent unemployment and interest rates skyrocketing.

In the two years between the end of 1978 and early 1980, all of the key interest rate-sensitive industries, led by construction and motor vehicles, were jolted. Domestic automobile and truck manufacture declined by 30 percent. Products related to the automobile, ranging from the steel and the machinery used in auto plants to the textiles and plastics used inside the car, soon followed. Tight money and cuts in government spending created a deep recession that began in the industrial Midwest and spread nationwide. The "misery index" for 1980—the sum of the rates of unemployment and inflation—reached almost 20 percent. A wave of plant closings and layoffs in one industry after another, rippling across the country, put labor on the defensive more than at any time since the Great Depression.

Moreover, there was the beginning of a great U-turn in policies affecting key sectors of industry. It was President Ford and then Carter—not Reagan, their successor—who initiated the deregulation of trucking and commercial aviation. This added enormously to the woes of labor in one industry after another. To Mr. Reagan fell the honor of completing the U-turn in policy—this time with gusto.

The Ideological Foundations of "Reaganomics"

Most economic planning—in particular, industrial policy—affects the "supply side" of investment and product markets. The intent is to promote industrial innovation, productivity, and output. Ultimately, an increase in output can solve the problem of stagflation, a condition that exists when inflation and unemployment occur simultaneously. Increases in output tend to reduce prices by satisfying demand; increases in output also usually entail increasing employment. Indeed, shifting attention to the supply side in a period of sluggish productivity, investment, and innovation is the only way to slay the twin dragons of inflation and unemployment.

Because of stagflation, by the late 1970s to early 1980s, emphasis on the supply side made sense. What did *not* make sense was the form it took, once conservative ideologues put it into practice. The argument of such "supply siders" as Arthur Laffer, Jude Wanniski, Paul Craig Roberts, and David Stockman was focused on the malfeasance of government instead of on the confusion within the private sector. According to Laffer, nothing so discourages work, savings, and investment as high tax rates and government regulation. Because of high taxes, workers are unwilling to put in longer hours or shift to better-paying jobs. Investors are unwilling to put more money into productive channels because the rate of return, after taxes, is so low that it makes more sense for potential investors to consume their savings or to speculate in tax-sheltered, usually unproductive investments such as gold, real estate, and antiques.

The same argument, that taxes discourage workers and investors, was easily used against government regulation. Government attempts to encourage opportunity for equal employment, a cleaner environment, safer workplaces, secure pensions, and protection for consumers have so burdened free enterprise, the argument goes, that there is no longer sufficient incentive to invest or reinvest in productive enterprise. For all the good intent of its framers, the supply siders asserted, regulation simply creates so much red tape that the entire economy loses its spontaneity and finally grinds to a halt. It becomes much more profitable to speculate in pork belly contracts or gold than to have to deal with the alphabet soup cooked up by government regulators.

The prescription of the supply-side school was elegant in its simplicity: deep cuts in taxes to spur work, savings, and investment, and massive deregulation to boost innovation and the productive spending of capital. If the medicine were swallowed, the supply siders promised, the economy would begin to grow again and America would regain its favored place in international markets. Tax cuts would create a greater supply of labor and more investment in plant and equipment, while deregulation would free up the innovative juices that could make U.S. producers competitive with foreign producers. Inflation would be squelched in the process through the expansion of supply to meet demand; unemployment would disappear through the creation of millions of new jobs; and international competition would be squarely met by the advances in productivity emanating from the newly oiled economic machinery. In the end, incomes would rise, revenue from taxes would be maintained for vital government programs, and nearly everyone would be able to take part in the American celebration. What more could anyone want? Change a number of tax forms, abolish a few government agencies, and a new era of prosperity would unfold.

The Reagan administration could not resist the appeal of such a simple solution to the complex economic problems it faced. With strong support from the business community, it wasted no time in adopting much of the supply-side prescription. Within seven months of President Reagan's inauguration, the broad outlines of the strategy were already in place. Reduced to its essentials, Reaganomics came to have five major components.[27]

The first involved a dramatic reduction in federal spending for other than military programs. For the first fiscal year, 1982, the administration proposed a $40 billion cut in the budget that President Carter had submitted to Congress only three months earlier. While Congress refused to make all the slashes in domestic programs that Reagan wanted, it went along with enough of them to realize a reduction of $16 billion by 1985 *plus* a reduction of $30 billion in entitlement programs, including Social Security benefits, farm price supports, food stamps, welfare assistance, and government pensions.

The second component was the enactment of deep cuts in federal taxes on individual incomes, businesses, gifts, and estates. By 1985, these were to amount to a reduction of personal income taxes of more than 25 percent, producing a decrease in income-tax liabilities of $124 billion.[28] The corporate sector benefited at least as much, as a consequence of reduced tax rates and a significant liberalization of allowances for depreciation on new investments.

Regulatory abatement was the third thrust of the new economic policy. Continuing a trend begun under Carter, Reagan moved to further deregulate the airlines, trucking, and telecommunications industries and called for a radical redefinition of the mandate of virtually all regulatory agencies. To do so, the administration adopted a strict "cost-benefit" type of analysis. Nowhere was this approach more evident than in regulations encompassing assessments of personal risk and risk management. Taking this type of cost analysis to its limit, the administration sought, in its own terms, to "improve consistency across federal regulations, to the extent permitted by law."[29] In practice, this meant using the price of a human life as the key determinant in deciding whether or not to regulate. For example, because it cost so many dollars to save a life by the proper disposal of dioxins, the new calculus of environmental control argued against any regulation at all.[30]

Finally—though altogether at odds with the first four policies—the administration greatly accelerated government spending on military research and development, and on the production of weapons. Even though this eventually led to making government spending *larger* rather than smaller, and to unprecedented budget deficits, Reagan's fear of what for most of his life he termed the "evil empire" (the Soviet Union) made military "preparedness" equally as important as economic recovery.[31] Since military production was, and continues to be, far more profitable to business than production for civilian consumption, the big defense contractors gladly went along for the ride. So did Congress and much of the rest of the country.

This was obviously an ambitious agenda. As economist Ezra Solomon, a former member of Nixon's Council of Economic Advisers wrote:

> The ultimate purpose of the Reagan economic program was to reverse two basic adverse developments that had taken place between 1965 and 1980—

a large and steady rise in the rate of inflation from 1½ percent prior to 1965 to 13½ percent in 1980, and a large and steady fall in the rate of productivity gain from the 3 percent level of 1965 to below zero by 1980.

Solomon added, "The success or failure of the 1981 turn in policy will depend on how well it spurs the economy on to improved performance on both of these fronts."[32]

Fiscal and Monetary Policy in the Reagan Administration

Volcker's and Reagan's initial experiment with strict monetary policy had mixed results. The prime rate—the interest rate that commercial banks charge their most creditworthy customers—soared to almost 20 percent as a direct consequence of tight money. As an inflation fighter, this policy worked like a charm. Annual price increases in consumer goods fell to 6.1 percent in 1982 and to 3.2 percent the following year. The war against inflation was won, and won quickly.

But the casualties were enormous. Four-and-one-half million more workers were unemployed in 1982 than in 1979, and entire cities, including Youngstown, Detroit, Buffalo, and Akron, were brought to the brink of bankruptcy. More than enough ice was added to the already frigid bath to bring inflation under control. The Reaganites turned out to be Keynesians in reverse. Depression became the cure for inflation—in the same way that the French had earlier discovered that the guillotine was the definitive cure for the migraine headache.

The recession of 1981–82 was deeper than any since the Great Depression. The gross national product fell by 4.9 percent in the fourth quarter of 1981 and by another 5.5 percent in the first quarter of 1982. Figures for the rest of 1982 were hardly better. If total output had increased by just 3 percent per year beginning in 1980, rather than following the downward path of the next three years, the United States would have enjoyed nearly $350 billion of additional output by the end of 1983. This would have been *more* than enough to solve the fiscal problems of the Social Security system, to expand primary and secondary-school programs all across the country, and to make a serious dent in the housing, transportation, and budgetary problems of the nation's cities.

But for business, the deep recession did precisely what it was designed to do. With more than ten million people unemployed in 1982, it was impossible for organized labor to maintain wage standards, let alone raise them. Reductions in wages rippled from one industry to the next and from the center of the country outward. The real average weekly wage fell by more than 8 percent between 1979 and 1982 and failed to recover at all in the next five years.[33] Essentially, with wage growth arrested by unemployment, what growth occurred in the economy during the rest of the Reagan revolution redounded mostly to the profits side of the capital-labor ledger.

It was only in 1983, after the recession had so seriously affected labor, that the Fed and the White House drastically switched course. Monetary policy was loosened, and budgetary allocations were shifted so as to even more sharply emphasize military spending, which by 1982–83 was growing by 10 percent a year.[34] The federal government suffered the first triple-digit deficit in history—all the while continuing to slow down, freeze, and in some cases eliminate domestic programs. While the defense and high-technology industries thrived, other sectors of the economy were devastated. For example, the federal provision of new units of public housing, which had peaked in 1978, plummeted, by 1984–85, to its lowest level since the program had been initiated in the late 1930s. Indeed, as the ranks of the homeless were growing, the number of public housing units in the United States demolished or turned over to private use from 1983–85 actually exceeded the number of new units constructed. While a new job training program was put into place—the Job Training and Partnership Act—it was drastically underfunded in relation to the magnitude of the need or even to its predecessor program, the Comprehensive Employment and Training Act, which the new president lost no time in eliminating. As a result, federal spending on all employment and training programs declined by 64 percent between 1978 and 1983.[35] By the following year, public spending for roads, bridges, sewers, airports, and other physical infrastructure, net of depreciation, had declined sharply, to only four-tenths of 1 percent of GNP. It had been as high as 2.3 percent in the late 1960s.[36]

Nor was the administration singling out the most vulnerable minority groups, those who depended so much on federal spending. Even entitlement programs that deeply affected the middle class were cut back. A good example is unemployment insurance, perhaps the longest-lasting and most popular legacy of the New Deal. Throughout most of the 1970s, a majority of the unemployed received unemployment insurance benefits (UIB) when they lost their jobs. In the recession of 1975, for example, nearly 80 percent of those eligible for UIB received them. In the 1980s, however, the program was limited—in many cases, severely. By October 1985, the percentage of the unemployed receiving unemployment benefits had plummeted to 25.8 percent, the lowest level in the program's history. Hence, nearly three out of every four jobless workers are now without benefits.[37] Again, the U-turn toward reducing the role of government in the civilian economy began under President Carter but accelerated after the election of Ronald Reagan.

In his book, *The Triumph of Politics,* David Stockman, past director of the president's Office of Management and Budget, frankly admitted that the massive tax cuts of 1981 (modified slightly by the tax reform act of the following year) were really intended to deprive the government of the resources which advocates of social spending needed to draw for the programs they were planning. Unabashedly, he wrote, "The Reagan Revolution, as I had defined it, required a frontal assault on the American welfare state. That was the only way to pay for the massive Kemp-Roth tax cut."[38] According to William Greider's famous interview with Stockman for the *Atlantic,* " 'Zero[ing] out' became a favorite phrase of Stockman's; it meant closing down a program 'cold turkey,' in one budget year."[39]

The tax cut was massive indeed. The 1981 cuts in business taxes were so generous that, to give only one example, the Center on Budget and Policy Priorities found that "the value of allowable deductions and actual credits actually exceeded the tax liability on the income that investment in a typical piece of equipment would generate."[40] This meant that investments in equipment had, because of the revised tax rules concerning depreciation, become fully subsidized by the government. In 1982, the Congress reduced some of these extraordinary subsidies to business. Nevertheless, the net effect of the changes in the tax codes of 1981 and 1982 was to reduce even further the government's receipt of taxes from business—a trend that has been more or

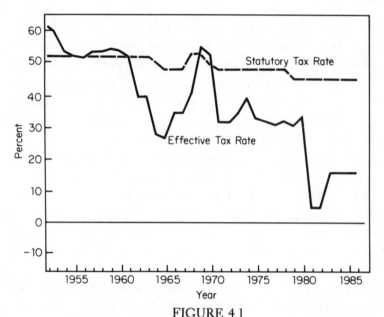

FIGURE 4.1

Statutory and Effective Marginal Corporate Tax Rates for Total
Nonresidential Business

SOURCE Charles R. Hulten and James W. Robertson, "Corporate Tax Policy and Economic Growth: An Analysis of the 1981 and 1982 Tax Acts: Changing Domestic Priorities," discussion paper (Washington, D.C.: The Urban Institute, December 1982).

less continuous since Richard Nixon became president back in 1969 (fig. 4.1). Not until 1986 did the Congress, desperate to reduce what by then had become an intolerably large and growing deficit, change these arrangements and eliminate some of the most flagrant loopholes. At the same time, however, it also reduced the statutory tax rates on profits, so that the long trend toward declining taxation of business continues.

Economic Deregulation

Huge cuts in taxes on business were the most direct way for the Reagan administration to boost corporate profits, while the custom-designed recession of 1981–82 was the most powerful indirect method. But the Reagan administration also set out to support corporate restructuring in three additional ways. One was to continue the trend toward *eco-*

nomic deregulation of specific sectors of the economy that had been initiated under President Carter. The second was to "privatize" much existing public enterprise by auctioning it off. And the third was to initiate a full-scale assault on the *social* regulations that had been constructed since the turn of the century to protect workers, consumers, and the environment. All of these policies played crucial roles either in inducing or reinforcing the restructuring of private industry, and all three contributed to the revival of corporate profits in the 1980s.

Economic deregulation was clearly intended to open previously regulated markets to more competition and to give businesses in those markets greater leeway to set wages, prices, and fees according to supply and demand. In theory, this would ultimately give consumers more choices among goods and services (or quality of service) and also lower the prices they paid. Although not usually trumpeted openly, deregulation might, it was hoped, also reimpose greater managerial discipline over day-to-day activities in the workplace. Taken together, said David Stockman, "sweeping regulatory relief was seen as a significant means to stimulate production by reducing costs and improving cash flow in the short run, and to improve productivity in the long run"—the essential goals of the supply-side theorists.[41]

Like other aspects of the revival of laissez-faire, deregulation began long before the inauguration of Ronald Reagan. Between 1968 and 1978, steps were taken toward the gradual deregulation of communications, banking, stock-market transactions, and airline transportation. Beginning in 1980, the pace quickened, as trucking and railroads, oil, cable television, and intercity bus travel were added to the list. Reagan was especially proud of the fact that, in the first year of his administration, nearly 24,000 fewer pages of new regulations were placed in the *Federal Register* than during the last year in office of his predecessor. A major milestone came in 1984 with the final breakup of the giant American Telephone and Telegraph Co. into nine regional firms.[42]

In many ways, transportation is the prototype of the deregulation movement.[43] For forty years, until its demise in 1978, the Civil Aeronautics Board (CAB) was responsible for setting the prices of commercial airline tickets and for regulating entry into the industry. It did this by stipulating which airlines could fly which routes and how frequently they could fly them. Essentially, the CAB established a network of monopolies and set prices to cover the actual costs of providing air travel, leaving a regulated profit for the carriers. Deregulation, under President Carter and then Reagan, permitted entrepreneurs to create new airline companies, to compete for customers on any routes they wished, and to charge whatever prices the market would bear. Young upstart companies like People Express and New York Air jumped into the market with discount airfares for "no-frills" air travel and forced the older carriers to compete by offering steep discounts of their own, "frequent flyer" programs, and more frequent flights. Profits at the older companies, including Eastern, Delta, American, and Trans World Airlines, tumbled as price wars erupted throughout the industry. In its initial stage, deregulation worked wonders for the customer who could take flights at off-peak hours, travel on weekends, or go by more circuitous routes.

The profit squeeze, reinforced by deregulation, worked to restructure managerial strategy in the airline industry in very much the same way that global competition had forced manufacturers to develop new cost-cutting measures. Airlines attempted to raise productivity by changing work rules and to recover profits by slashing the cost of labor. They introduced two-tiered wage structures, froze those salaries which they did not actually cut, and increased the number of hours of flight time required of many of their employees. (This last is known as "speedup" to blue-collar workers.) The airlines also subcontracted much of their maintenance work.

Deregulation of banking has been less thorough, but it too has radically changed the face of the industry. The major changes in banking law, codified in the Depository Institutions Deregulation and Monetary Control Act of 1980, ultimately eliminated all regulation of interest rates and loosened restrictions on the geographic areas served and the services offered by individual banks.[44] The Act also permitted savings and loan associations to become more like commercial banks by giving them the right to issue credit cards and lend money to consumers for other purposes than home mortgage, to which they had previously been restricted. The Garn–St. Germain Depository Institutions Act that followed in 1982 went a step further by authorizing "super-NOW" checking accounts (interest-bearing checking accounts) and by permitting commercial banks to sell life insurance. The culmination of all this deregulatory activity has been the introduction of the "non-bank bank"—firms such as Sears, Roebuck that now offer financial services ranging from life insurance and real-estate brokerage to national credit cards and stock brokerage. As it did in the airline industry, the heightened competition in banking sent managers scurrying to develop strategies to maintain profits, in part by the imposition of many of the cost-cutting measures we described in chapter 2.[45]

While there is widespread disagreement over the precise economic effect of deregulation, most experts acknowledge that it has greatly facilitated corporate mergers, acquisitions, and joint ventures involving companies that would otherwise have been blocked from such close co-operation by the old antitrust laws.[46] The initial flurry of new entrants into commercial aviation has died down. The no-frills airlines, such as People Express and New York Air, are either bankrupt or have been absorbed by other corporations. And, ironically, the federal government has had to take a giant step back in the banking industry in order to facilitate the acquisition of failed banks such as Continental Illinois by other, financially healthy banking corporations. What is not to be denied is that deregulation has directly reinforced the restructuring of the private sector—particularly in regard to labor and corporate mergers.

The Privatization of the Public Sector

The Reagan administration borrowed one of its favorite strategies from Margaret Thatcher, Britain's prime minister. During the first seven years of rule by the Conservative Party of Britain, more than two dozen businesses owned by the government were sold to the private sector, for some $28 billion. Included in this world's largest fire sale were British Telecom, Jaguar, and British Aerospace.[47]

In March 1987, after several false starts, the Reagan administration held its own sale. At a price of more than $1.6 billion, the federal government sold the Consolidated Rail Corporation—Conrail, the nation's leading rail carrier of freight,—to a consortium of private railroads and investment banks.[48] Although it had lost money in each of the first five years after the government took over the bankrupt Penn Central Railroad and forged Conrail out of the entrails, the system was profitable every year after 1981.[49] In 1986 alone, it made a highly respectable profit of $431 million on revenues of $3.1 billion.[50] Conservatives point to the U.S. Postal Service when they wish to "prove" that public enterprise cannot possibly be profitable; the Conrail story teaches otherwise.

Partly to reduce the deficit, but mainly to remove government from any competition with private industry that might challenge profitability, the White House proposed to sell off hydroelectric power plants, airports, more passenger rail service, and even radio frequencies—all to the highest bidder.[51] If Reagan's laissez-faire advisors had had their way, even such hallmarks of the New Deal era as the Bonneville and Grand Coulee dams would have been privatized. So would Washington National and Dulles Airports; the Naval Petroleum Reserves at Elk Hills, California and at Teapot Dome, Wyoming; AMTRAK, the government-owned passenger railway system; additional public housing units; and loans previously issued by the U.S. Small Business Administration, the Rural Housing Administration, and the Department of Education. This last idea entailed selling the loans to private banks and other financial institutions at 50 cents on the dollar, so that Wall Street and commercial bankers would, in the words of the editors of *Business Week*, "all stand to reap a windfall from sales."[52]

In privatizing government operations, the Reagan administration has broken more new ground than even Margaret Thatcher. For example, the Department of Agriculture has sold off its rural data base to Martin Marietta, the aerospace firm, which now sells information from these files to farmers and agricultural researchers. Similarly, the National Institutes of Health have sold their Medline service to Mead Data Central, and the Federal Election Commission has turned over its data base to a company owned by McClatchy newspapers.[53] All of these firms have profited by raising the on-line price to customers by as much as 3,000 percent.

According to Washington conservatives, privatization can and should also be used to shift traditional responsibilities of state and local governments to the commercial sector. The introduction of vouchers for primary and secondary education, health care, housing, and welfare, as well as privately operated prisons have all been under consideration. Thus, for example, the government would allow companies to establish corrections facilities and then pay them for each prisoner they agree to incarcerate. Medicare and Medicaid already effectively operate on this principle—which is why they in no way constitute "socialized medicine," as conservatives often charge. This is not to say that public enterprise is always efficient and cost-effective. But it does suggest that the conservative approach to the improvement of these services is to regard business as the savior—whereas in the past we normally turned to the government to protect the nation from the inefficiency or excesses of free enterprise.

Social Deregulation

In contrast to economic deregulation and privatization, social deregulation was, from the beginning, the innovation of the Reagan administration. Between 1964 and 1979, Congress had passed sixty-two health and safety laws to protect consumers and workers, and an additional thirty-two measures to regulate the use of energy and the environment.[54] Thus the Council on Economic Quality, the Environmental Protection Agency (EPA) and the Occupational Safety and Health Administration (OSHA) all came into existence in 1970, while the Consumer Product Safety Commission was brought into being under a 1972 congressional mandate to protect the public against unreasonable risks of injury associated with consumer products.

In general, these regulatory bodies were established to intervene in cases of what economists call "market failure," for example, when unregulated competition would result in pollution or unsafe working conditions, even under the most enlightened management. The object of social regulation has always been to force businesses to operate in a fashion that minimizes such "negative externalities" or to compensate society for any that the firm cannot avoid.

Almost by definition, then, social regulation is costly to companies. It requires them to pay for and install scrubbers on their smokestacks and safety equipment in their workplaces. According to Robert Litan and William Nordhaus of the Brookings Institution, the control of pollution alone has cost American firms anywhere from $13 to $38 billion, and provisions for health and safety have cost industry between

$7 and $17 billion.[55] Not surprisingly, the business community has bandied about even higher estimates in its lobbying for relief.

The Reagan administration has obliged these lobbyists by softening regulations in one area after another. Reductions in the budgets of regulatory agencies, changes in personnel, eased rules, and increased delegation of regulatory responsibilities to state legislatures, where the business lobbies are if anything even more powerful, have all helped to reduce effective regulation. In constant dollars, the budgets of regulatory agencies were cut by 8 percent between 1981 and 1985. In the same period, personnel at the Consumer Product Safety Commission—including the investigative staff—was reduced by more than a third, and OSHA's staff was slashed almost a quarter.[56] The National Highway Traffic Safety Administration, the EPA, the Equal Employment Opportunity Commission, and a host of other agencies have all met a similar fate. While there are no detailed estimates of the actual savings to business, a reasonable guess would be in the billions of dollars.

Social deregulation has also entered the area of labor law. The simple refusal to increase the legal minimum wage from $3.35 per hour, set in 1981, has reduced its real cost to employers by 25 percent. The administration has also weakened the bargaining power of organized labor by changing the ideological stance of the National Labor Relations Board (NLRB). That story also began long before the election of Ronald Reagan in 1980. Gordon Clark, an economic geographer and political economist at Carnegie-Mellon University, has pointed out that:

> From the moment the Wagner Act was passed, campaigns were begun to repeal, amend, and revise the Act. . . . By amendment, judicial interpretation, and passage of new labor laws, organized labor's legal environment has become [increasingly] more conservative over the past fifty years . . . the judiciary systematically "deradicalized" the Wagner Act by limiting the applicability of the Act and failing to vigorously enforce decisions by the National Labor Relations Board (NLRB).[57]

Clark cites as milestones in the undoing of federal support for labor the passage of the pro-business Taft-Hartley amendments in 1947, the Landrum-Griffin Act of 1959, failure of the 1965–66 campaign by labor to win congressional repeal of the Title 14(b) of Taft-Hartley "right to work" provision, and the failure to reform labor legislation during the Carter years.

The Reagan administration greatly accelerated the shift against federal protection of the rights of workers, and especially of unions. The terrain on which most of the battles of the 1980s was fought is the NLRB. Thus, for example, in 1982, in the case of *Milwaukee Spring vs. United Auto Workers of America* (UAW), an NLRB still dominated by President Carter's appointees ruled that an employer could *not* relocate production from a unionized plant to a nonunion site during the term of a collective bargaining agreement—which the company had tried to do after a local of the UAW refused to grant concessions. The company appealed the decision to a federal district court, which remanded it to the NLRB for a rehearing in 1984. By that time, the Board was dominated by Reagan's appointees, much as the U.S. Supreme Court itself has undergone a profound ideological shift through new appointments. The revamped Board promptly ruled that, since the contract did not contain explicit language prohibiting such a relocation, the Milwaukee Spring Company was indeed within its rights to run away from its union, contract or no contract.

In a related case, the Supreme Court had ruled, in 1981, in *First National Maintenance Corp. vs. NLRB,* that a company could run away from a union while a collective bargaining agreement was still in force only if prompted by some "economic necessity" other than the cost of labor per se. In 1984, the NLRB cited this case as the basis for its decision, in *Otis Elevator,* that a company *did* have the right to relocate its property wherever and whenever it pleased. In doing so, the Board dramatically changed long-standing rules governing collective bargaining. In Clark's words, "the Board has narrowed the scope of collective bargaining by narrowing the legitimate interests of labor to issues of compensation."[58] The legal right to a secure job protected by a legal contract with an employer is now in a state of limbo.

In 1984, Congress held hearings on the question: "Has Labor Law Failed?" Prominent among those giving testimony were two Harvard professors, economist Richard Freeman and legal scholar Paul Weiler. Freeman emphasized the explosive growth of unfair practices by managers, especially the peremptory dismissal of union organizers. Weiler pointed out that not only were there material incentives to companies to break the law (union wages are still somewhat higher than wages in nonunion settings), but that the law itself was no longer being enforced, especially in the 1980s.[59]

All of this deregulation of labor law affects unionization by imposing a "chilling effect" on the act of organizing itself. Indeed, in the long run this may prove to be the Reagan administration's single greatest gift to the business community, as a recent study of clerical workers has made clear. The legal and regulatory confusion over whether firms will be allowed to relocate if their workers organize has had a measurable effect on elections in offices where unions are trying to organize clerical workers. It has been found that "clerical workers in offices that were judged to be easier to relocate were found to be more likely to report that the fear of job loss was important to their voting decision," and that "those who voted against the union were most likely to report that the fear that they would lose their jobs was a significant consideration." Finally, "workers in units judged to be most easily relocat[able] were found to have a 7 to 30 percent lower probability of voting union than those who were in less mobile jobs."[60]

Government Promotion of the Use of Contingent Labor

The Reagan government's attitude toward labor was made patently clear well before the NLRB handed down its decision to reverse *Milwaukee Spring*. When the president summarily fired the nation's entire complement of striking air-traffic controllers, members of PATCO, the White House sent a strong signal to the private sector that it considered "getting tough with the unions" acceptable, if not downright patriotic. New full-time controllers were hired by the Federal Aviation Administration—the nature of the work precluded using part-timers—but everyone involved understood that it would be dangerous for the new employees to attempt to reassert control over the "quality of their working life"—at least for a while.

A more direct government assault on the principal of full-time, permanent employment came in August 1983 with the promulgation by the Office of Management and Budget of Circular no. A-76. This rule ordered all agencies to increase their reliance on businesses for commercially available services, unless the agency could demonstrate that it could provide the services more economically. As a consequence of A-76, services such as food preparation, building maintenance, warehousing, and data processing have been subcontracted at an increasing rate. The commercial suppliers of these services have proven to be far more likely than the government to employ part-time or temporary labor.[61]

Still another step was taken in the direction of advocating more "flexible" work schedules in 1984. In that year, the administration imposed on the U.S. Postal Service a second tier of wages that was 25 percent below the previous standard. This was at a time when the two-tier system was spreading well beyond troubled industries to more and more segments of the American economy.[62]

Then, on New Year's Day of 1985, the federal government gave itself the right to hire temporary workers, at all levels, for up to four years. In doing so, the administration severely eroded the Civil Service's precedent of guaranteeing permanent employment following a short probationary period. Justifying the order to substitute temporary for permanent employees "whenever possible," the Federal Office of Personnel Management claimed that it would reduce costs. "Temporary employees are not eligible for federal health benefits, may be dismissed 'at will,' and have no appeal rights or other protection against adverse personnel actions," explained a memo prepared for the director of that agency in support of the new policy.[63]

The administration struck a blow for laissez-faire in yet another labor matter. Since 1979, a debate has been under way within the U.S. Department of Labor, which regulates conditions of work under the Fair Labor Standards Act of 1937. The controversy is over the legality of "homework." Employers (and some homeworkers, especially in rural areas) have argued that unsupervised piece work at home introduces a much-needed degree of flexibility into the labor market. Unions and many individual workers fear that homework will escape the reach of minimum-wage, health-and-safety, child-labor, and other laws designed to guarantee at least a minimal quality of working life. The Reagan administration enthusiastically entered this ongoing fray on the side of deregulating homework, and in 1986 promulgated new regulations that substantially increase the freedom of companies to organize production in this fashion.[64] For a number of industries in both manufacturing and services, this presumably small change in regulation produced windfall profits.

Local Government Subsidies for Urban Revitalization

Government relief to business has by no means been a monopoly of the federal government. States and localities have joined the parade in record numbers. Thus, the public was subjected to such spectacles as governors and prominent legislators from more than a dozen states making the pilgrimage to Michigan, hat (and wallet) in hand, to beg General Motors to locate its new assembly plant for Saturn automobiles in their jurisdiction (GM eventually chose Tennessee).

Nowhere has government support for private business interests been more visible than in the subsidization of urban real estate development by municipalities. In the last chapter, we saw that the country's major urban centers have been undergoing a commercial revitalization in response to the need of global corporations and their suppliers for a new physical environment of office towers, convention facilities, restaurants, and hotels within which to carry on their trade. The most formidable obstacle to the transformation of the urban environment into a space amenable to the needs of multinational corporations and their contractors, suppliers, and advisers (not to mention their employees, who are searching for safe and comfortable housing) was the social and physical structure of the existing city. Downtown areas were either crowded or abandoned—often both, at different times of the day. Sanitation was deteriorating. Electricity was not completely reliable. Pollution of the air and water was increasing. Good housing was becoming more scarce, even as the slums were spreading over more of the inner city. Municipal budgets were inadequate, and more and more cities faced potential bankruptcy.[65]

Making the cities safe and physically suitable for the central activities of the multinational corporations became a major objective of what John Mollenkopf has aptly termed the "growth coalitions" that began to emerge in one large American city after another during the 1970s.[66]

Real-estate developers, leading architectural firms, big banks and insurance companies, corporation executives, unions of construction workers, and a new breed of mayors who cast themselves as the true architects of the "new city"—all worked together to raise the money and prepare the ground for the restructuring of the social and (as the city planners say) "built" environment.

This agenda was far too important to business to be held hostage to any ideological consistency. The watchword of the era may have been laissez-faire, but urban redevelopment was too big a matter to be conducted without government assistance. Thus, as they did for the military buildup, conservatives closed their eyes and jumped in to help business in a major way.

Consider the scope of the subsidies in just one place: New York City.

Eager to push development, city government gave tax breaks to all sorts of projects with little regard for social purpose or need for subsidy. A conspicuous example is the glittering Trump Tower on Fifth Avenue, with its million-dollar condos and peach-colored marble atrium encircled by six levels of some of the most costly retail space in America—all subsidized with $100 million worth of tax abatements. The city also gave $7.2 million in tax abatements for IBM's new headquarters, and $20 million for AT&T's. And it kept tax assessments far below current market values for choice commercial buildings. Official policy is to assess commercial property at 60 percent of fair market value. The Pan Am Building, however, which sold for $400 million in 1980, carried an assessed value of less than 25 percent of what it brought on the market; and the Manufacturers Hanover Trust building, sold for $161 million in 1981, had an assessment of less than 20 percent of its sale price. When Rockefeller Center offered common stock to the public for the first time in 1985, its management commissioned an independent appraisal which valued the property at $1.6 billion; yet the Center's assessed value was only 22 percent of the appraisal figure.[67]

Professors Lynn Sagalyn and Bernard Frieden, urban planners at M.I.T., point out that these new growth coalitions were also highly successful in managing the *politics* of development—especially the inevitable conflicts between downtown commercial and neighborhood (poor and working-class) interests. Thus, by the mid-1980s, what had been described only twenty years earlier as a "battleground"—the downtown core of the large American metropolis—was being transformed into an apparently thriving new "post-industrial city." The only problem was that the transformation was leaving a good share of the resident population out of the bargain, creating an increasing gap between the living standards of the haves and the have-nots.[68]

As urban wastelands were torn down and rebuilt to fit the needs of the global corporations, their suppliers, and the middle-class workers who would be employed in the office towers, property values that had been stagnant (if not falling) for years began to rise. Acting on inside information about new construction being conceived at some city hall or executive dining room, speculators entered the scene, further driving up rents. Just as in an earlier era, when an ostensibly socially constructive program (urban renewal) came to acquire a pejorative monicker ("Negro removal"), so the present wave of young urban professionals, or "yuppies," invaded one low-income community of minority residents after another in the 1980s, leading to the new complaint of "gentrification."[69] Between the developers, with their new or rehabilitated towers, and the affluent middle-class professionals returning to the city as a location of choice, housing prices and rents were driven higher and higher. The escalation was heightened still further by foreign capital, especially from the Middle East, as oil profits were invested in urban real estate. More recently, the Japanese have become major investors in urban real estate in the U.S.

Thus, even though the deep recession of 1982 and the massive growth of foreign imports effectively halted inflation at the national level, the cost of living skyrocketed in the big cities. In one metropolitan area after another, the explosion in real-estate prices drove the middle class out of the city into lower-cost suburbs, leaving the city with larger proportions of both the rich and the poor. In this way the polarization of urban America, which began in the changing workplace, has been reinforced.

The Laissez-Faire Affair in Retrospect

There can be little doubt that the fiscal and monetary policies of the last decade, the wave of deregulation, the government's assault on workers' rights, and urban revitalization have speeded the restructuring of the private sector as a whole. This is true even if more than a few individual companies have been driven to the brink of financial disaster by the reinforcement of competition by the government.

In 1984, eight hundred executives of large and medium-sized corporations were surveyed by the *Wall Street Journal*. They agreed "recession had been a good thing for the country" by bringing about "the control of inflation and the imbuing of workers and management with a more realistic sense." They also liked the "more rational federal tax and regulatory structure." Another survey, conducted by the Urban Institute, revealed that business executives thought that the deterioration of basic industries such as steel, auto, machine tools, and rubber was "inevitable" and that Reagan's policies were the "medicine we need" to make business and labor more "realistic."[70]

To be sure, the "medicine" did revitalize parts of the economy, rebuild profits, and send the stock market soaring—at least until the crash of October 1987. But it also had a terrible downside. The strategies adopted by business and reinforced by the U-turn in government policy have had a profound impact on the labor market—the foundation of the typical family's standard of living. We have seen a growing fragmentation of work; a revival of dual labor markets, both within large firms and in the economy as a whole; the proliferation of contingent forms of employment, which create greater inequality in the amount and stability of employment to which workers have access; a weakening of the bargaining and political power of labor; a further shift of capital from productive to largely financial and speculative pursuits; the emergence of a node of growth—urban revitalization—which creates a demand for a dual supply of labor; and a series of deregulatory actions by government which actually heightens the intense competition that triggered the disastrous experiments in corporate restructuring in the first place.

On the one hand, government leaders claim to be endorsing a return to laissez-faire. And federally mandated social programs of all kinds have indeed been slowed down and, in some cases, reduced in scale. Yet, at the same time, enormous public resources have been used to subsidize the restructuring process, especially the physical reconstruction of the headquarters cities of the largest global companies. Leaders may call these deals "public-private partnerships" and attempt to fold them under the ideological umbrella of laissez-faire. But they must be seen for what they really are: the re-allocation of public resources to fit a new agenda. That agenda is no longer redistribution, or even economic growth as conventionally defined. Rather, that agenda entails nothing less than the restructuring of the relations of production and the balance of power in the American economy. In the pursuit of these dubious goals, the public sector continues to play a crucial role.

5

The Crisis of
the American Dream

AS WE HAVE SEEN, ever since the early 1970s, corporate managers have been attempting to carry out strategies to rebuild sagging profits, and it is at least since the end of the 1970s that the federal government has been working in earnest to help them do it. Enough time has passed that we might reasonably ask: how have these joint efforts at restructuring worked out? Have they restored corporate profits? Have they raised wages and family incomes? Have they contributed to social equality?

A mountain of data provides a disturbingly clear answer. At very best, we have batted 1 for 3. The strategies *have* improved the corporations' bottom line, but at enormous cost to much of the nation. Average wages and family incomes continue to stagnate, and the maldistribution of well-being becomes more distressing each year. No longer is the cost of rebuilding profits merely a burden on the poor; it is increasingly falling on the middle class as well.

The Bottom Line and the Unemployment Line

During the 1980s, both the level of profits and the rate of return on real assets—the two most common ways we measure corporate success—began to recover from their low points at the end of the 1970s. By 1984, according to Bowles, Gordon, and Weisskopf, after-tax profits had rebounded to more than 7 percent, about the level that prevailed back in 1969.[1] This was far better than the 4.5 percent achieved in 1980 and substantially better than the average of 5.7 percent in the 1970s. After 1984, profits continued to build, although the pace slowed (fig. 5.1). From the trough of the recession of 1982 through the end of 1986, the owners of American corporations enjoyed an increase, adjusted for inflation, of 92 percent in the level of profits *before taxes.* *After-tax* profits, benefiting from falling corporate tax rates, grew even faster—by 118 percent.[2]

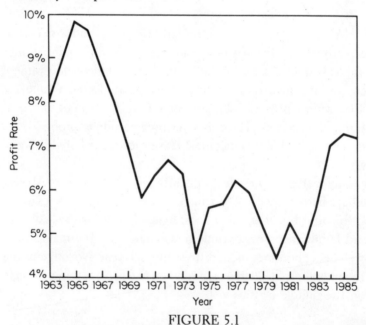

FIGURE 5.1

U.S. Corporate Profitability, 1963–86 Net After-Tax Rate of Return

Source Samuel Bowles, David Gordon, and Thomas Weisskopf, "Power and Profits: The Social Structure of Accumulation and the Profitability of the Postwar U.S. Economy," *Review of Radical Political Economics* 18, nos. 1 and 2, Spring and Summer 1986, as revised by Weisskopf in December 1987 to reflect new government capital stock series.

Stockholders, who had become so disillusioned with corporate performance during the 1970s, had reason to be pleased with the turn of events. In many cases, their dividends more than quadrupled, while the opportunities to make huge capital gains were never better. Reassured of management's rejuvenated competence, investors poured money into the stock market, pushing the Dow-Jones Industrial Average up to 2700 before the crash of October 1987. Even after the speculative bubble had burst, the Dow-Jones average at the end of 1987 was still more than 230 percent above its level in 1978. Foreign investors joined in the financial frolic, investing billions in the stock market, buying up Fortune–500 firms and Manhattan skyscrapers lock, stock, and barrel, and assuming partial ownership of one Wall Street securities firm after another.[3] Corporate profits continued to set new records throughout 1987, despite the stock exchange's "meltdown." The U-turn in corporate strategy had generated an auspicious U-turn in the corporate bottom line.

Moreover, the cost-containment strategies adopted by business to boost profits—from domestic plant closings and wage cutbacks to more "flexible" labor relations—certainly have not inhibited the creation of new jobs. Far from it. For more than a decade the United States has been creating more new jobs than the rest of the industrialized world combined. Indeed, all of Western Europe—with a total population exceeding ours—had zero growth in employment between 1973 and 1986, while the United States was adding nearly 26 million new jobs.[4] Given this extraordinary track record, America has been aptly enshrined as "the Great Jobs Machine." The economy generated employment for millions in the "baby-boom" generation and for an unprecedented number of women who entered and remained in the labor force. The official unemployment rate, nearly 11 percent at the end of 1982, dropped to below 6 percent. Instead of nearly twelve million people on unemployment lines, at the end of 1987 there were only seven million.

The American Jobs Machine has been the envy of Europe and even Japan. Leaders of the European Common Market have been so impressed by these gains in employment that they have sent one delegation after another across the Atlantic with explicit orders to learn everything they can about the secret of our success. With increasing frequency, they have returned home to advocate many of the restructuring strategies pioneered by American corporate managers. Increasingly, they are succumbing to the lure of the flexible workplace as the best way to restore profits and opportunities for investment in a competitive world. In the words of one International Labour Office official, who in fact does not share this view, the current problem in Europe is seen as

> "Eurosclerosis"—conjuring up an image of [an] arthritic tightening of sinews, a virulent disease supposedly ravaging the boardrooms, union headquarters and government departments all over Europe.[5]

This notion of ossified and overregulated labor markets has been derived primarily from the shocking contrast between expanding employment in the United States and growing unemployment in Europe. A key theme of those advocating the adoption of American-style flexible use of labor in Europe is that somehow the United States has accomplished a jobs miracle precisely *because* it has flexible labor markets.

What Kinds of Jobs Is the United States Creating?

To be sure, compared to Europe, the American Jobs Machine has an enviable record. But as a deeper plumbing of the data proves, this is true only so long as one deals only with the sheer number of the employed. The dark side of the American story, which enthusiastic European and Japanese colleagues might consider before plunging in to adopt the newest "American plan," is that, since the 1970s, the job market in the United States has itself taken a series of U-turns. Unfortunately, *all* of them—with the single exception of the overall level of employment—have been in the wrong direction. We have created jobs, but at lower wages; more family members are in the work force, but family income is stagnating.

Recall the statistics cited at the beginning of this book. After improving steadily since the 1950s, the real (adjusted-for-inflation) weekly wage of the average American worker peaked in 1973, and has been falling or stagnating ever since.[6] In 1986, the average wage in the

United States bought nearly 14 percent less than it had thirteen years earlier. Similarly, beginning in the mid-1970s, the distribution of annual wages and salaries became increasingly unequal, after a long period of movement toward greater equality. This has occurred, at least partially, as a result of a growing polarization of wages: the proportion of jobs that are low-paid has been mushrooming since 1979, while among the year-round, usually full-time employees who form the core of the work force, the proportion of the best-paid jobs in the economy has also been on the rise. Thus, the nation *is* producing jobs by the bushel, but corporate restructuring, aided and abetted by permissive government policy, is producing a startling deterioration in the quality of those jobs and consequently in the standard of living of a growing proportion of our citizens.

What has been happening to the labor market ultimately affects the well-being of families. Wages, after all, make up the lion's share of a family's resources, whether the earner be a high-priced systems engineer or the local high-school custodian. Wages alone (not counting the value of fringe benefits) are responsible for more than three-fifths of our total national income. When benefits are added, the labor share accounts for nearly three-fourths. Hence, underlying trends in individual wages strongly influence trends in household income.

Of course, other factors beside wage rates affect the family's economic well-being. It has become increasingly true, for example, that the typical household contains two or more members who contribute to the family's support. Moreover, unearned income has become increasingly important, as a result of more favorable tax treatment of income from property and of the Wall Street boom of 1985–87 that sent the value of stocks, bonds, and real estate skyrocketing. Indeed, it is conceivable that the bull market in stocks was so powerful that by itself it could have offset the decline in wages, thus in principle producing an overall increase in family well-being.

In fact that did not occur. Just the opposite happened. As figure 1.3 in chapter 1 illustrated so vividly, median annual family income—the best single indicator of the typical family's standard of living that we can construct—rose steadily from the end of World War II until 1973.[7] Since then, it has gone nowhere; rising and falling with every turn of the business cycle but no longer with any underlying positive trend. The equality of family income has also undergone a U-turn (as we demonstrated in chapter 1)—from improvement over the long period between the late 1940s and the end of the 1960s to a sharp downward turn which, if anything, has been exacerbated since 1980. The old adage seems to be true yet again: the rich are getting richer while the poor get poorer. One thing, however, is very different in the present era. For the first time at least since the Great Depression, the "poor" are coming to include millions who have been taught to think of themselves as middle-class.

To understand how serious these trends are, we need to explore in more detail a slew of reversals, including the U-Turn in wages, in equality of earnings, in family income, and in the equality of family income. Along the way, we shall discover that the conventional economic wisdom on these matters—that the trends (if they exist at all) are attributable simply to business cycles and demographic changes—is simply wrong. The U-turns are *not* temporary. Because they are not, the problems of the growing inequality of income and the proliferation of low-paid work in America are likely to outlast the presidency of Ronald Reagan and plague us well into the last decade of the century.

The Decline in Real Annual Wages

In the first section of this book, we saw how American corporate managers tried to boost short-term profits by shifting from productive to speculative investments in the casino economy—thereby radically altering the *kinds* of jobs being created and destroyed—and by making the reduction of the cost of labor the target of *all* of their activities. Sometimes this was done through "rationalization": the reduction of employment through automation, subcontracting of work to plants in foreign countries, and the closing down of entire factories. In other cases, managers undertook a wide range of experiments to transform the remaining work in order to reduce the wages of those still employed. This so-called restructuring has taken the form of freezes and cuts in wages, the introduction of two-tiered wage systems, the substitution of floating bonuses for fixed wages, the proliferation of part-time work and "home" work, and the shifting of work previously performed by regular (often unionized) employees to independent, typically nonunion subcontractors. Even this list does not exhaust the number of devices being pursued by managers to cut costs and to utilize labor more flexibly.

One way of sizing up the influence of these factors on workers is to investigate changes in the *total hourly wage bill*—the total amount of wages paid to the work force for each hour of work. Using data from the U.S. Bureau of Labor Statistics, we can see how the wage bill has changed in each sector of the economy and divide this change into an "employment effect" and a "wage effect." The former reflects the change in hourly earnings due to company decisions to hire or lay off workers, while the latter reflects changes in the real wage paid workers for each hour they work. Essentially, this apportioning of the wage bill indicates how much of the actual change in earnings is due to the growth or decline in employment and how much is due to increases or decreases in wages. Table A.1. in the appendix contains the information needed for this assessment.

The first thing that becomes clear is the depth of the crisis in the manufacturing sector. Between 1973 and 1986, the total real wage bill for the manufacture of durable goods—such as automobiles, steel, machinery, and electrical equipment—declined by more than $16 million per hour of work, or 17.5 percent. The total wage bill for the manufacture of nondurable goods—such as apparel, textiles, and shoes—fell by more than $5 million per hour, or 9.7 percent, in 1986 dollars. As a whole, then, manufacturers in the United States were paying out in wages in 1986 nearly $22 million *less each hour* than they had been in 1973. From the point of view of workers, that amounts to from $15 to $17 million per hour less in the pay envelope, after deducting income taxes and Social Security payments.

How much of this decline in the wage bill for manufacturing can we attribute to falling employment, and how much to reductions in hourly wages for those lucky enough to hold on to their jobs? In durable manufacturing, the answer is that $13 million of the $16 million lost in real wages was a direct result of cutbacks in employment. Between 1973 and 1986, manufacturers of durable goods "saved" $13 million an hour in wages by eliminating more than 1.2 million jobs. Firms in the nondurable-goods sector saved another $4.7 million by eliminating 500,000 jobs. We might call this getting "lean."

But these were not the only savings in the cost of labor that corporate managers were able to generate. An additional $3.1 million was salvaged each hour by producers of durable goods by forcing the average real hourly wage down from $10.75 an hour in 1973 to $10.33 an hour in 1986.[8] Manufacturers of nondurable goods were not quite so successful, but even they were able to pay 13 cents an hour less to their employees by the end of this thirteen year period. From the typical worker's point of view, employers were getting "mean."

In manufacturing, slimming down the wage bill by reducing employment clearly accounted for most of the direct reduction in wages. The relative strength of unions in this sector of the economy and the nature of traditional collective-bargaining agreements explain this. Unions have some control over wages but little over the level of employment. By resisting, as much they could, reductions in wages and, in major industries, insisting on the maintenance of cost-of-living-adjustment (COLA) clauses in their contracts, unions played a key role in maintaining real hourly wages. But they could not restrain management from rationalizing the factory—downsizing its labor force. As a result, in the manufacturing sector, the decline in the wage bill was accomplished much more through shutdowns, relocating work overseas, subcontracting, and automation than through the restructuring of wages in the course of bargaining for concessions from the unions.

Outside of manufacturing, the story is very different. Employment increased in every other part of the economy between 1973 and 1986, making possible potential increases in total wages of anywhere from 8 percent in mining to nearly 78 percent in producers' and consumers' services. Yet, as a result of shifts in employment between industries and the restructuring of American business, the actual increases in wages available for spending by American workers, adjusted for inflation, were much less. This was true because *real hourly wage rates fell in every sector* except mining. In the construction industry, management policies, including the shift to nonunion, lower-paid contractors, actually turned a potential 19 percent increase in total wage payments into a 5 percent *decline* in the sector's bill for wages. In the retail trade sector, the potential growth of wages was cut almost in half by reductions in real hourly pay.

These data show clearly that shifts in employment from generally higher-paying to generally lower-paying industries—for example, from manufacturing to services—constitute only one part of the reason for declining average wages in America. Much of the problem is the result of changes *within* industrial sectors, particularly in the retail trade and service industries. At the highly aggregated level of analysis presented here, average wage rates fell in most industries, but especially in those outside of manufacturing.

More detailed studies of the changing distribution of wages have shown that our declining average masks a more disconcerting underlying development: the tendency for average wages to rise in the highest-paying industries and to fall in those paying the lowest wages. This tendency toward a *polarization* of the distribution of wages was first reported by Linda Bell and Richard Freeman, using a variety of data sources and wage measures, and confirmed by researchers in Paris at the Organization for European Cooperation and Development (OECD).[9] In fact, the European researchers discovered that the inequality in different industries, after declining throughout the 1960s, began to grow sometime between 1970 and 1973, presenting us with yet another of those seemingly ubiquitous U-turns. The OECD's data revealed that average wages were declining in the poorest-paying industries and increasing in the highest-paying ones—the not-so-very-rich getting richer, the poor getting poorer once more.[10]

The U-Turn and the Individual American Worker

So much for industry aggregates. These are averages and, as such, they provide only a clue as to what might be happening to individual workers. To find out more, one must probe into the data on households and persons. Fortunately, the U.S. Bureau of Labor Statistics' *Current Population Survey (CPS)* provides data back to 1963 with which to accomplish this task.

We already know that real average weekly earnings have been falling since 1973. That is bad news in itself, but what has been happening to the distribution of earnings could make the situation even worse. One method of studying this is to measure the overall degree of inequality of wages with a standard measure of wage dispersion used by labor economists. This measure is the "variance in the logarithm of annual earnings," or what we might call for short, the earnings inequality index.*

The higher this index, the greater the overall disparity or inequality in earnings. From repeated experiments, we know that even relatively small changes in the index can signify rather large shifts in the distribution. Figure 5.2, based on our own analysis of data from the *CPS*, indicates that the annual dispersion of wages has made a U-turn of its own. After moving toward greater equality from at least the early 1960s through the mid-1970s, the distribution of earnings suddenly began to move in the opposite direction. Since 1975, after accounting for movements in the business cycle, the *in*equality of wages has tended to increase. In fact, the index of inequality used here increased by 18 percent between 1975 and 1986.

Since this must be a rather abstract sort of number to most readers, let us put it into perspective. A simple way to digest this statistic is to view it historically. The increase in inequality since 1975 has been so great that the index has returned all the way back to the level that existed in 1966.[11] Virtually all the movement toward greater equality made between the mid-1960s and the mid-1970s was wiped out by 1986. Clearly we are talking about quite a substantial increase in inequality.[12]

What factors led to this phenomenal U-turn in the trend toward greater equality of wages? Let us consider first how much of the increase in inequality among workers resulted from the growing dispersion of their hourly pay and how much was due to the growing dispersion in the amount of time people worked—what the government statisticians call "work experience." When we analyze the data, we find that at least two-thirds of the growing inequality can be attributed to the increasing dispersion of hourly wage rates. The remaining third is the result of increasingly unequal hours worked.[13] In short, the growth of inequality is due to two factors. First and foremost, some workers have been able to climb up the hourly pay ladder while others have fallen down a few rungs; and second, some workers have benefited from

---

*A measure of inequality known as the "Gini coefficient" is described in more detail later in the chapter and in note 30.

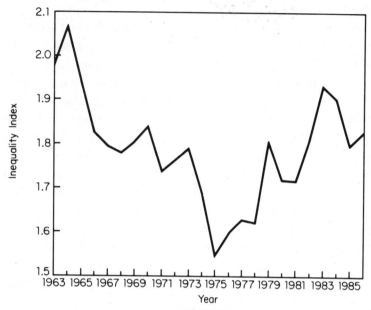

FIGURE 5.2

Inequality in Annual Wages and Salaries, 1963–86
(decycled)

Note: The data reflect the variance in the logarithm of annual wages and salaries of all U.S. workers aged 16 and over. The raw data on the variance in wages drawn directly from computer analysis of the data from *CPS* have been adjusted for variations in the business cycle so that the figure represents underlying trends rather than simply the fluctuations associated with years of expansion and recession. This economic decycling was accomplished in a two-stage regression: the logarithm of GNP was first regressed against a straight time trend, and the resulting residuals were then used to decycle the earnings data.

SOURCE Special tabulations from the March issues of the U.S. Census Bureau, *Current Population Survey* (Washington, D.C.: U.S. Government Printing Office, 1964–1987).

more overtime hours while others are increasingly trapped in part-time or seasonal jobs. This is fully consistent with the reports about entire industries from Bell and Freeman and from the OECD researchers in Paris.

What about more conventional explanations for growing inequality, such as the entry of the baby-boom generation into the work force of the 1970s and the rising number of women workers? Such generational and gender "crowding," widely postulated by mainstream economists and journalists, could obviously cause an increase in the gap between the wages of older and younger workers and between men and women. That in itself could be the reason for the growing overall inequality.

It could be, but it is not. When we consider crowding on its own (that is, not simultaneously accounting for other factors such as the shift of workers from the manufacturing to the service sector and from full-time to part-time work), we discover that the baby boom and the growth in the number of female workers have had *no significant impact whatsoever* on the increase in the inequality of wages. Indeed, men's and women's wages actually converged slightly in this period—owing more to declines in the average wage of males than to increases in the wages of women. The wages of white women and women of color are now almost indistinguishable. Put another way, all of the increase in inequality since 1975 must have occurred *within* age, race, and sex groups, not among them. Inequality is growing among whites as well as nonwhites, among the old as well as the young, and among women as well as men.

Similarly—and perhaps surprisingly—changes in the level of education of the work force, in the amount of training workers receive, and in their years of experience on the job contribute practically nothing to an explanation of the growing inequality of wages. It may well be that the much-discussed deteriorating quality of American education and the failure of private industry to provide adequate training on the job are depressing the productivity of the American labor force and impairing our competitive position in international trade. But whatever their effects on "competitiveness" and on the overall *level* of wages, changes in education and training are not making the *distribution* of income from labor more unequal. Something else must be going on.

One thing is the shift of workers from the manufacturing to the services sector. When we studied to what extent inequality might be due to a shift in employment from the generally high-paying, durable-goods manufacturing sector to the lower-paying service sector, we found, sure enough, about a fifth of the increase in the overall inequality of wages since 1978 is attributable to this shift. Jobs in the durable manufacturing sector pay much more equitably than jobs in the service sector. The other four-fifths of the increase in the inequality of wages occurred *within* industries. We believe this was due to the internal restructuring of wages and hours of work that we discussed at length in chapters 2 and 3. These research findings provide both direct and indirect support for the hypothesis that it is a combination of deindustrialization and the restructuring of industrial relations within companies that has produced the growing inequality among American workers.

The Polarization of the Job Market

What we know so far is that the distribution of workers' earnings is becoming more unequal, and we know something about why. But this does not tell us the whole story. We can learn even more about the U-turn in the labor market by looking specifically at the trends in low-paying, average wage and high-paying jobs. Again we find that the trend is toward polarization, at least among the roughly 60 percent of the American labor force that works year-round and usually full-time (YRFT).* Since the late 1970s, the proportion of the labor force earning low wages has grown steadily, the proportion at the top of the distribution has also expanded (but not as much), and the middle group has shrunk. This may not imply literally an economy with a "missing middle" but it certainly shows an economy in which the center is contracting.

Nowhere is the U-turn in the job market more evident than in the trend toward low-paying jobs, as shown in fig. 5.3. Here we have plotted the percentage of the YRFT labor force that earned the equivalent of about $11,000 a year or less (in dollars adjusted for inflation as of 1986) in every year from 1963 to 1986.** Note that, from 1963 until 1970, the share of low-paid workers plummeted. While more than one out of five (21.3 percent) YRFT workers earned low wages at the beginning of this period, that proportion fell to only about one in eight, 12.4 percent, by the dawn of the 1970s.

*Originally, we had thought to study the distribution of wages among *all* workers.[14] Critics pointed out that this was akin to mixing apples and oranges. The total work force includes those employed most of the year and people who, either by choice or because of circumstances beyond their control, work only part of each week or year. Since the size of the latter group fluctuates greatly over the business cycle, it was (said our critics) misleading to lump both groups together. The best way to get a glimpse of the underlying wage structure of *jobs*, they said, would be to focus on the YRFT workers. We have followed their advice.

**The data for these computations come from the same official U.S. government *Current Population Surveys* that we used to study the "variance" in annual earnings. We chose $11,000 (more precisely, $11,103) as our measure of low-wage employment on the basis that it represents *half* the prevailing wage of all YRFT workers in 1973, adjusted each year for inflation by the Consumer Price Index (CPI). The year 1973 was chosen as the base for this calculation since, as we saw in chapter 1, average wages reached their highest point in history in that year. While any given percentage of the median wage could have sufficed, 50 seems as appropriate as any. In 1986, according to this measure, a worker who was employed all 52 weeks of the year and was paid for 40 hours each week would have had to earn no more than $5.34 an hour to be included in the low-wage category.

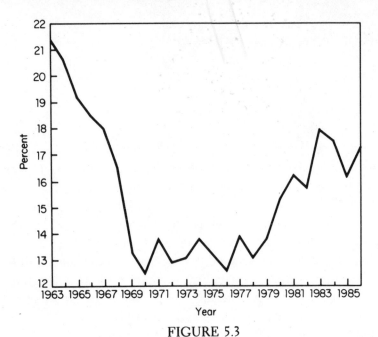

FIGURE 5.3

Low-Wage Share of Total Employment, 1963–86
(Year-Round, Full-Time Workers Earning a Maximum of $11,103 in 1986
Dollars)

Source Special tabulations from the March issues of U.S. Bureau of the Census, *Current Population Survey* (Washington, D.C.: U.S. Government Printing Office, 1964–87).

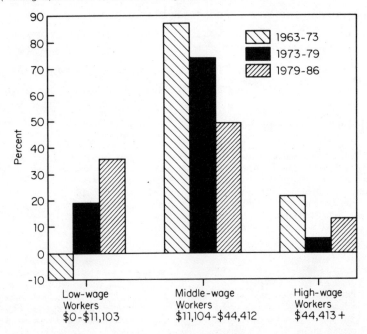

FIGURE 5.4

Net Change in Employment by Wage Stratum, 1963–86
(Year-Round, Full-Time Workers)

Source Special tabulations from the March issues, U.S. Bureau of the Census, *Current Population Survey* (Washington, D.C.: U.S. Government Printing Office, 1964–87).

During the next eight years, the low-wage share remained essentially unchanged. The oil crisis of 1973 did not budge it, nor did the deep recession of 1975. The dramatic improvement of the previous eight years was over, but the labor market did not deteriorate. This era came to an end sometime around 1978. Ever since, the Great American Jobs Machine has been churning out low-wage jobs at a record pace. By 1986, the percentage of low-wage workers had risen back up to 17.2— the 1967 level. More than one in six YRFT workers was again in the low-wage bracket.[15]

And what about the rest of the distribution—the high and middle strata of the labor market? Of the net number of workers added to the labor market since the early 1960s, how many have been paid low wages, how many high wages, and how many fell into the middle?* Figure 5.4 sums up the answer to this question.

Look at the columns reporting new low-wage workers. The percentage of net additional YRFT workers earning low wages rose steadily over the three periods shown in the chart—roughly the 1960s, 1970s, and 1980s.[16] At the other end of the wage spectrum—encompassing jobs paying roughly $44,000 or more per year—the percentage of net additional workers declined sharply in the middle years but rose again after 1979. This expansion of new workers at the bottom and the top of the wage distribution had to devastate the middle. Nearly nine out of ten of the net new jobs generated between 1963 and 1973 had fallen into the middle of the distribution. In the period ending in 1986, that proportion sank to only one in two!

---

*Following the methodology used to choose a low-wage cutoff, we set the threshold for high wages at twice the 1973 median annual wage for YRFT workers, adjusted for inflation by the CPI. (We use twice the median instead of just 50 percent above, because like all income distributions, this one is skewed to the right. A "50 percent above the median" cutoff would exaggerate the size of the high-wage group.) This procedure provided our three wage categories or strata (in 1986 dollars):

Low-Wage Stratum	Middle-Wage Stratum	High-Wage Stratum
$0–$11,103	$11,104–$44,412	$44,413 or more

What Caused the Boom in Low Wages?

Many critics assert that what we have been measuring is nothing more than a movement of wages normally associated with the ups and downs of the business cycle. Robert J. Samuelson, economics columnist for *Newsweek* and the *Washington Post,* argued that the "low-wage explosion is mostly a statistical illusion, reflecting the impact of inflation and recession on workers' earnings."[17] In a similar vein, Janet L. Norwood, the commissioner of the BLS, reasoned that lack of progress toward reducing low-wage employment "reflects the impact of the 1981 to 1982 recession rather than a general inability to generate good jobs."[18] And Warren Brookes, a conservative newspaper columnist based at the Heritage Foundation, called the finding of low-wage proliferation nothing more than a "Big Lie."[19]

Others have argued that, while the trends are not in real dispute, the cause is. Downplaying any structural change in the economy, researchers, including Robert Lawrence of the Brookings Institution, have dismissed the low-wage phenomenon as simply a temporary demographic quirk caused by the extraordinary number of inexperienced baby boomers who flooded the labor market during the 1970s.[20] To these observers, the aging of the baby-boom generation will be sufficient to eliminate the low wage "bubble."

To test these hypotheses, we subjected the raw YRFT data on wage trends to a series of statistical tests.[21] The first of these involved an investigation of how much of the pattern could be explained by the business cycle. To do this, we decycled the data using six different variables.[22] No matter which variable we used, the U-turn remained strongly in evidence. Of the six decycling terms, only one proved statistically significant, and that one explained less than 30 percent of the total variation in the low-wage trend. Furthermore, *after* the data were decycled, the rise in the low-wage share beginning in 1979 turned out to be even greater than the rise in the raw numbers! Hence, an increasing national trend toward lower wages remains evident despite at least four years of economic expansion and falling unemployment.

Another part of the analysis involved three factors that might explain changes in the decycled low-wage share: growth or decline in productivity, in the proportion of the labor force aged 25 to 34, and in the share of the labor force employed in the manufacturing sector. We reasoned that low productivity could easily cause lower real wages (either by holding down wages in the pay envelope or by pushing up prices), that the baby boomers could depress wages either as a result of their inexperience or by their sheer numbers, and finally that the shift from a manufacturing economy to a postindustrial service economy could depress wages by eliminating highly paid manufacturing jobs and substituting poorer-paid service employment.

The results were quite clear. Productivity matters. The lack of growth in productivity during much of the 1970s and its slow growth in the 1980s are at least partially responsible for the proliferation of low-wage employment. Specifically, a 1 percent decline in productivity, others things remaining equal, produces approximately a 2 percent increase in the proportion of low-paid workers. Deindustrialization also matters. Declines in the proportion of workers employed in manufacturing are associated with increases in the proportion of workers earning low wages. Here, a 1 percent decline in the percentage of jobs in manufacturing yields a 1 percent increase in the size of the low-wage stratum.

And what about the claim that the baby boomers account for the rise in the low-wage part of the distribution? The answer seems to be in the negative. After accounting for the business cycle, for productivity, and for the shrinkage of manufacturing jobs, the growing proportion of baby boomers in the total work force contributes nothing to an explanation of low wages. While it is true that they include the largest proportion of earners of low wages, they are not alone. Older workers have experienced a U-turn in their fortunes as well, so that age itself provides no clear explanation of the changing wage pattern. It therefore seems likely that the key factors are, after all, those that we explored in chapters 2 and 3—the global economic challenge, industry's inability to meet that challenge by increasing productivity and by marketing quality products, and corporate management's decision to adopt a desperate policy of reversing the slide of profits by becoming lean and mean with regard to its work force.

The Democratization of Polarization

What we have found out about the labor force as a whole turns out to be true of virtually all groups within it. This pattern of the proliferation of low wages and the polarization of jobs is by no means confined to only a few subpopulations. The polarization of jobs is becoming increasingly universal, no matter what the color of workers' skin, their sex, their age, or for that matter, the industry within which they work. Table A.2 in the appendix conveys a sense of just how widely the problem is shared. All of the eighteen groups shown separately in this table experienced a trend toward polarization between 1979 and 1986, and most show an even longer-term trend toward the proliferation of low-wage jobs.

Consider, for example, the position of men—historically the most privileged group in the work force. Men comprise approximately three-fifths of the year-round, full-time work force. In 1973, fewer than 7.4 percent of them earned the equivalent of $11,000 per year or less. By 1986, the percentage had risen to 11.7. Moreover, the proportion of net new employment that paid middle-level earnings to male workers—between $11,000 and $44,000 a year—has literally crashed, from nearly 78 percent between 1963 and 1973 to only 26 percent in the period ending in 1986. This is polarization with a vengeance.

In at least one sense, women who are employed YRFT have fared better than men. The proportion earning low wages dropped dramatically, from more than 40 percent in 1963 to 25 percent in 1973, and it has remained at that level. The fact that the incidence of low wages among these women workers has not risen since 1973 is, by contrast to men, good news. So is the rise in the percentage of such women earning high wages, which has more than tripled since 1973. We could be more enthusiastic about this improvement if the underlying numbers were not so minuscule. The proportion of women earning $44,000 or more a year (in real dollars) increased from a grand total of less than two-hundredths of 1 percent of all YRFT workers in 1963 to nearly nine-tenths of 1 percent by 1986!

Tragically, low-wage employment rose sharply among workers of color beginning around 1979, after more than a decade-and-a-half of improvement. Indeed, virtually all of the improvement experienced by black, Hispanic, and Asian workers between 1973 and 1979 disappeared in the 1980s. Younger workers were also hard hit after 1979. Almost three-fifths of the net new YRFT employment that went to workers under the age of 35 since then has paid less than $11,000 a year. Those without high-school diplomas also suffered disproportionately. By 1986, more than a third of the dropouts were low-wage earners, the highest percentage of any group enumerated in table A.2.

The remaining panels of the table show how the patterns vary among the major regions and industries of the country. Not unexpectedly, the condition of the old industrial Midwest is the most extreme. It leads the nation in generating new low-wage jobs. What new employment has been created is *all* in the extremes of the distribution of wages—and fully 96 percent is in the bottom. There are no new jobs in the middle stratum at all! Deindustrialization, more prevalent in the Midwest than anywhere else, is plainly taking its toll. As well-paying manufacturing jobs disappear, new employment is almost entirely in the poorly paid jobs in the service sector, with a handful of new workers at the top. The Northeast, South, and West also all show a U-turn in the proportion of poorly paid workers although, in the Northeast and South, after 1979, the proportion of well-paid workers rose as well.

Who Are the Low-Wage Workers?[23]

Just who *are* these people who worked year-round, full-time and yet still earned wages that placed them below even the government's meager poverty level for the average family of four persons? An investigation of this question only reinforces the picture that has been emerging throughout our discussion. The low-wage work force in America increasingly includes a large contingent of middle-class citizens—or, at least, citizens who have up to now thought of themselves as middle-class. To be sure, the pool of poorly paid workers in 1986 still contained a disproportionate number of women and members of minority groups, the young, and the poorly educated. But large percentages of other groups are also earning low wages. Nearly three million people with college training were among the ranks of YRFT low-wage workers in 1986, amounting to more than a quarter of the total. Nor are the workers in the low-wage pool mainly young and inexperienced, or people facing retirement. A full three-fifths were of prime working age, 25 to 54.

What is more, the *trend* in the low-wage population since 1963 suggests that those workers traditionally most favored in the U.S. labor market—whites, men, and workers in the high-wage Midwest—are joining the low-wage segment in record numbers. In this sense, the low-wage work force is far more heterogeneous than had previously been thought—more of a socioeconomic rainbow.

One last point is in order. So far, all of the statistics that we have presented refer to year-round, full-time workers. Yet there are nearly fifty million workers in America who for any number of reasons work less than year round or full time. Their earnings are even more precarious. Nearly 80 percent earn less than the $11,000 established as the low-wage cutoff for YRFT workers. And only four hundred thousand of those nearly fifty million earn above our high-wage standard. With involuntary part-time employment growing in the nation, this is truly an important reminder of just how many flaws there are in the Great American Jobs Machine.

Family Income and Another Great U-Turn

What is troublesome for individuals in the labor market is reflected in the family. After all, in any economy—with perhaps the exception of a few rich oil sheikdoms—the most important source of a family's income is wages from work. If wages are stagnating and becoming more unequal, one can pretty safely bet that family incomes are stagnating and becoming more unequal as well.

But family income is affected by more than just the job market. The wages of every single worker in the economy could decline and family income could still rise, if more members of more families entered the work force. In large numbers of households, this is precisely what has been happening since the mid-1960s.[24] The distribution of family income could also be affected by changes in the "structure" of families. If, indeed, we are moving toward a nation of families of "DINKs" (dual-income, no-kids) and divorcés (single parents), one might well expect the distribution of family income to veer further and further toward the extremes.

Transfers of income in the form of Social Security, veterans' payments, workers compensation for illness or injuries on the job, unemployment insurance, and AFDC are also counted as family income. This makes it possible that, even as wages stagnate and earnings become more unequal, government transfer payments could buoy average family living standards and offset the polarization of wages. Despite the sharp cutbacks in a number of important transfer programs during the Reagan administration, the total level of federal transfer payments to persons has doubled since 1979, while state and local government assistance has expanded by nearly 90 percent. By early 1987, the combined sum reached, for the first time in history, more than half-a-trillion dollars.[25]

Family income also includes interest, dividends, and rent paid to households. Since 1979, these have grown nearly twice as fast as wages, and therefore have also served to buttress family coffers.[26] However, unlike Social Security payments, such "property income" is very unequally divided. According to a report of the Congressional Budget Office, the upper 20 percent of all families received more than seven tenths of all property income generated in the country and the very richest 5 percent received half the entire pool.[27]

How has this all worked out? If we add up the effect of falling average wages, the growing polarization of earnings, the changing demographic data, and the growth of transfer payments, interest, dividends, and rent, what has happened to family income and its distribution?

We saw part of the answer in chapter 1. Median family income has stagnated ever since 1973 (recall fig. 1.2), and the inequality of family income has followed the same course as wages—it has taken a sharp U-turn toward ever greater inequality, in this case starting in the late 1960s (recall fig. 1.3).[28] This U-turn in the equality of family income has been confirmed by a host of researchers, using a variety of methods, definitions, and data.[29]

The measure of inequality that we used in figure 1.3 was the "Gini" index, named after the nineteenth-century Italian mathematician who developed it. It is today the official measure of inequality adopted by the U.S. Census Bureau. The higher the Gini index, the greater the degree of inequality; the lower the index, the more equal the distribution.[30]

Back at the end of World War II, the index stood at .376. The poorest two-fifths of all families in the nation received only 16.9 percent of total family income while the richest fifth received 43.0 percent. By 1968, after years of strong economic growth, the War on Poverty, and the Great Society programs, the Gini had fallen to .348. The share of income received by the low-income group had increased to 17.7 percent while that of the high-income group had shrunk to 40.5 percent. While hardly a revolution in the income distribution, the income of the bottom 80 percent of the population rose faster than that of the richest 20 percent.

This shift in the distribution of family income did not occur smoothly during the early years, but was instead closely related to the business cycle. During recessions in 1954 and 1961, family incomes became more unequal. But, owing to the nation's economic growth during most of the postwar era, and especially between 1961 and 1968, the general direction was toward growing equality.

After 1968, however, any effect that the business cycle had was swamped by the reverse movement—a virtually incessant tendency toward growing *in*equality. From 1968 until 1980, the Gini rose at a modest pace. Then inequality accelerated. By 1984, the Gini was at its highest level since the end of World War II and continued to rise despite the economic recovery of 1983 through 1987. It exceeded .390 in 1986, the highest, as far as we know, since the Great Depression.[31] Put in its starkest terms, every bit of the progress made toward American equality during the first twenty years after World War II was wiped out in the next decade-and-a-half. The gains made during President Truman's Fair Deal, Kennedy's New Frontier, and Johnson's Great Society, were all reversed. The equality of family income underwent a 180-degree U-turn.

Gini coefficients are tiny numbers, and not easy to grasp intuitively. They are likely to convey the impression that not much has really changed, while nothing could be further from the truth. Look at the numbers in table 5.1. In 1986, the average annual income of the

TABLE 5.1

The Impact of Changing Income Distribution on Rich and Poor Families in 1968 and 1986[a]

	Poorest Fifth of All Families	Richest Fifth of All Families
Average Family Income in 1986 Under the 1968 Distribution	$ 9,779	$ 70,722
Average Family Income in 1986 under the 1986 Distribution	$ 8,033	$ 76,310
Gain or Loss ($)	−1,746	+5,588
Gain or Loss (%)	−17.9	+7.9

[a]This table is based on the number of families in the United States in 1968 and 1986, and on the distribution of total family income in those years.

Source Computed from data in U.S. Department of Commerce, Bureau of the Census, "Money Income of Households, Families, and Persons in the United States: 1984," *Consumer Income Series* P-60, no. 151 (Washington, D.C.: Government Printing Office, April 1986), table 12, p. 37, and special tabulations for 1986 provided by the U.S. Bureau of the Census. See endnote 32 for a more detailed explanation.

poorest fifth of all families was $8,033. This was more than $1,740 *less* than they would have received had their share of national income remained the same as in 1968. By contrast, the wealthiest fifth of all families were the prime beneficiaries of the great U-turn. By 1986, they were receiving nearly $5,600 *more* per year (on top of an average $71,700 income) than they would have received under the 1968 distribution.[32]

In summary, the growth of families with more than one wage earner, together with the increase in income from property and government transfers, has been, at best, just sufficient to maintain the value of the median family's income in the face of falling wages, but any equalizing due to transfer payments has apparently been overshadowed by the sharp disparities in the distribution of wages, interest, dividends, and rent. What is more, none of the statistics regarding family income include capital gains—the profits made by selling stocks, bonds, or real estate. Given the boom in the prices of stocks and bonds and the soaring real-estate market, the growth in inequality would surely be even greater if these were included in the income estimates. Virtually all capital gains go to a tiny segment of the well-to-do in America. In a moment we will return to the measurement of growing inequality in the distribution of wealth.

The "Declining Middle"

What we—and many other researchers—have discovered is a striking redistribution of family well-being. A debate continues over whether the trend toward greater financial inequality is taking the form of a relative decline in the size of the so-called middle class.[33] Moreover, there still remain a number of unanswered questions concerning the *causes* of this growing polarization of incomes.

The idea that such developments as the shift from manufacturing to services might be leading to a disproportionate decline in the size of the middle class was first advanced in a widely quoted article published in 1983 by the journalist, Robert Kuttner.[34] Such a discomforting picture of President Reagan's "new morning" in America could not go unrebutted. A host of other journalists, as well as academic and government critics, emerged to describe Kuttner's "missing middle" as a statistical illusion.[35] The trends were either nonexistent or simply a consequence of business cycles or demographic change. With the battle lines drawn, in quick succession others entered the fray. After several years of wrangling, it now appears that the preponderance of the research tends to support Kuttner's idea.[36]

A definitive study of the question was prepared at the Federal Reserve Bank of Boston by senior economist, Katherine Bradbury.[37] Comparing data for 1973 and 1984, Bradbury finds a substantial decline in the share of income going to middle-income families. The size of America's middle class—which she defines as consisting of families with incomes between $20,000 and $50,000—declined from 53 percent of the population in 1973 to 47.9 percent in 1984. And what has happened to the middle? Of the 5.1 percentage point decline, 4.3 percent *slid down* the income spectrum to the bottom bracket and less than 1 percent moved up to the top bracket. More recent research, conducted by the U.S. Congressional Office of Technology Assessment, broadly confirms Bradbury's findings.[38]

Bradbury's work also helps us to understand what was responsible for this trend—or at least what was *not* to blame. Following the lead of Robert Lawrence of the Brookings Institution, many of the critics of the thesis that the middle class is declining have suggested that, to the extent statistical evidence *can* be adduced in its behalf, the explanation would turn out to be mainly demographic. But when Bradbury examined her data for indications of any conspicuous demographic correlates of a declining median family income and increasing inequality of income, she found precious little. As table 5.2 indicates, all of the leading demographic explanations for the declining middle can account for no more than four-tenths of 1 percentage point of the 5.1 point drop in the middle class. Changes in the size of the family have contributed modestly at best to the decline, as has the changing regional location of families. The expansion of DINKs at one end of the distribution and single-parent families at the other contributes more to the decline, but this factor is countermanded and outweighed by the growing participation in the labor force of spouses and the aging of the overall population. In the end, Bradbury concluded that a definitive explanation of the shrinking middle class still eludes statistical verification, but she believed we will eventually find part of the answer in the deindustrialization and restructuring of the economy. In the final analysis, she suggested a hypothesis close to our own:

> Declines in the middle class were biggest (6 to 7 percentage points) in the Middle Atlantic and East North Central divisions—the nation's heavy industrial heartland—lending some credence to the view that the decline in the middle class is related to the decline in traditional manufacturing.[39]

Who suffered the greatest relative deterioration in their standard of living from the economic developments of the 1970s and 1980s? Ac-

TABLE 5.2

Change in the Size of the U.S. Middle Class from 1973 to 1984

	Change in Percentage of Families with Middle-Class ($20,000–$50,000) Incomes
Estimated Change Attributable to Shifts in:	
Family Size	−0.3
Region	−0.2
Age of Head	+0.3
Family Type	−1.4
Labor Force Status of Spouse	+1.2
Sum of Demographic Factors	−0.4
Change To be Explained by Other Factors	−4.7
Total Change	−5.1

SOURCE Katherine L. Bradbury, "The Shrinking Middle Class," *New England Economic Review*, September–October 1986, adapted from table 3, p. 52.

cording to Bradbury, it was the stereotypical middle class household—what she calls the "Ozzie and Harriet" family, after the 1950s television program created to depict a "typical suburban household" of the period. It consists of a male head of household aged 35–44, a nonworking spouse, and two dependent children. Between 1973 and 1984, the real median annual income of such families fell by 7.4 percent. And the fraction of such families earning middle-class incomes fell by 8 percentage points, compared to a 5-point decline for all families. In general, older families are now doing somewhat better, particularly because of the expansion in Social Security. Younger families are doing worse.

That the baby boomers are in particular trouble has been demonstrated by Frank Levy and Richard Michel of the Urban Institute. According to their careful research, the typical young male baby boomer in the 1980s has not come anywhere close to enjoying the same rising living standards as his parents did when they were the same age. The 25-year-old in 1950 could expect to see his real income more than double by age 35. The same was true of 25-year-olds in 1960. But in the 1970s, the gain in income between the ages of 25 and 35 was a mere 16 percent.[40] Levy's forecast is for negative income growth among this cohort in the decade of the 1980s.[41]

Still, the hardest hit by the restructuring strategies of the business sector and the policies of the federal government continue to be the poor, whose numbers have swollen since the mid-1970s. Earlier we observed that no one-to-one connection can be drawn between low wages per se and poverty. Poverty is a *family*, not an individual condition. Now is the moment for re-examining that connection. After all, poor families are simply the group making up the lower end of the distribution of income among all families in society.

Figure 5.5 shows the federal government's own calculations of the number of persons living in poverty since 1960. Its pattern is one with which we are now familiar. The incidence of poverty declined rapidly during the 1960s, stagnated until the late 1970s, and has shot up since then. The overall expansion of the economy beginning in 1983 has reduced poverty a trace; nevertheless, by 1986 there were nine million more poor people in the nation than there were in 1973.

At the University of Wisconsin's Poverty Institute, Peter Gottschalk and Sheldon Danziger have studied some of the factors responsible for

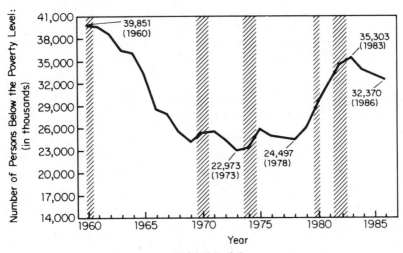

FIGURE 5.5

Number of Persons Below the Poverty Level: 1960–1986

Note. Shaded areas are periods of recession.

SOURCE U.S. Department of Commerce, Bureau of the Census, "Money Income and Poverty Status of Families and Persons in the United States: 1986," *Current Population Reports,* Consumer Income (Washington, D.C.: Government Printing Office, July 1987), Series P-60, no. 157.

this increase in poverty in an America that at one time had challenged itself to wage an all out "war" to eliminate the problem altogether. They conclude that, during the period from 1967 to 1979, increases in transfer payments from the government (such as food stamps) and increases in wages were equally influential in reducing poverty, while the gradual increase in inequality in the overall national distribution of income cut the other way, acting to increase the incidence of poverty. By 1979, with wages falling and the government actively seeking to slow down (and eventually to reduce) some income grants to poor people, the negative effect of a worsening distribution of family income had become dominant. The explosion in the rate of poverty since 1979 has been the result.[42]

The Growing Inequality in the Distribution of Wealth

Finally, we can take a brief look at what has been happening to wealth—the accumulated assets of families. Unhappily, the story is once again the same: a turn toward growing inequality, beginning in the late 1970s. From the "Survey of Consumer Finances" conducted in 1983 by the staff of the Board of Governors of the Federal Reserve System, we learn that the proportion of nonfarm American families owning their homes increased from 62 percent in 1970 to 65 percent in 1977, but then fell back to 60 percent by 1983.[43] And small wonder, given the astronomical increase in mortgage rates in the late 1970s to early 1980s and the continued slide in real take-home wages. As late as 1973, the typical 30-year-old male with average earnings required 21 percent of his salary to finance the mortgage on the median-priced home. In 1983, a similar 30-year-old needed 44 percent of his monthly pay to afford an equivalently priced house.[44] Without assistance from parents—or two full incomes—home ownership has become only a dream to a large segment of the baby-boom generation.

Ownership of financial assets—checking and savings accounts, stocks and bonds, certificates of deposit, and money-market accounts—has also taken a U-Turn in the direction of increasing inequality. The proportion of families with more than $2,000 worth of financial and liquid assets (adjusted for inflation) rose between 1970 and 1977 from 53 percent to 56 percent. Sometime after 1977, this ratio fell, so that by 1983 only 52 percent of American families held assets of more than $2,000. During the same periods, the real median financial and liquid assets of the family also rose and then fell, from $2,307 per year to $3,033 and then back to $2,300.[45]

The staff of the Federal Reserve Board found the concentration of wealth "striking." For example, in 1983 the most prosperous 10 percent of families owned 41 percent of all the dollars sitting in checking accounts, 72 percent of all the dollars invested in stocks, 50 percent of the value of all physical property, and 78 percent of the value of all businesses.[46] No data are available for a later year, but it is likely that the merger-and-acquisition driven stock-market boom of the mid-1980s, together with continued high real interest rates, have made the contemporary distribution of wealth even more unequal than these numbers indicate.[47] Thus, it is not only income, but also the savings that families can rely upon in a time of need that have taken a U-turn toward growing inequality.

An End to the American Dream?

From the end of World War II until the late 1960s and early 1970s, average real wages and incomes rose steadily, and both individual wages and family incomes became distributed more and more equally. Moreover, the economy created a steady stream of jobs that permitted workers and their families to escape poverty and become part of a growing and vibrant middle class.

Then, just when the Vietnam War was drawing to a close, wages started to fall, family income deteriorated, and inequality of wages and income began to grow again. Inequality has been growing ever since. Especially dramatic has been the proliferation of low-wage employment, even among persons working year-round and usually full-time. When one has compiled and digested all of this statistical evidence, it is hard to avoid the conclusion that the average standard of living and the degree of equality among workers and families are both deteriorating.

These developments appear to be neither cyclical nor temporary. The ups and downs of the business cycle explain little of the U-turns in real wages, the inequality of wages, and family income. Demographic factors cannot explain lower wages or the decline in the size of the middle class. What we are led to believe is that this overall deterioration in the living standards of many Americans is traceable mainly to deeper structural causes: the increasingly vulnerable position of the United States in the volatile global economic system, the particular strategies adopted by corporate managers to reduce the cost of labor in an effort to cope with the profit squeeze engendered by this heightened competition, and the many ways in which the U.S. government has encouraged those corporate experiments in restructuring.

Does all this portend an end to the middle class in America? Of course not. But as all these statistics prove, the standard of living of low and middle-income workers and families is definitely under attack—perhaps the most forceful and concerted since the Great Depression. Still, the middle class in America is resilient. Workers struggle to maintain their wages against the forces of deindustrialization and restructuring through both individual and collective action. Families cope in a hundred-and-one ways, all to maintain their standard of living.

What the U-turns tell us is that America's families today find themselves on a treadmill. They must run as fast as possible—and work harder than ever—to sustain a standard of living no greater than that which prevailed in 1973. The global challenge to their skills and their talents would certainly have been enough to force them to find new ways of earning a living. But what makes the going so much harder is that America's corporate leaders and the nation's elected officials have adopted an explicit set of private and public policies that have further handicapped those still in the race. These policies may have proven effective in rebuilding profit rates, but they are wreaking havoc with the American dream.

6

The Illusion of Solid Growth

THERE ARE MANY CONSERVATIVES who might agree—at least in private—that the corporate and government policies of the 1970s and 1980s contributed to falling real wages and rising income inequality. But they would be quick to add that such outcomes, although painful, were unavoidable side effects of a fundamentally sound economic program—a program designed to increase savings and investment, boost productivity, and ultimately contribute to international competitiveness. After all, on the eve of Ronald Reagan's ascendancy to the White House, economic matters were, by anyone's calculus, exceedingly grim. Unemployment was rising past the 7 percent level and inflation was threatening to linger in double digits. GNP was falling, the country's merchandise trade balance had shifted into what would soon appear to be virtually permanent deficit, and productivity in the business sector had declined two years in a row. Something drastic had to be done.

Politicians, economists, journalists, and corporate officers agreed that sacrifice would be needed to put America's financial house back in order and to assure a reversal of the economic malaise associated with the stagflation of the 1970s. The days of paying lip service to the "equality of short-term sacrifice" (much less fretting about it) were over. David Stockman, Reagan's chief architect for the administration's revolutionary changes in policies governing taxes, transfer payments, and expenditures was the most honest of all, admitting in his best-selling memoirs that "his blueprint for sweeping, wrenching change in national economic governance . . . required the ruthless dispensation of short-run pain in the name of long-run gain."[1] Today, no one denies the pain. The question is, what is the nature of the gain?

In his first address to Congress on February 18, 1981, the new president confidently outlined a plan to "put the nation on a fundamentally different course—a course leading to less inflation, more growth, and a brighter future for all of our citizens."[2] As we saw in chapter 4, the basic tenet of the new supply-side strategy was that private initiative and unfettered markets were the only feasible roads to economic recovery. Workers, entrepreneurs, and corporations would have to be offered lower taxes and regulatory relief in order to unleash work, savings, investment, and innovation. Those who had become indolent in their protected markets and listless on the dole would change their ways in the wake of deregulated markets and shrinking public assistance.

Many believe that Reagan's economic strategy worked. Economic growth, which had stumbled in 1980 and in 1981–82, began to surge in 1983. For more than five years, the GNP kept growing month after month, compiling a more durable record than at any time since the extraordinary decade of the '60s. Along with growth came jobs—more than twelve million since 1981. And as we saw in the last chapter, there was also a substantial recovery in corporate profits.

But did Reaganomics actually work? Is the growth we enjoyed sustainable? Can the doctrine of laissez-faire, deregulation, and devolution of the welfare state ultimately reverse the trends toward lower standards of living and more inequality? The answer to all three questions is no. Instead of exchanging short-term sacrifice for long-term prosperity and more equality, America has been doing just the opposite: buying short-term economic recovery at the exorbitant price of forfeiting long-term social and economic security.

The Illusion of Solid Growth

Reassessing the Reagan Economic Recovery

A multiple-choice question about the Reagan revolution might read as follows: Which of the following statements were true of the American economy in the 1980s?

(a) The economy experienced a substantial recovery after the dark days of 1980–82.
(b) Reagan's policies were largely responsible for the growth in GNP and new employment.
(c) The supply-side mechanisms that Reagan hoped would spur the economy were dismal failures.
(d) Reagan's policies set in motion long-term economic consequences that threatened the very standard of living in the United States.

The answer to the quiz is that all four statements are true. To understand this, we need to take a look at Reagan's economic record.

By early 1987, in spite of the Republican Party's setback in the previous November's midterm elections and the growing scandal over Iran and aid to the contras in Nicaragua, the Reagan administration was gloating over its economic successes. In his economic report to the Congress, the president announced:

> Our market-oriented policies have paid off. The economic expansion is now in its fifth year, and the growth rate of the gross national product, adjusted for inflation, should accelerate to 3.2 percent in 1987. By October, the current expansion will become the longest peacetime expansion in the postwar era.
>
> Our efforts to reduce taxes and inflation and to eliminate excessive regulation have created a favorable climate for investing in new plant and equipment. Business fixed investment set records as a share of real gross national product in 1984 and 1985, and remains high by historical standards. Despite the economy's tremendous gains in employment and production, inflation has remained below or near 4 percent for the past 5 years.
>
> In short, since 1982, we have avoided the economic problems that plagued our recent past—accelerating inflation, rising interest rates, and severe recessions. Production and employment have grown significantly, while inflation has remained low and interest rates have declined. This

expansion already has achieved substantial progress toward our long-term goals of sustainable economic growth and price stability.[3]

The president's report was submitted to Congress in the midst of a financial boom unprecedented in the postwar era. On the very day of its release, January 23, 1987, Wall Street had one of its most bizarre days ever. In a span of less than two hours, the Dow Jones Industrial Average soared by 65 points, and then, in the next forty-five minutes, plunged by more than 115. The market lost $30 billion in value in the time it takes to play a set of tennis.

That night on ABC's news program *"Nightline,"* host Ted Koppel asked Robert Prechter, whom *Business Week* had proclaimed the most prescient stock-market analyst of 1986, "What's going on?"[4] Prechter predicted, as he had before, that the Dow Jones average would climb to 2,800 by the end of 1987 and would continue on to 3,600 by late 1988. "And then?" Koppel asked. Without batting an eyelash, Prechter looked into the TV camera and forecast six years of substantial declines. "The best analogy," the analyst suggested, "is that the market is where it was in early 1928." The Dow Jones average still had a pretty good ride ahead, but then there would be something very much akin to the crash of 1929. Koppel and his audience were stunned.[5] As it turned out, Prechter's forecast of a second great stock-market crash in this century was on the mark, but his timing was off, costing some of his clients a fortune.

In large measure, the reason for such an alarming forecast lies in the very nature of the economic recovery that began in 1983. On the surface, the recovery looked real enough.[6] The GNP, which had declined in 1980 and 1982, rebounded smartly. In 1983, its real rate of growth was 3.6 percent; the next year it weighed in at a hefty 6.4 percent, the most since the mobilization for the Korean War in 1951. Unemployment, after peaking at 10.8 percent in December 1982, fell steadily through 1987. Corporate profits, which had been moribund in 1982, bounced back by 1984, rising by 45 percent in two years. And as we have seen, double-digit inflation was completely defeated, owing largely to a consistently overvalued dollar which cheapened the cost of all imported goods coming into the United States. Looking at the statistics in the first two years of the recovery, one could certainly ask of the Reagan critic, "So what's the beef?"

The Illusion of Solid Growth

To see the problem with this recovery, one must recall the steps by which the supply-side resurgence was supposed to take place. Step 1: The personal tax cuts were to encourage work and personal savings, while corporate tax cuts and deregulation would presumably lead to a boom in short-term investments and innovation. Step 2: The additional work plus new investment were supposed to increase productivity and thereby boost the United States' global competitiveness. Step 3: The increased productivity and new-found competitiveness would permit an increase in exports, GNP, wages, profits, and family incomes. Finally, Step 4: Rising wages and increased profits would put the national economy on a trajectory of steady, inflation-free economic growth and enhanced economic security. In short, the temporal *order* of the recovery was to proceed from government-induced tax cuts and market deregulation to increased savings, investment, and innovation, to increased productivity, and then to renewed international competitiveness, and finally to rising wages and a higher standard of living.

But the plan did not work out this way at all. To be sure, GNP, employment, and profits all went up in the short run and inflation did come down. But the deep cuts in personal taxes did not create a boom in savings. Just the opposite occurred. The rate of savings plummeted after 1981 (fig. 6.1), declined steadily thereafter, and by 1986 was at its lowest since 1939.[7] Rather than behaving as the supply-siders wanted, the American public refused to save its tax cuts and instead went on a spending spree. Domestically generated dollars for investment were, in consequence, not forthcoming from the household sector. If it wished to invest, business would be forced to find sources of finance capital abroad.

This it did, and net investment in new business equipment increased after 1982. But this small boom was short-lived and hardly a direct consequence of reduced taxes on profits or the increased allowances for the depreciation on capital. It took until 1985, well after the tax cuts were in force, for the rate of spending on capital to exceed the level of 1978 and 1979—and just one year later, the investment boomlet petered out.[8] In fact, total expenditures for all new plant and equipment in the manufacturing sector actually declined—in current dollars—by 5.7 percent in 1986, and hardly grew at all in 1987. Even investment *outside* the manufacturing sector stopped growing by 1986.[9]

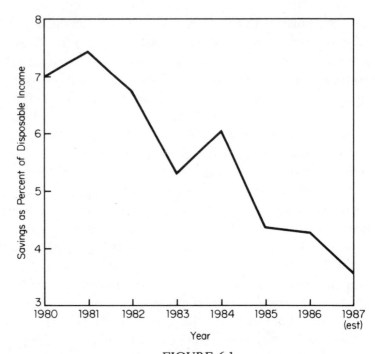

FIGURE 6.1
The Savings Rate Keeps Sinking
Data: Commerce Dept., Data Resources Inc.

Source Council of Economic Advisers, "Economic Indicators" (Washington, D.C.: Government Printing Office, March 1988), p. 6.

Using another standard indicator of U.S. private capital spending— the ratio of nonresidential fixed investment to GNP—Benjamin Friedman, an economist at Harvard University, has shown that the rebound in investment by mid-1985 only brought the United States back to where it had been in the mid-1950s. The 1985–86 rate of 2.9 percent was far below the nearly 5 percent achieved by the middle of the presidential term of Lyndon Johnson.[10] Moreover, what investment did occur was limited to a narrow range of goods. Between 1979 and 1984, 93 percent of all business investments were either for computerized office equipment or the replacement of autos and trucks in company transportation fleets. Only about 7 percent of the investment dollar was spent on new productive equipment to be placed in operation on factory floors.[11]

To predict the impact of this anemic and skewed investment pattern on productivity hardly requires a complicated model. Labor productivity for the economy as a whole—the very centerpiece of Reagan's program—never rebounded at all. In fact, it crashed. From a high of 3.3 percent in 1983, the growth of productivity fell to 2.1 percent in 1984, 1.2 percent in 1985, and turned negative in the last two quarters of 1986.[12] Even during those first nine strong quarters, from early 1983 through the spring of 1985, the Reagan recovery ranks last among all postwar recoveries in terms of productivity growth.[13] That is hardly the type of boom in productivity the supply siders promised when they took up the reins of economic policy back in 1981.

As we have learned, profits did rebound in the wake of the 1982 recession. One might have expected this to fuel a new wave of productive investment. But, in many industries, it did not. At least part of the reason is that greater profitability, which in theory *could* finance productive new investment, does not automatically *compel* that investment to take place. If there is already sufficient capital in place, it is unlikely that much more will be added. And such has frequently been the case. In spite of five years of recovery, the average rate of capacity utilization in American industry—the economist's best measure of the "unemployment rate" of factories and workshops—is still below the 85 percent level of 1979.[14] Indeed, as fig. 6.2 shows, in terms of capacity utilization the Reagan recovery compares quite unfavorably with past recoveries lasting a comparable length of time. With existing productive capacity still relatively underutilized, it is hardly surprising that so many companies have been unwilling to invest in even *more*. Indeed, a major reason for what higher utilization rates have occurred is the continued rash of plant closings that reduce production capacity.

It is also true that, after eight years of Reaganomics, American corporate managers continued to be more intrigued with short-term returns than long-term investment. The new federal tax code that took effect on January 1, 1987 should have reduced the financial incentives for mergers and acquisitions by substantially increasing the tax rate on capital gains. Yet even this did not change entrepreneurial behavior. The number of completed mergers and buyouts in the first half of 1987 was actually higher than in the first half of 1986.[15] The casino economy continued apace even as the decade of the 1980s was becoming history.

There is still a third reason why the restoration of profitability did not lead to a comparable wave of new long-term investment throughout American industry—and this goes to the very core of Reagan's eco-

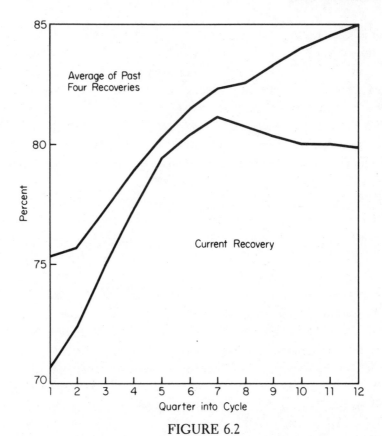

FIGURE 6.2

*Rates of Utilization of Manufacturing Capacity in the Reagan Recovery,
Compared with the Four Post–WW II Recoveries That Also Lasted 36
Months or Longer (seasonally adjusted)*

SOURCE *Business Week,* 17 March 1986, 72; based on data from Morgan Stanley & Co. and U.S. Department of Commerce.

nomic legacy. The rebound in profits has been the product of spending by consumers and the government that was virtually all financed by debt. The government has gone farther into debt than ever before, mostly to pay for the biggest so-called "peacetime" military buildup in history. Consumers, whose average wages had long since stopped growing, found themselves with almost no choice but to go deeper and deeper into debt simply to maintain their standard of living. Fear that all this debt would eventually lead to a sharp curtailment of spending both by government and consumers has kept managers from investing in new capital. No manager wants to invest in capacity that may ultimately sit idle as the economy moves into a recession.

The Sources of Economic Recovery: Defense and Debt

The enormous growth in debt during Reagan's years in the White House explains much more than just the slowdown in investment. It explains most of the macroeconomic trends we have observed since the end of the 1981–82 recession. One might ask, for example, if savings rates fell, investment petered out, and productivity plunged, what magic did Reagan call upon to sustain the growth in GNP and employment through the mid-1980s? The answer turns out to be quite simple. The president, with a good deal of support from the Congress, led the public sector on a military-spending spree financed by deficits, while the private sector—particularly households—went on a credit-card binge of its own. The mammoth debt created by both was sufficient to fuel at least a continuous, if not buoyant, short-term recovery.

The Department of Defense (DOD) led the way. Spending for defense more than doubled, from $134 billion in 1980 to $282 billion in 1987, in the process coming to consume nearly 60 cents out of every personal and corporate dollar raised by the federal government through income taxes.[16] Even after accounting for inflation, this amounted to an average growth rate of over 7 percent a year—nearly three-and-a-half times the real growth rate of GNP.[17] Since 1979, the country's military production has expanded by more than 80 percent, while production of business equipment grew by only 15 percent and the manufacture of such consumer goods as cars, refrigerators, and lawn mowers grew by at most 20 percent. (See fig. 6.3) This meant that by fiscal year 1986, direct outlays for national defense comprised more than 6.8 percent of the total national output, compared to 5.2 percent when Jimmy Carter left the White House.

As a result of all of this defense activity, more and more American manufacturers were becoming increasingly dependent on the Pentagon as a customer for their wares. Table A.3 in the appendix provides a sense of the magnitudes involved. By way of example, consider the radio and television communications industry. In 1977, about 36 cents out of each dollar of goods sold by companies in this industry went to the Defense Department, to its prime contractors, or to *their* suppliers. By 1980, the figure was 42 cents and, by 1985, fully 50 cents out of

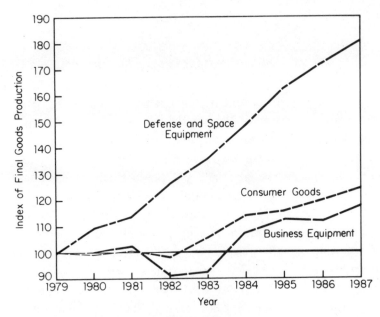

FIGURE 6.3
Industrial Growth, by Economic Sector
(1977 = 100)

Source Council of Economic Advisers, *Economic Indicators* (Washington, D.C.: Government Printing Office, October 1987), 17.

every dollar's worth of radio and television equipment were being sold directly or indirectly to the Pentagon.[18] Looking at projected DOD budgets prepared by the Reagan administration, Charles Schultze, an economist at the Brookings Institution, found that the growth in military procurement "implies the rather startling conclusion that some 30 percent of the increase in the 'goods-producing' GNP over the next four years (1982–1986) will go to the military."[19] In one sense, we can be thankful for this development. Increased military spending is the major reason why America's manufacturing sector did not become even more deindustrialized during the 1980s.[20]

It is hardly surprising that the private sector went along for the ride. After all, from 1970 to 1979 and from 1980 to 1983, periods during which the average annual rate of return on assets invested in durable goods as a whole (machinery, cars, and so forth) was falling from 14.4 to 10.6 percent, profits for arms suppliers rose from 19.4 percent to 23.3 percent. In short, "the profits gap between commercial and military businesses widened enormously."[21] As a result, the average rise in the prices of the stock of the country's fifteen leading defense contractors was consistently greater than that of the Dow Jones Industrial Average.

In the wake of the military buildup, American workers have unquestionably become more dependent on military spending for their jobs. Defense-related employment in all sectors of the economy grew by less than 4 percent from 1977 to 1980. But between 1980 and 1985, the total number of defense-related jobs (including those in the armed services) increased by more than a fifth, while employment in the private sector attributable to military procurement rose by 45 percent. All in all, the military buildup created at least 1.2 million new jobs in the United States just during the first five years of the Reagan presidency.[22] We say "at least" because these Commerce Department estimates do not include either sales abroad by the U.S. government of military goods or licensed commercial exports of military items. No one knows how much larger the buildup would look if these flows could be measured accurately.

If military spending is the first of the twin pillars on which the Reagan recovery was erected, the second—and equally strong—pillar was the literally unprecedented levels of consumer, business, and government debt accrued since 1982.

Without necessarily recognizing their own contribution, consumers played an enormous role in the recovery. In a desperate attempt to protect their standard of living from stagnating wages and increasing unemployment, families became more resourceful. They sent extra members out into the labor force to supplement the household's earnings, and a growing number of those who were already working increased their moonlighting (holding extra jobs) in an effort to stay afloat.[23] Many dug deep into their savings, often simply to survive financially. In the devastated Midwest, more than 70 percent of laid-off Michigan auto workers used up one-third or more of their savings, and more than two-fifths depleted *all* their savings.[24]

But most of all, during the Reagan years, people went into debt. The total amount borrowed by consumers nearly doubled between 1981 and 1986, from $394 billion to $739 billion. Families expanded their use of "plastic money" even faster. Revolving installment credit, via Mastercard, Visa, and the likes of the Sears credit card grew from $55 billion in 1980 to more than $128 billion in 1986. The total, including loans for automobiles, passed the half-trillion dollar mark in 1985, and kept growing nearly a $100 billion a year.[25]

As the prominent Wall Street economist, A. Gary Shilling, demonstrated, no postwar recovery has ever been fueled to such an extent by consumer debt. The ratio of such new debt to the net growth in disposable income ranged from 24 to 29 percent in the four economic recoveries previous to the one that began in 1983. In contrast, in this one the ratio grew to 44 percent.[26]

The same rush into unprecedented indebtedness was also true in the business sector. Nonfinancial corporations converted enormous amounts of equity into debt in order to finance the leveraged takeovers and buyouts they undertook during the 1980s. In fact, according to Shilling, "the value of equity withdrawn in 1984 and 1985 [alone] equals, in real terms, three quarters of all the corporate equity issued from 1959 to 1983."[27] In the same vein, economists at Manufacturers Hanover Bank in New York found that the debt-to-equity ratios of nonfinancial corporations took 13 years—1970 to 1983—to rise from under 2 to just below 4. During the following three years, this key ratio nearly doubled again. That is how rapidly the new corporate indebtedness grew.[28]

Still, it has been the behavior of the federal government that has been the most extraordinary, especially given Reagan's expressed abhorrence of public debt. The doubling of military spending between 1980 and 1986, in combination with tax cuts that reached more than $124 billion by 1985 (in personal taxes alone), made triple-digit deficits inevitable despite the administration's rhetorical support for an amendment to the Constitution to balance the budget. During his eight years in office, President Reagan presided over a federal government that spent more than $1.3 *trillion* more than it captured in taxes and other government receipts.[29]

It has been precisely this debt engendered by government, business, and private households—not increases in productivity or enhanced international competitiveness—that has been responsible for the short-term recovery of the national economy. Simply adding together the new consumer debt and the new federal debt since 1982 (and excluding new corporate debt) produces a dollar figure that is 25 percent higher than the total net growth in GNP (see fig. 6.4). Put another way, the sacrifices in wages, incomes, and inequality that we measured in the

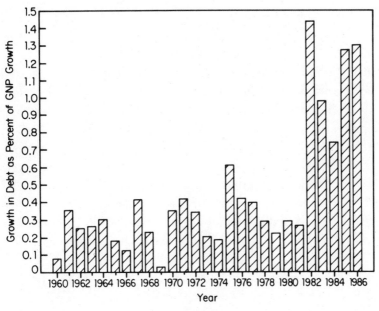

FIGURE 6.4
Ratio of New Debt to New GNP
1960–1986

SOURCE Authors' calculations from Council of Economic Advisers, *Economic Report of the President, 1987* (Washington D.C.: Government Printing Office, 1987), 330–31.

previous chapter did not produce a new wave of growth in GNP or enhance the basic soundness of the economy. All of the growth in the economy since the last recession was borrowed from the future.

From Recovery to Crisis

It is precisely the fact that all of the much-heralded growth has come from borrowed funds that makes the Reagan recovery such a Faustian proposition. This is true for families, for business, and for government. By 1986, the average family in the United States was saddled with personal debts of more than $11,500, excluding their mortgages. If the typical loan is for three years and the annual interest charge is 12 percent, the monthly installment payment for the average family amounted to roughly $380 in 1986.[30] Considering that after-tax monthly household income averaged $1,930 in that year, the typical family in the United States was spending one-fifth of its monthly income simply to pay off past purchases.[31]

That is future income that cannot be used to buy new goods and services. It is also why the number of bankruptcies declared by individuals and families under Chapter 13 of the Bankruptcy Code grew from an average of less than 39,000 per year between 1975 and 1980 to almost 95,000 a year between 1981 and 1984.[32] The federal government itself is feeling the weight of family indebtedness and bankruptcy. According to the deputy director of the Office of Management and Budget, the government, in early 1987, contracted with private collection agencies to track down and dun 1.4 million people (described by the deputy director as "deadbeats") who had defaulted on federal loans worth $7 billion.[33]

The growth of business debt adds to the instability of the economy. Martin Feldstein, a Harvard economist and former chair of Reagan's Council of Economic Advisers, warned repeatedly, before leaving office in 1985, that too much corporate income was being dedicated to the payment of interest, thereby threatening the liquidity of companies. These warnings in turn spurred Stephen S. Roach of Morgan, Stanley and Co. to observe: "These are extraordinary [corporate financial] vulnerabilities for this stage of the business cycle."[34]

The mushrooming national debt represents claims against future income, as well, and therefore a potential crisis. More and more future tax dollars need be set aside for servicing debts rather than for the production of additional public goods and services. A dollar spent on interest payments cannot be used to buy improvements in schools, public health, highways, or any of the thousand things that government should provide for society (including a reasonable level of military security). In 1980, less than 20 percent of personal income tax revenue was needed to service debt; by 1986, the proportion had nearly doubled, to 38 percent. Hence, almost $2 of every $5 we pay in federal personal income tax now goes for nothing more than interest payments. At the present rate, our grandchildren will still be paying for the Reagan recovery we bought on credit in the mid-1980s.

Along one other dimension, the picture is even grimmer. Besides the mounting personal, corporate, and federal debt, the economic policies of the Federal Reserve Board and the Reagan administration have contributed directly to the infamous trade debt. The intricacies of international finance suggest just how this came about.

In the all-out struggle against inflation, the Fed allowed domestic interest rates to rise well above the rates prevailing in other nations. For example, after accounting for inflation, the prevailing interest rate on six-month U.S. Treasury bills rose to nearly 9 percent in late 1981. The best an investor in West Germany could do was less than 5 percent.[35] As a result, large German investors, including banks, insurance companies, and trustees of pension funds traded their deutschemarks for dollars in order to invest them in U.S. securities. This additional demand for dollars naturally drove up the exchange rate. The differential in interest rates between the dollar and most other currencies became so great that investors from Japan to Saudi Arabia began to demand dollars in record amounts in order to take advantage of the investment bonanza here in the United States. Consequently, by 1985 the real trade-weighted value of the dollar had risen 32 percent above its value in 1981. Essentially, this meant that American exports were now one-third more expensive and that foreign imports were one-third cheaper. Already damaged in international markets by goods of poor quality and by poor productivity, American manufacturers were doomed by the run-up in the value of the dollar. The rest of the world flooded our markets with what had become cheaper imports.

Once the balance of trade began to move against the United States, the trade picture deteriorated rapidly and dramatically. As fig. 6.5 indicates, a long history of trade surpluses came to an end in 1981. The trade balance on current account went from a surplus of $6 billion in that year to a deficit of more than $140 billion by the end of 1986.[36] By the mid-1980s, few foreigners wanted our overpriced products and Americans were desperate for foreign currencies with which to buy imports.[37] What began as voluntary investment in the United States by foreigners became a necessity for Americans.*

To obtain the Japanese yen, the German marks, the South Korean

---

*What is so disconcerting about the trade deficit is that even after the dollar began to decline in early 1985, the trade deficit continued to balloon. By late 1987 the dollar was trading at half its February 1985 value against the Japanese yen and the German mark. Nonetheless, trade deficits, even with these two countries, did not decline significantly. Foreign firms, eager to maintain their market share, cut their profit margins and increased their productivity in order to limit the rise in prices caused by the collapsing dollar. By early 1988, the volume of U.S.–manufactured exports was finally showing signs of growth. Yet imports were still so expensive that, on balance, the total trade debt continued to rise at a pace of more than $100 billion a year.

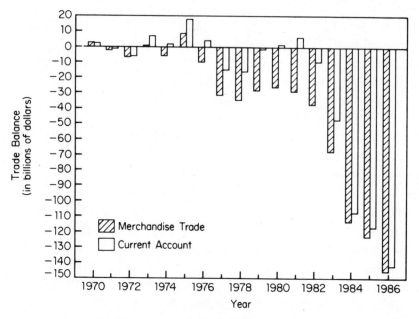

FIGURE 6.5

U.S. Balance of Trade
(in billions of dollars)

Source Council of Economic Advisers, *Economic Report of the President, 1987* (Washington, D.C.: Government Printing Office, 1987).

won, and the Canadian dollars to pay for the merchandise we were purchasing from abroad, it became necessary to get foreigners to invest more and more dollars in the United States. For example, in order to balance our $100 billion merchandise trade deficit we accumulated in 1985, foreigners bought more than this amount of American assets—almost $20 billion of high-rise office buildings, hotels, restaurants, and factories; $26 billion of U.S. Treasury securities (thus buying more of the national debt); and nearly $50 billion of corporate bonds and $30 billion worth of corporate stock.[38]

The Japanese have been the largest foreign investors. Net purchases of equity by Japanese firms came to $5.6 billion in 1986, and they spent another $6 billion on a Manhattan real-estate spree. Japanese investors bought the Exxon Building, ABC headquarters, and the Tiffany Building as well as a half interest in Eastdil Realty, one of the nation's first real-estate investment banks. So much foreign investment was necessary to finance the trade deficit that, by 1985, the United States—for the first time in modern history—became a debtor nation. As of 1985, the United States had essentially liquidated its $141 billion positive world asset position that it held in 1981, and had turned it into a debt of $107 billion.[39]

Such piling up of debt cannot go on forever. Sooner or later, the rest of the world will stop lending at current rates of interest. When that happens—when foreigners call in their loans—Americans will have to pay in one or both of the following ways. First, we may try to induce the rest of the world to keep letting us run up an international tab. The only way to do this will be to keep interest rates high, or increase them still further, in order to lure foreigners into lending us more money. This will ultimately stifle domestic consumption and investment. There is no surer way to create a deep recession and, with it, a further worsening of both the level and distribution of income.

The alternative is to induce foreigners to accept our goods and services by cutting our prices—through devaluation. This has its cost to us, as well. Devaluation means that foreign goods will become ever more expensive and that inflation induced by exchange rates will gnaw away at our real incomes. Imports are close to 15 percent of our GNP. Thus, a 33-percent devaluation means an average increase in prices of 5 percent. If incomes rise by 3 percent when devaluation occurs, real incomes will fall by 2 percent almost immediately. The worst might still be to come. If the United States continues to lag behind the rest of the world in productivity, it will be necessary for the dollar to fall steadily against foreign currencies in order for us to pay off foreign debt. If this goes on very long, the standard of living in America will gradually, but surely, fall further behind that of our trading partners. We will fall prey to the notorious "British disease."

In effect, during its years in the White House, the Reagan administration bought short-term recovery by means of a colossal debt-driven "Ponzi scheme"—an ingenious fraud *almost* perfected in 1919 by Charles Ponzi, who set up business in the heart of Boston's financial district.[40] His offer to an eager war-weary public was simple: invest any sum with him for forty-five days and he would return the money plus 50 percent interest. Invest for ninety days and realize a profit of 100 percent. He claimed that he was speculating in a sure market—the market for International Reply Coupons. These were vouchers for postage stamps that could be redeemed in any country belonging to the International Postal Union. Ponzi told his customers that, with the money they invested with him, he intended to buy the coupons in European countries where the exchange rate was low and then redeem them for stamps where the exchange rate was high. By selling the stamps he had purchased in this way, he promised his investors a fortune.

Ponzi never did buy any reply coupons or attempt to arbitrage them. But he guessed that people who were offered a chance at a geometrically increasing return would probably leave their money with him indefinitely. He was almost right. He seduced twenty thousand Bostonians into giving him $14 million in the first few months of his operation. By paying off early investors with money given to him by new ones, he built up a pyramid whose early success earned him cheers on the streets of Beantown.

The fatal flaw of pyramids, however, is that they have to be perpetual-motion machines in order to work. Ponzi's, of course, was not. It was stopped by his arrest and conviction for fraud in 1920. It took auditors until 1931 to untangle his finances, the end result being that his hapless investors received only 30 cents on the dollar. Ponzi eventually went to jail in Massachusetts, later jumped bail, and started a venture in Florida swampland. In 1934, the U.S. government deported him to Italy.

There is a lesson here. Building a recovery almost purely on borrowed funds, as the United States has been doing since at least 1983, is equivalent to a publicly sanctioned, multibillion-dollar Ponzi scheme. Without the gains in productivity required to increase the size of the economic pie, the only way to keep the recovery going is to build the pyramid of debt ever higher. When the creditors finally ask for their money back, the entire edifice will come clattering down.

As if the Gordian knot which the policies of the conservatives have tied around the U.S. economy were not bad enough, the whole situation has been made increasingly dangerous—more unstable and certainly more intractable—by yet another aspect of the debt crisis: the inability of the Third World to prosper sufficiently to provide a market for the goods produced by the developed countries. Martin Carnoy and Manuel Castells have summarized the nature of the problem of global debt so well that we quote them at length:

If the U.S. deficit is viewed in light of current economic trends world-wide, it is evident how fragile the world economy has become as a result of neo-conservative policies. The current U.S. recovery is based upon military spending and private consumption stimulated by tax cuts for the upper middle class; both are financed by government borrowing and deficit spending. [Early in the recovery] this . . . pushed up [real] interest rates and the value of the dollar, attracting capital from all over the world. But it . . . also dried up financial sources for investment elsewhere, dramatically plunging much of the Third World into debt and seriously slowing the pace of the international recovery.

The basis for a sustained international expansion is limited to a small portion of the U.S. market (middle- and high-income households), for which there is increasing international competition, and to the military in both the United States and the Third World. But these sectors are precisely those that benefit most from the two factors underlying the budget deficit—tax cuts and defense spending. Thus the U.S. deficit is sucking in capital resources from the entire world, and it has to keep doing so to prevent a collapse of the markets it has so decisively expanded. In sum, the world's economic equilibrium rests on a fragile foundation of rich consumers and wasteful government expenditure. We are engaged in a hysterical race to keep afloat until the benefits of the new [potential] productivity that is being spurred by the technological revolution can be realized. Yet these benefits cannot be realized as long as the technology is channeled into military uses. Nor can technological change be fruitfully assimilated into the economy without a different kind of social and political organization, one that would conflict with the authoritarian and bureaucratic postulates of the neo-conservatives.[41]

The Contradictions of Deregulation

As if a growing debt, a worsening distribution of income, and erratic growth were not enough to warrant strong criticism of conservative economic policy, there is mounting evidence that deregulation, the central pillar of the administration's laissez-faire philosophy, has itself produced a host of outcomes that reinforce slower growth and worsening inequality.

Consider the impact of financial deregulation on interest rates. The conventional economic wisdom lays the blame for high interest rates on deficits in the federal budget. When the government spends more than it receives in revenue, it is claimed, the U.S. Treasury's floating of bonds to finance the resulting deficit "crowds out" private opportunities to borrow, thereby driving interest rates up. The implication is that interest rates can only be lowered by cutting the federal budget deficit itself. Such economic reasoning was of course attractive to the Reagan administration, since it supported its basic desire to cut the domestic budget anyway.

The large and apparently intractable budget deficits *do* have real and deleterious effects on the economy. But the production of high interest rates is not one of them. According to a recent study conducted by the Washington-based Economic Policy Institute, since at least 1964 the Fed's prime rate, the leading indicator of interest rates, has consistently moved *counter* to changes in the budget deficit, expressed as a percentage of GNP.[42] This conclusion is fully supported by the generally conservative Federal Reserve Bank of St. Louis.[43]

A better explanation links higher interest rates to the deregulation of banks and to merger mania. Allowing banks to pay interest on checking accounts, and permitting money-market funds, insurance companies, and "non-bank banks" (such as Sears, Roebuck) to offer interest to attract lenders, set in motion a competitive spiral which surely contributed to an upward bias in interest rates in the 1980s. In order to attract and retain savings, all of these financial institutions were forced to offer higher interest rates to their depositors. To cover these higher rates, however, the institutions turned around and charged higher rates to their borrowers. The surge in business borrowing to finance mergers and acquisitions added to the upward pressure on interest rates.

While interest rates have fallen from what were astronomical heights in 1981—the prime rate charged the most credit-worthy corporate customer reached nearly 19 percent—interest rates in real terms remain well above the levels that prevailed before deregulation. These higher rates have certainly discouraged some borrowing for investment in new technology. They have kept borrowing for mortgages and home building less than it would otherwise be. And as we have just seen, by attracting foreign investors who want to purchase interest-bearing assets in this country, higher interest rates have also contributed to an excessive demand for U.S. currency. Between 1980 and 1986, this drove up exchange rates and thus cut deeply into American exports of goods and services. The result? Financial deregulation has actually inhibited economic growth.

Financial deregulation produced other problems as well. For example, it led to considerably greater *instability* in domestic and foreign financial markets. The violent roller-coaster ride in the prices of stocks and bonds attests to this development. At home, reduced governmental supervision of the investments and loans of banks made it much easier for bankers to make quick and often foolish decisions. These led to losses for consumers when the banks failed or had to be bailed out by the government's Federal Deposit Insurance Corporation, the U.S. Treasury, or by the arrangement of a shotgun merger with some healthy bank willing to take over management of the essentially bankrupt bank.[44] Internationally, the emergence of new and almost entirely unregulated inter-bank transactions—which now account for upwards of 70 percent of the market in Eurocurrency—allowed excess savings in one part of the world to be moved quickly to borrowers located somewhere else. That is certainly a healthy development. But as Karen Lissakers wrote in the *New York Times:*

> . . . many banking experts have come to regard the interbank market as the Achilles heel of the international financial system. For if the interbank market can swiftly transmit funds from one part of the system to the other, it can just as rapidly transmit—and spread through the system—the problems of any one bank.[45]

The excesses of financial deregulation have not gone unnoticed even by conservative bankers. As a result of the stock-market debacle in October 1987, the Fed moved rapidly to support re-regulation of the financial community. Republican Alan Greenspan, who replaced Paul Volcker as chair of the Federal Reserve Board, welcomed legislation sponsored by the Democratic Party that would create a financial services oversight commission to coordinate the activities of the Securities and Exchange Commission, the Commodity Futures Trading Commission, the government's banking agencies, and even state insurance commissioners. In testimony before the Senate Banking Committee in late 1987, Greenspan asserted:

> The need for greater regulatory coordination could not have been brought out more clearly than in the recent stock market developments, where we saw the complex interactions of securities, commodities and banking markets.[46]

Deregulation also adversely affected other parts of the economy, particularly the workplace. Cuts in the budget of the Occupational Safety and Health Administration (OSHA) have shown up in the most grisly form: increased maiming, illness, and death on the job. Nowhere was this more true than in the meatpacking industry, where in 1985 more than 30 percent of the work force incurred occupational injuries or illness. In other industries, including sawmill products and the manufacture of mobile homes, the rate was more than 25 percent.[47] With fewer OSHA inspectors, managers were able to speed up the pace of work, leading to a greater number of accidents. The head of the union's safety committee at one large meatpacker noted that the beef chain moved 84 percent faster than it did in 1979. In that time, the injury rate also increased—by 76 percent.[48] In all of manufacturing, days lost owing to injury and illness per hundred workers, according to the BLS, bottomed out in 1982 and has been rising ever since.[49] Here we have perhaps the most deadly U-turn of all.

A good case can also be made that even the quality of many services within the country has been damaged by deregulation. Especially dramatic is the way in which the Federal Communications Commission (FCC), during the Reagan administration, went about deregulating the television broadcasting industry. Consider these developments:

- **Children's programs**—the FCC has relaxed the rules requiring broadcasters to air "informative" children's programming, and rejected restrictions on the showing of cartoons that feature expensive toys
- **Public service**—The FCC has loosened guidelines requiring nonentertainment programming, such as coverage of community issues
- **Commercials**—The government has eliminated the limits on the time and frequency on TV commercials, allowing more commercials per hour
- **Station ownership**—The limit to how many TV, AM and FM stations which any group of investors may own has been raised from seven to twelve
- **Fairness doctrine**—The FCC has abolished the fairness doctrine, which required radio and TV stations to provide time for competing points of view[50]

The effect of the deregulation of airlines on the quality of service is now well known. The combination of delayed flights, cancelled flights, lost baggage, and increases in the number of reported "near misses"—a rather strange term for barely avoided midair collisions—resulted in a soaring number of complaints from passengers to the Department of Transportation (DOT). In the first six months of 1987, the DOT received more than fifteen thousand complaints, nearly two-and-a-half times the number received in the same period in 1986.[51]

Finally, and perhaps most paradoxically, deregulation seems, in many industries, to lead to a *stifling* of competition. Since 1978, the concentration of ownership has actually increased—that is, the number of major firms has diminished—in trucking, airlines, and railroads. While in theory small enterprises are legally free to enter any local market they wish, most simply cannot afford to compete with the local branch of a national, and often multinational, giant. In the rather understated words of Alfred Kahn, an economist at Cornell University and one of the original architects of airline deregulation: "When you have the same six carriers meeting each other in market after market, there is danger of softer competition."[52]

The movement toward privatization of public services is also a mixed blessing. The eminent sociologist Paul Starr, of Princeton University, has argued that privatization may save less public money than expected, while generating greater social cost.[53] A number of studies have demonstrated rather conclusively that, for example, public utility companies are no less efficient or competitive than private ones.[54] At the same time, privatization often reduces public accountability and skews benefits away from individuals and families of limited means. When costs are lowered, it is almost invariably done by paying lower wages and using part-time or contigent workers in place of full-time, regular staff.

This itself has created a mounting problem in cities that have attempted to privatize social services. New York City has contracts of more than $1 billion with private nonprofit agencies to provide such vital services as day care, foster care, health care at home, and emergency food and shelter.[55] Because of low wages, the rate of employee turnover has been so high in these agencies that the delivery of services was impaired. This is true of low-level service workers, and of professionals as well. As the *New York Times* discovered in 1987, the salary of a social worker with a master's degree ranged from a minimum of $24,967 to a maximum of $30,865 at a city agency. The average salary of comparable workers in the private sector was only $21,806. It is no wonder then that turnover in the private agencies reached 24 percent per year. So much for the efficiency of the supply side.

The Effect of Conservative Fiscal and Monetary Policy on Distribution

The failure of Reaganomics to solve macroeconomic problems is only half the story. The administration's tax, expenditure, and welfare policies were also responsible for directly redistributing income from the poor to the rich and from one region to another. Reagan turned out to be Robin Hood in reverse.

As early chroniclers of Reagan's experiment put it,

> In the short run, some degree of public sacrifice was inevitable if the Reagan administration was to deal effectively with problems such as high inflation and inadequate defense that faced the nation in 1981. Yet the magnitude, duration, and distribution of the needed sacrifices . . . were unclear and a cause for great concern.[56]

To see how the Reagan administration's priorities actually affected the overall distribution of income, the Social Welfare Research Institute at Boston College carried out a computerized simulation of the key fiscal elements of the Reagan program from fiscal year 1981 to fiscal year 1985.[57] The analysis was accomplished using the Multi-Regional Policy Impact Simulation model (MRPIS) developed at the Institute.

The MRPIS analysis is based on estimates of line-item revenues and expenditures in both fiscal year 1981 and fiscal year 1985, obtained from the U.S. Congressional Budget Office (CBO).[58] These estimates were initially prepared by the CBO in order to isolate the sources of the increased federal deficit between 1981 and 1985. To produce these estimates for congressional budget committees, the CBO first forecast what tax revenues and federal spending on procurement and entitlement programs would have been if the policies governing taxes and expenditures in the fiscal year 1981 (President Carter's last budget) had been carried forward to future years without alteration. These "counterfactual" estimates were then compared with actual taxes and expenditures in 1985, during the Reagan administration. The "line item" *differences* between the 1981 and 1985 budgets were used as the data for the MRPIS simulation. These are shown in table 6.1.

Essentially, defense spending was $35 billion greater in 1985, nondefense procurement was down by $16 billion, and funds for entitlement programs (such as Social Security benefits, food stamps, and Aid to Families with Dependent Children) were cut by close to $30 billion.[59] On the revenue side, the Economic Recovery Tax Act of 1981, the Tax Equity and Fiscal Responsibility Act of 1982, and the Social Security Amendments of 1983 reduced personal taxes by $117 billion, but increased Social Security taxes by $11 billion.

The MRPIS analysis confirms that the overall effect of Reagan's budget was expansionary. Disposable family income (after taxes) in 1985 was 7 percent greater than it would have been in the absence of the tax cuts and the military spending spree. Families spent so much of this windfall that overall production increased by more than $250 billion. The simulation demonstrated that in the course of this boom, 3.4 million additional jobs were created, enough to account for half of the total growth of jobs between 1981 and 1985.

But there was a less sanguine aspect of the new policies, besides the massive runup in federal debt. As a package, the creation of deficits in the early 1980s—given the method by which it was carried out—

TABLE 6.1

*Differences between Actual FY 1985 Federal
Expenditures and Spending That Would Have
Occurred If FY 1981 Policies Had Continued*

Revenue or Expenditure	Increase or Decrease (in Billions of Dollars)
Defense spending	+35.0
Nondefense discretionary spending	−16.0
Entitlement programs	−29.9
Personal income taxes	−117.0
Social Security taxes	+11.0

generated sharply increased inequalities in income. Those already at the top of the income ladder received disproportionately large gains from the shifts in taxes and benefits, while those at the bottom—despite the national boom in income—either benefited very little or sustained losses.

The most comprehensive measure of the effect of the redistribution can be found in the changes in disposable family income in various family income categories (see table 6.2). The disposable income of the average family in the top group rose more than 10 percent, while that of the lowest group fell by 2 percent. Cumulatively, 96 percent of the increase in disposable income went to the 55 percent of all families in the top two categories, and more than 63 percent accrued to the top fifth of the population alone. This is an enormous shift in income, even compared with the 44 percent of total income that initially accrued (in 1981) to the most privileged fifth of the population. The deficit-creating policies of 1982–85 increased the average disposable income of these high-income families by more than $5,300 each. Families with incomes in the lowest category suffered an average *loss* of $67.

The tendency of these tax and spending policies to create substantially greater inequality is confirmed by changes in the Gini index. During the Carter administration, that index averaged .369. By themselves, Reagan's new policies boosted the Gini index to .383. Considering that the official Gini index for the economy as a whole rose from

TABLE 6.2

Changes in Disposable Family Income
Due to Changes in Fiscal Policy,
1981 and 1985 (in 1985 dollars)

Income	Percentage of All Families	Percentage Change in Disposable Income
$ 0–5,500	9.1	−2.1
5,501–8,500	8.6	−1.0
8,501–11,250	8.9	1.1
11,251–14,000	9.3	2.2
14,001–16,750	8.6	3.5
16,751–33,500	36.0	6.1
33,501+	19.5	10.1
All Families	100.0	7.0

SOURCE John Havens et al., "The Microeconomic Impacts of Macroeconomic Fiscal Policy, 1981–1985," *MRPIS Project,* Social Welfare Research Institute, Boston College, November 1985, table 14, p. 36.

.364 to .381 between 1981 and 1984, this policy-induced rise is quite substantial. Indeed, something on the order of *four-fifths* [(.383 − .369)/(.381 − .364)] of all of the net increase in the inequality of family incomes between 1981 and 1984 was directly due to the policies regarding taxation, transfer payments and spending decided upon by the Reagan administration.

At the very low end of the income distribution, we find perhaps the most disturbing news of all. While 413,000 families initially below the official poverty line rose above it by reason of the new policies, at the same time more than one million new families were forced below it. This net increase of 636,000 poor families led to an increase in the proportion of American families in poverty, from 13.5 percent in 1981 to 14.1 under the new administration. Moreover, those families originally below the poverty line (and who remained below) suffered a further erosion of 3.4 percent of their already depressingly low disposable incomes. Again, this all occurred despite the fact that the government was pumping up the economy with hundreds of billions of dollars of deficit spending.

These federal policies also created substantial regional inequalities. The New England and Pacific census regions both averaged gains of 8.2 percent in family income, nearly 60 percent more than the states of the farm belt. Increased procurement of high-technology defense goods was the main reason for the gains on the East and West coasts, and relative cuts in agricultural subsidies were mainly responsible for the smallness of the gains in the Midwest. Farm families were adversely affected by more than just the declining world price of grain. The revisions in federal farm programs that began in 1982 left the average farm family with 0.5 percent less disposable income while families, overall, gained 7 percent. Others lost as well. The income of families dependent on transfer income (such as AFDC, food stamps, veteran's compensation) fell an average of 1.3 percent; those who started out poorest, especially families headed by women who were dependent on welfare for at least half of their income, lost almost 5 percent of their pitifully small resources.

No one understands better than family farmers and unemployed single parents what David Stockman had in mind when he developed a blueprint requiring a "ruthless dispensation of short-run pain." According to his budget director, however, Reagan "proved too kind, gentle, and sentimental" for the real revolution in American economic policy that Stockman demanded.[60] Nevertheless, the cuts Reagan *did* approve and the tax changes that he *did* sign into law shifted the distribution of income more toward the rich and away from the poor than any other set of federal policies since World War II.

"No Binge Lasts Forever"

The long-term trend toward stagnation that made its appearance in the late 1960s and early 1970s with the collapse of the postwar social contract and the opening up of the American economy to global economic forces was still there in 1988. The only difference is that it became well masked. For a time, that great American invention, the postindustrial service sector, created enough jobs to put the baby-boom generation to work and keep unemployment at bay. Then came the twin pillars of the Reagan recovery: a splurge of military spending and unprecedented indebtedness. These were sufficient to provide the illusion of solid growth. Yet in spite of the many glowing reports about the successes of the Reagan revolution, by the end of his presidency, the essential underlying vulnerability of the American economy was being recognized. More and more observers were summoning up the courage to take a close look at what eight years of an affair with laissez-faire had wrought.

Knowing what we now know, what can we expect in the near future? Economic growth will continue to stagger along, and long-run growth in productivity, especially in the service sector, looks anemic. Edward Denison, of the Brookings Institution, reports that, in each successive business cycle, the actual GNP has fallen farther and farther below the level of output which our growing labor force and new technologies *ought* to permit us to produce.[61] The result is a stagnating or even falling standard of living. Indeed, many of the long-run indicators of working-class hardship continue to show a rise: the average duration of a spell of unemployment, the ratio of layoffs to presumably voluntary quits, and the overall "marginality index"—a summary statistic made up of those who are unemployed entirely, those who work part-time because they cannot find full-time jobs, and those who have become discouraged by repeatedly unsuccessful searches for jobs and have dropped out of the labor market altogether.[62]

That the structural economic crisis is *not* over is also indicated by the continuing shakeout of business establishments. The upward trend in business failures that began back in the late 1970s, after declining earlier in that decade, accelerated sharply during the Reagan administration, far outpacing the rate of new incorporations. Between 1979 and 1985, the rate of business failures almost doubled, while new incorporations rose by less than 25 percent; the Commerce Department's index of net business formations actually declined by 14 percent. The financial sector was in trouble even before the stock market crash of October 1987. By the end of 1986, the Federal Deposit Insurance Corporation's list of "problem banks" totaled twelve hundred—more than one of every twelve banks in the country. Just three years earlier, there had been only 250 banks on the danger list. All of this can now be added to the trends we mapped in the last chapter— the U-turns in the level and distribution of real wages and family income.[63]

Alan Blinder, an economist at Princeton University, has no doubts whatever that, on balance, the Reagan revolution was an economic disaster.

No binge lasts forever. The drunk eventually sobers up. Sooner or later America will awaken to the hangover of Reaganomics. No nation can long consume more than it produces. Since our spending now greatly exceeds our output, and since we are piling up international debt on which interest must be paid, America is headed for a painful adjustment period during which spending will grow more slowly than GNP.

How much slower? During the past six years, spending expanded at a 3.4 percent annual rate while GNP grew at a 2.4 percent rate. If the one-percentage-point difference reverses itself over the next six years, 2 percent to 3 percent real GNP growth will yield only 1 percent to 2 percent growth in real spending. Such will be the unpleasant legacy of Reaganomics.

It is hard to resist the conclusion that we've been had.[64]

There is an age-old debate in economics over whether an economy should be judged on the basis of its contribution to growth or to equality. Some have argued that the two are often incompatible.[65]

Others, like Robert Kuttner, in his superb account of what he terms the "economic illusion"—the belief that social justice is bad for economic growth—argue just the reverse.[66] Social justice, to this way of thinking, is a necessary condition for long-term economic growth.

To assess the Reagan revolution, it is unnecessary to resolve this debate. The policies that Reagan and the conservative supply siders brought to government in the early 1980s have failed on both grounds. To be sure, inflation was brought under control and the basic statistics on GNP and the growth of employment look much better than those of the stagflation-prone 1970s or the recession years of the early 1980s. But the real test of these policies is whether they have contributed to rebuilding the basic engine of the economy so that it can grow over the long term, regain its competitiveness, assure a rising standard of living, and ultimately provide greater economic opportunity for ever-greater numbers of people. This, Reaganomics has not done. Instead it mortgaged the future of the economy to pay for the mirage of recovery today, and in the process created a society more deeply divided by income and social class than at any time since the end of World War II.

During the 1980 presidential campaign, then-candidate George Bush referred to the supply-side proposals put forth by candidate Ronald Reagan as "voodoo economics." In retrospect, Bush seems to have been right, after all.

7

Swings of the Pendulum

WITH THE END of the Reagan presidency, it is possible to look back and assess the two great social experiments of the twentieth century. One was the welfare state, which developed from the Great Depression, went through its heyday during the 1960s, and began to unravel by the middle of the next decade. The other is the laissez-faire affair which we have studied at length. As we enter the last decade of the century, it seems clear that neither of the two great experiments lived up to its advance billing. The welfare state, that seemed to promote and distribute material gain so well from the end of World War II to the early 1970s, finally ran out of steam. It could no longer assure economic growth or stable prices, and without these the widespread popular support necessary for the further redistribution of wealth to root out poverty and promote equality evaporated.

The expansion of the welfare state was never high on the agenda of the rich. But by the middle of the 1970s, it had lost its glamour for much of the middle class and the working class as well. Forty-two percent of unionized auto workers voted for Ronald Reagan during the recession of 1980. About the same number voted for him in 1984, despite the fact that industry employed many thousands fewer of them than in 1979. Reagan's landslide presidential victory over Walter Mondale in 1984 was not so much an embracing of laissez-faire as a rejection of what were seen as the shopworn welfare policies of an earlier era.

The same message heard in the United States reverberated in the United Kingdom, where Margaret Thatcher campaigned successfully time and time again on an avowedly antiwelfare platform.

But this is not to say that the American people, or for that matter the British, have embraced the supply-side policies of government or the cost-containment strategies of the private sector. The Democratic Party regained a majority of the U.S. Senate in 1986—at least one piece of evidence that unrestricted laissez-faire will not sell forever.

To our way of thinking, as more and more citizens become aware of the instability of the economy and of their own growing insecurity within it, the door is opened—at least a crack—to a radical departure from both the standard policies of the Democrats and the supply-side nostrums of the conservatives. What could such a radical departure be like? Would it hold out a better promise of increasing productivity, boosting wages and incomes, and distributing the fruits of this growth more equitably?

The Failure of the Democrats

The allure of the Democratic Party agenda that included antipoverty programs, subsidized housing for those with low incomes, public transit for those without autos, welfare for those without jobs, and affirmative action for those of the "wrong" color or sex did not pale because Americans became more selfish and greedy or more racist and chauvinist. Its appeal diminished when the agenda had to be financed by the redistribution of wealth rather than by growth—and when what was financed was not broad-based social programs such as Social Security, the G.I. Bill, and federally funded mortgages but programs designed almost exclusively to help the poorest of the poor. We can trace the end of the great welfare state to the early 1970s, when earnings and family income stopped growing and low-wage employment began to dominate the American Jobs Machine.

What the Democrats lacked most were not plans for education, health, housing, or transportation, but for restoring productivity and economic growth. By the time Jimmy Carter moved into the White

House, the administration had neither a macroeconomic plan to use government spending and tax cuts to stimulate industry nor industrial policies to restructure capital and labor markets to run more effectively. In place of bold initiative, the Democrats turned to what was fundamentally an end-game strategy: hold the fort with existing policies, at least until the ammunition runs out.

By the end of the 1970s, the American people more than sensed that there was no more ammunition left in the Democratic Party's arsenal. They were ready for the first time in nearly half a century to take a big risk: not to merely change parties, but to take a chance on an entirely new economic and political philosophy. It was therefore with some excitement and not a little relief that the American public awaited the new Reagan administration, with its bold promise of a grand experiment in laissez-faire. The economy, it was said, was *too* planned. Government was *too* big and intrusive. It was time for another swing of the pendulum, this time back from the welfare-state experiment that had begun a half-century earlier with the election of Franklin Delano Roosevelt in 1932. The name of the new game in town was to be "competition."

The Reagan revolution offered a single, simple solution to any and all of society's problems: *more competition.* If management were inefficient, unbridled international competition would force it to reform. If profits lagged, the competition of workers for wages would boost them. If the airlines' services were poor, deregulation would force them to compete with new airlines and to offer cheaper fares and better service. If public schools failed to educate students, privatizing them through a voucher system would boost literacy and scores on college-entrance examinations. "The Gipper" knew how competition on the playing field sharpened performance. If it could work in football, why not in everything else?

The Failure of the Conservatives

It did not take long for the problems of laissez-faire to become apparent. Competition works as long as you sometimes win the game. But for an increasing pool of Americans, numbering in the millions, competition did not mean opportunity, it meant they played the game and they lost. The game turned out to be a sort of Darwinian struggle of worker against worker, community against community, and region against region. Perhaps more rapid growth would have turned the contest into a positive-sum game in which the overwhelming majority improved their lot. But this has most decidedly not been the legacy of the supply-side experiment.

The conservatives failed to take two things into consideration. First, human beings tend to be averse to risk. Second, even in the roughest of sports, there *are* rules. For these two reasons, the pure "competitive solution" is always destined to fail—leaving the social pendulum to swing back toward a greater balance between economic competition and social planning. Reaganomics was doomed from the beginning, not because of some technical malfunction in policy but because of a much deeper fundamental flaw: it violated basic tenets of human nature. To understand this, we need to examine more closely the essentials of conservative ideology.

The true conservative takes issue with virtually everything the federal government provides, outside of the activities of the departments of Defense, State, and Justice. Milton Friedman, the dean of contemporary American conservatives, for example, has steadfastly opposed—with no exceptions—price supports for farmers, tariffs and import quotas, rent control, minimum wages, detailed regulation of industry, occupational licensing, public housing, national parks, publicly owned-and-operated toll roads, and Social Security.[1] In each case, the conservative argues that individuals are denied their freedom when they are forced to pay more for commodities because of price supports, tariffs, and quotas; when they are barred from renting their property and selling their labor without restriction as to price and without being required to have a license, and when they are forced to pay for services—such as pensions and recreation—that they can provide for themselves.

Laissez-faire, according to its adherents, not only maximizes individual liberty and is therefore ideal in its own right, but it has one additional attractive property. It promotes economic efficiency. Unbridled competition guarantees consumers the lowest possible prices and the highest quality. Similarly, competition guarantees employers the best labor at the lowest wage. As long as people are willing to offer their services at a lower price, employers are free to hire them. Anyone who wishes to work in such a world is virtually guaranteed a job. Simply ask for less pay, agree to work harder or longer, or improve your skills, and some employer will hire you in order to make a profit from your effort. What is more, the conservative argues that laissez-faire enforces civil rights. Any firm that discriminates against minorities or women will soon find that it must pay higher wages for the labor it is willing to employ, and the higher wages will destroy their profits. Hence, the free market and perfect competition not only bequeath liberty to the individual, but implicitly combat inflation, unemployment, and discrimination. What more could anyone ask of a social system?

The answer is: peace of mind.

The type of competition that conservatives postulate amounts to a Hobbsian world in which there is a war of all against all. Firms must be constantly on guard against losing their entire market to a new domestic or foreign entrepreneur with essentially the same product but a slightly lower price. And workers must continually keep an eye cocked to see which young upstarts are perched to take away their jobs simply by offering equivalent work for ten cents less an hour. In such a world, there is a bullish market in Maalox and valium. It is a world of stress and depression, ulcers and cardiac arrest. As the political scientist, Charles Lindblom, wrote:

> Because [market] exchange is usually abruptly terminable, what one wins in exchange is at risk. . . . Market-oriented systems may have prospered historically only because subtly working social mechanisms have restrained the total demands put upon them. If these constraints are eroding, we may have to look forward to decades of growing economic disorder in market systems.[2]

The age-old defense against Hobbsian war is collective action. Firms form industrial associations in order to set quality standards and lobby for legislative protection of their market. Professionals form associations to set licensing requirements and to lobby for standards that protect their occupations. And workers form trade unions to protect themselves from managerial strategies of divide and conquer. Associations—recently castigated by conservatives as "special interest groups"—have always been the white cells of human society. They ward off the unhealthy competition that threatens the very lifeblood of civilization. They provide the foundation for individual security and social civility by placing bounds on competition and keeping it in its place. Collectivities promote freedom from perpetual risk.

One implausible, but revealing, social experiment—or better yet, magic trick—might be to wipe out, in a single stroke, every association, club, and organization that serves the purpose of promoting the interests of a particular segment of society. The National Association of Manufacturers (NAM) would disappear, as would the Chamber of Commerce, the Machine Tool Builders Association, and the Associated Industries of Massachusetts. The American Medical Association (AMA) and the American Bar Association would be dissolved, along with the American Association of University Professors and the College of Barbers. Gone would be the United Auto Workers and the Service Employees International Union.

What would happen if such magic could be wrought? Would everyone begin to compete as individuals, driving down prices, improving quality, and generating full employment? Of course not. Within a matter of weeks, if not days, new associations would arise in response to the enormous insecurity throughout society. Instead of the NAM, we would likely find an AMS—the American Manufacturers Society— holding an inaugural convention. Instead of the AMA, doctors would soon be forming the NPO—the National Physicians Order. And those who toil in automobile assembly plants and work in post industrial service jobs would also form new organizations—perhaps the National Car Builders and the Service Workers Collectives.*

Within a few months, each of these organizations would assume most of the standard setting and lobbying of their predecessors. Instead of undiluted competition, a whole set of associations and unions with the same functions as the ones that now exist would be built. Likewise, if a conservative magician could wipe out half the federal laws and emasculate two-thirds of the nation's regulations, these would surely be reinstated as individuals rediscovered their usefulness.

---

*Indeed, we already have one example of this very thing occurring. Within four years of the abolition of the Professional Air Traffic Controllers Organization (PATCO) by executive order of President Reagan, a new formal union was organized to press the grievances of overworked and overstressed controllers. The new organization has nearly the unanimous support of its occupational group.

In a strange sense, perhaps, the Reagan revolution (and the conservative ideology underlying it) is utopian. It is dynamically unstable. It requires selfless individuals, who—contrary to all of history—believe that individual competition in a totally unfettered market will serve their interests best and who accept self-defeat with perfect equanimity, blaming no one but themselves and seeking no allies. With the exception of a few "Rambo" characters here and there, the human race simply does not behave this way. This is not to say that people are not competitive. Naturally, they are. But they are competitive in the same way that most of us are willing to wager an occasional $10 on the state lottery, but few of us will bet our homes, our cars, or our jobs. We are all gamblers to some extent, but we value basic security even more. What is it then that requires fundamental change in the Reagan revolution, that makes one believe the political pendulum will swing back? Simply that the revolution has created too much personal and family insecurity and too much social and economic instability.[3] As long as unemployment remains generally in check and as long as those who finance consumer, government, and trade deficits continue to extend credit no matter how indebted we become, Reagan's policy of deregulation and delegitimation of government could continue. But, as the business cycle plays itself out, as joblessness creeps up again and indebtedness comes home to roost, the collective demand that government rein in competition will be difficult to ignore. What people want is both economic growth and a modicum of economic security. The question is, what can be done to achieve it?

A "Revenue-Side" Alternative to Conservative Supply-Side Austerity

In the context of the Reagan revolution, supply-side ideology essentially became "cost-side" economics. To counter heightened competition from abroad, the Reagan revolution entailed not so much a counter-assault on foreign markets as the deliberate encouragement of heightened competition at home. Lip service was paid to the enhancement of productivity that could also enhance international competitiveness, but the real thrust of the supply-side theory was to augment corporate attempts to reduce the cost of labor and the price paid for government.

Could there have been a "revenue-side" alternative—one that did not require such indiscriminate sacrifice by so many workers, families, and communities? We believe the answer is yes. Such a revenue-side alternative would stress increases in output and demand as an alternative to the wholesale reduction of costs. Instead of shrinking wages and incomes, which only reduce the size of the world market, a revenue-side policy for the United States must be founded on global reflation and a greater stress on raising productivity at home. Both require more public planning than ideological conservatives will abide—or, for that matter, many traditional Democrats.

While there is much to be done at the level of the individual firm, reversing wage stagnation and thereby rebuilding living standards will require a continuing expansionary macroeconomic policy both at home and abroad. With the U.S. economy limping along at an average real growth of well below 3 percent per year—and virtually all of this sustained by debt—there is simply not enough demand to raise living standards. If total output rises at a rate no higher than the growth of the population, average income cannot rise. We must therefore find ways to accelerate growth. This can only be done by boosting consumption, investment, government spending, or net exports—the constituent components of the GNP.

With consumer debts at such high levels, any boost in consumption will require substantial increases in the income of consumers. Given the enormous national debt and the continuing string of triple-digit federal deficits, another round of tax cuts to increase the income of consumers is clearly out of the question. The alternative, of course, is to raise family income by raising wages. Instead of the reductions in wages we have suffered since the early 1970s, we need the opposite: wage and salary increases that outrun inflation.

Investment also requires a sharp boost. After healthy growth in 1983 and 1984, real domestic investment actually declined in 1985 and then rose an anemic 1.8 percent in 1986. That figure was not much better in 1987. With domestic buying weakening and real interest rates rising still higher, corporate managers have little incentive to make new productive investments. A combination of higher wages and lower interest rates is needed to reverse this situation. A forth-right move by the Federal Reserve Bank to counter rising interest rates is in order.

Ordinarily, if government deficits were not already so large, expansion could be fueled by more government spending. In the current climate, politics, if not economics, precludes any such stimulus. This does not mean that we cannot have more spending on education, research and development, health care, housing, and other socially beneficial programs. But to do so we must reduce other slices of the federal pie—especially the well-stocked defense budget. Compared to its key trading partners, the American government spends little on research and development for industrial productivity and energy, less on housing, and much less on health care. In a recent study of the United States, West Germany, Japan, and Sweden, America scored lowest on all of these accounts.[4] Improving our record in these fields will not only help to maintain our output, but will help to increase productivity and our international competitiveness.

Switching away from our heavy reliance on military spending and redirecting these dollars into other areas will help boost productivity directly. This is particularly true because the Department of Defense (DOD) budget is increasingly concentrated in research and development with limited commercial applicability. The share of federal spending going to the development of high-technology manufacturing related to the military is now enormous, and by itself is distorting any pretense of balanced economic growth. More than 70 percent of all federally funded research and development is now tied to military programs, up from 50 percent as recently as the last year of the Carter Administration.[5] Almost the entire development (perhaps 70 to 80 percent) of such "cutting-edge" technologies as lasers, artificial intelligence, fuel-efficient jumbo jet engines, superspeed computers, high-density semiconductors, vision-equipped robots, computer-aided manufacturing systems, and advanced synthetic materials is now controlled by military policy. A new Pentagon office is expected to account, by 1990, for a full fifth of the nation's high-technology venture capital. And none of these statistics include President Reagan's Strategic Defense Initiative (SDI) which, according to plan, would eventually enroll more scientists and engineers than either the Apollo space program or the development of the atomic bomb.

In the past, many observers have felt that, while perhaps politically distasteful, military-driven research and development provided a source of optimism for the long run, on the assumption that it would have other significant applications which would eventually lead to the emergence of entirely new manufacturing processes and products that might restore the international competitiveness of U.S.–made goods. Others simply thought that the whole thing made for a splendid political arrangement—especially for senators and representatives from states and districts benefiting from contracts from the Pentagon.

But now a major reassessment of the benefits spun off from military-driven research and development is under way.[6] From Paul Sweezy and Harry Magdoff on the left, writing in *Monthly Review,* to Murray Weidenbaum, President Reagan's first chair of the Council of Economic Advisers, and the late Arthur Burns on the right, more and more analysts ranging across the ideological spectrum are raising doubts about the long-term benefits of military research and development. Indeed, such students of the subject as Ann Markusen, Mary Kaldor, Seymour Melman, James Fallows, and Lester Thurow now believe that massive defense spending actually *harms* high technology by creating bottlenecks in production, encouraging inefficiency, and diverting human and capital resources away from pressing social problems. Jay Stowsky of the University of California at Berkeley offers several compelling examples:

> The list is long of defense contractors that have failed to blend defense and commercial technologies successfully: Rockwell International and its Admiral T.V. sets; Grumman's flexible urban buses; Rohr's subway cars; Boeing Vertol's trolley cars; McDonnell Douglas' jet-powered fire fighting platform.[7]

Moreover, preoccupied with their contracts with the Pentagon, "American small aircraft manufacturers, including Beech, Cessna, and Piper, have failed to invest in the technology necessary to develop an aircraft that can compete effectively in the fast-growing commuter airline market. Defense technology has become so exotic that its transferability is increasingly limited even in the aircraft industry, our premier source of export earnings. Hence, America's commuter airlines are turning to Canadian, French, and Brazilian firms to fill their needs."[8]

This indicates the last, but perhaps most important, way to boost demand: increasing exports. Reversing the massive trade deficits that have plagued the country since 1982 could do more to bolster the GNP than any conceivable turnaround in domestic investment or consumption. The $112 billion trade deficit in 1984 is estimated to have reduced the GNP in that year by as much as 2.5 percent and cost the economy as many as 2.4 million jobs.[9] The trade deficit has since grown, presumably costing the nation even more in output and income.

Balancing our international trade will require much more than simply depreciating the dollar (in any case, that only lowers domestic purchasing power at home even further). Managing exchange rates so that they better reflect real production costs in each country is certainly one part of better planning. But given any reasonable set of international exchange rates, two changes will still be necessary if exports are to assist in reviving economic growth. First, the United States will need to offer products and services of better quality; second, the rest of the world will need to expand—reflate—its own economies in order to buy what we have to sell.

The sluggish growth of the European Economic Community (EEC) and the devastation of Third World economies both contribute to our stagnation. The EEC, comprised of the major countries of Western Europe, has experienced a continuing decline in the growth rate of its GNP. Its average growth of 4.7 percent between 1961 and 1965 and 4.5 percent between 1966 and 1970 rate fell to 2.8 percent during the following five years, revived slightly to 3.0 percent between 1976 and 1980, and has been lethargic ever since. For the past six years, the Community's average growth, 1.4 percent, has fallen substantially behind ours (2.4 percent). An equally dramatic decline in the growth rates of developing countries has occurred as well. Between 1961 and 1980, their real GNP grew by an average annual rate of nearly 6.4 percent; since then, the rate has barely reached 1.9 percent.[10]

Global reflation will require other developed countries to accelerate their own economies through expansionary fiscal and monetary policies. The recent announcement that the Japanese will speed up their investment in public infrastructure is a move in this direction. The expansion of foreign money supplies would be another.[11] But each nation is reluctant to expand its economy in the absence of an agreement by all to do the same. Each fears that unilateral expansion would lead to inflation and a surge in imports that would harm its own industries. Hence, an explicit agreement among the leading developed countries is needed to solve the dilemma that each nation faces.

Reflating the Third World is, perhaps, even harder to accomplish. Saddled with billions in debt, the world banking community, led by the World Bank and the International Monetary Fund (IMF), has forced one less-developed country after another to promote internal austerity as a condition of further life-sustaining loans. As one might imagine, in a Third World country with little hard currency the first austere measure is to reduce foreign imports, thus ironically contributing to the trade deficit in the United States.

Before such indebted Third World countries as Mexico, Brazil, and Venezuela can contribute to global reflation, they need to have much of their current debt forgiven. Private banks in the United States are slowly moving in this direction, writing off "bad debts" and thus freeing their Third World customers from some of the huge interest payments that would otherwise make them insolvent. Still, the amount of "forgiveness" in the global banking system is insufficient to the task. Only a resurgence of economic growth that equals that of the 1960s and 1970s can enable the less-developed nations to pay off their remaining indebtedness. For this to happen, reflation of the developed countries is necessary, for without a substantially expanded market for their exports, the Third World cannot generate sufficient income to make even a dent in its debts.

The second condition for the economic expansion of the Third World is the liberation of workers' organizations in these countries from the heavy hand of state suppression. Trade unions, co-operatives, and the community-based economic organizations typically created by national liberation movements all have as their common objective the raising of the living standards of poor and working people in these countries. Just as an organized labor movement played a central role in the economic expansion of our country, so too must it be allowed to flourish in the Third World. The United States can promote such developments actively, through preferential trade policies and technical assistance.* At the very least, our government can get out of the way of genuine nationalist and even socialist movements already struggling for breathing space. Too often, the U.S. government (and, unhappily, the leadership of some U.S. unions and the AFL–CIO) can be detected behind the scenes where some second-rate military dictatorship is trying to quash a local labor movement.[12]

The Need for a Strategy for the Domestic Economy

Global reflation and a solution to Third World debt are necessary but not sufficient conditions for a successful revenue-side recovery in the United States. Indeed, the centerpiece of a progressive program for re-igniting economic growth and providing a renewed basis for redistribution must be a strategy for boosting productivity in the manufacturing sector and, perhaps even more, in large segments of the service economy.

While it is premature to lay out, say, a twenty point program for resurrecting an equitable, fast-growing economy, there are some unmistakable guideposts for our consideration. The central proposition is straightforward. If we are to achieve the twin objectives of growth with equity, then *American companies must learn to operate in a climate of a rising standard of living. Wage (and benefit) cutting have got to end.* More specifically, we imagine seven general themes that must be addressed in order to deal with the dual issue of productivity and distribution. These include: (1) industrial policy; (2) democracy in the workplace; (3) a new commitment by existing or newly created labor unions to organizing the unorganized; (4) the reconstitution of public infra-

---

*In a surprising move just before Christmas 1987, the Reagan administration actually took the first hesitant steps toward penalizing nations that violate internationally accepted standards of workers' rights. Citing a "retrogression" in workers' rights in Chile, and following the arrest of more than three hundred union members in the country for engaging in a labor strike, the United States withdrew Chile's privileges to sell certain products in the United States free of customs duty. Chile is actually the sixth country to be suspended from duty-free access, the fourth because of insufficient attention to workers' rights.[13]

structure; (5) the public fulfillment of the promise of universal social benefits, including health insurance, day care, and care for senior citizens; (6) re-regulation of specific private market activities, especially in the runaway financial sector (these we have already discussed); and, finally (7) managed international trade. Let us deal with each in turn, suggesting the roles that both the public and private sectors must play.

INDUSTRIAL POLICY

The debate over national industrial strategy between 1978 and 1984 was focused on two policies: the creation of a government development bank to provide investment funds to firms starved for capital; and the conscious use of government to "pick winners and losers" and treat these industries accordingly. Curiously, the counterattack was led not by a conservative Republican, but by a well-respected Democratic Keynesian, Charles Schultze of the Brookings Institution. In an oft-quoted article, Schultze launched a broadside against industrial policy.[14] His attack was based on four propositions. The first was that deindustrialization was a myth. Manufacturing, outside of a few obvious sectors, was *not* in serious trouble and consequently, U.S. industrial policy was a solution in search of a nonexistent problem. Schultze went on to argue that, even if American industry were truly in trouble, industrial policy was not the answer. Third, according to Schultze, no country, including Japan, had a successful industrial policy. This was because, by assumption (or just plain assertion), no government can make better decisions than the private sector. And, finally, even if planners could do better than the market, any industrial plan would fall prey to political wrangling that would destroy its worth well before it was put into action.

Schultze's arguments might be valid if the issue at hand were Soviet-style central planning. But this was clearly a red herring. Indeed, the types of industrial policy—or "industrial strategy," the term in vogue after "industrial policy" became politically discredited—relevant to the debate were ones that were subsequently laid out, at least in part, by President Reagan's own Commission on Industrial Competitiveness. In its 1985 report, the Commission, composed of hand-picked corporate executives, union leaders, and a smattering of established academics and chaired by John Young, president of the Hewlett-Packard

Company, urged the White House to create an economic security council to plot U.S. global economic strategy.[15]

In its report, the Commission called for all of the following:

- the creation of a federal department of science and technology to promote national policies for research and innovation including the assurance of effective funding for research and development
- enhanced tax credits for research and development to "maximize innovation"
- the elimination of antitrust barriers to joint research and development
- the streamlining of patent laws to promote the development of new products
- the expansion of Export-Import Bank services to assist U.S. industries in foreign markets
- the initiation of an export promotion campaign by the executive branch
- the encouragement of state and local government initiatives in the area of joint management–labor–government programs to enhance competitiveness and promote exports.

To be sure, the Commission avoided any mention of a national development bank and said nothing about "winners and losers." Nonetheless, the president totally ignored the report, presumably finding even this level of government intervention ideologically unacceptable.

What the Commission was attempting to do was replicate in the United States some of the public policies used successfully in other countries, especially Japan. The Japanese Ministry of Industry and Trade (MITI) describes "its own industrial policies as 'first' a matter of 'vision.' "[16] Industrial policies in Japan are for the most part analytical (or, in technical parlance, "indicative"), providing the private sector with the best information available about how technology and human needs are going to alter the industrial structure and how business and labor, working with government, can best meet the global competition. Instead of a sinister plot against private enterprise, industrial policies— as implied by the Commission—should be the product of ongoing day-to-day tripartite interaction among representatives of the corporate and labor communities and officials of the government. Hence, strategic long-term plans for dealing with both healthy and sick industries can be generated as a substitute for ad-hoc policies that become highly politicized in the heat of crisis. Instead of relying on eleventh-hour bailouts of multibillion corporations—the Chrysler Corporation, Lockheed, and Continental Illinois come to mind—the government should develop a regularized system for dealing with the crises that inevitably arise within a global economy.

The centerpiece of such industrial policies must be "conditionality." Corporations and workers who approach the government for assistance must be prepared to devise a set of quid pro quos, assuring that, in return for assistance in development or reconstruction, the company will commit resources to new investment and new jobs and that workers will commit themselves to working with management to develop strategies for improving their skills, improving the quality of the product (or service), enhancing productivity, and expanding the company's share of the market. Assistance should not be an inalienable right, but an incentive or reward for behavior in the private sector that provides domestic and foreign consumers with better products at competitive prices while improving job prospects in the United States and boosting American standards of living.

Many in the labor community have expressed deep skepticism about entering into such tripartite planning agreements. Their fears are not unfounded. As we saw in chapter 2, the record of American corporate managers when it comes to co-operating with labor is not such as to inspire confidence. But this only makes it doubly important for labor to create mechanisms for holding its representatives to the new planning committees accountable to the rank and file. At the very least, all proposed industrial policies should be freely and widely debated *within* labor—at the plant, store, office, local, regional, and national levels— *before* a "labor position" is put forth in Washington. And unions, like other associations of workers, must have the right to withhold their co-operation if the planning seems to be heading back toward lower wages and speedups. After all, business will insist on its own "right to strike." In a system of truly democratic planning, the right to strike need not be inconsistent with the genuine progress of a program of socially constructive restructuring. Indeed, it is probably indispensable.[17]

WORKPLACE DEMOCRACY

While government can play a crucial role in devising national (and in some cases, state and local) strategies for improving productivity and income, much of what is needed must occur *within* the firm. Essentially, the role of workers and unions must be greatly expanded in literally every enterprise within the nation. This is not so much an issue of economic justice or the dignity of labor as it is a matter of cold, hard-headed economics. Corporate management alone does not hold the secret of how to produce high-quality, competitive products. It must increasingly rely on the entire range of employees within the firm to develop new techniques of production, judge the applicability and usefulness of new technology, assure quality control, and forge new labor-management relations that enhance productivity and equity within the firm.

To do all of this, workers and their representatives need to possess much more information about their industries and the decision-making process within their firms. They must ultimately share in decisions, not just about wages and working conditions, but about the entire panoply of functions that management has traditionally controlled. This goes well beyond so-called "quality-of-work-life" programs that are ostensibly intended to upgrade the workers' contributions on the plant floor. It encompasses control over the introduction of new technology, decisions about new investments and locations of plants, subcontracting, the design of new products, and even the pricing of products. Today, perhaps more than ever, the decisions that management makes unilaterally about the design, quality, and price of products affect the job security of workers and the nation's standard of living substantially more than contractual language governing wages, vacation time, job classifications, and the like. Yet, workers have yet to share sufficient control over these business matters.

Like industrial policy, the extension of democracy in the workplace should be negotiated in the context of conditionality. In return for greater control over the key decisions of the corporation and justifiable guarantees of greater job security, workers and unions should be willing to sit down with management to bargain over job classifications, work rules, and new definitions of work that can strengthen the health and productivity of the firm. This obviously requires, as a first step, that management give up its attempts to secure a union-free environment.

While the content of a new democratic social contract between managers and workers may seem a radical departure from past practice, the process of advancing workers' interests in this manner is hardly new. All of the modern history of labor-management relations has been a story of workers striving to reduce the purview of the "management rights" clauses in collectively bargained agreements. What democracy in the workplace means is that workers win a meaningful share of decision-making power not only on the plant floor, but in the upper office suites as well.[18]

Here, again, there is considerable skepticism and much disagreement within the labor movement. Especially as so many Quality of Work Life programs have been accompanied by deteriorating wages and (in some cases) cutbacks in benefits as well, many workers have dropped out of programs ostensibly aimed at promoting democracy in the workplace. These programs include the currently fashionable solution of having workers acquire ownership of failing companies as a last-ditch way to prevent a shutdown.

This internal debate is healthy and vital. Only through such self-criticism can a revitalized labor movement become strong enough to hold its own in the broader arena which a new swing of the pendulum toward more planning is going to bring to America.

ORGANIZING THE UNORGANIZED

Increases in productivity are not automatically translated into higher wages or family incomes. In fact, since 1982, while productivity as measured by output per person per hour in the business sector grew by 9.2 percent, real compensation per hour increased a paltry 3.8 percent.[19] The difference explains the rise in profits that business has been experiencing since the end of the recession of 1981–82. But in one of those famous contradictions of free enterprise, the lagging growth in wages is responsible for the slowdown in consumer spending and hence, in economic growth. Somehow, the distribution of the gains from increased productivity must be better balanced between capital and labor.

Why has the gap between productivity and wages widened? One likely suspect is the diminished strength of trade unions. Deindustrialization and restructuring have drastically undermined the sectors of the economy in which labor unions had their traditional strongholds. Within even these industries, the influence of unions has been weakened. Virtually all of the growth in employment now occurs in the services and trades (especially in business services, health, education, and hotels and restaurants) where unions are weak or nonexistent.* While high-technology manufacturing is unlikely to generate enough jobs and income to constitute the basis for a new long wave of economic growth, these activities are by no means trivial. Yet unions have hardly made a dent in organizing this sector, either.

Without representation, it is unlikely that workers will get their share of the dividends resulting from increased productivity. Particularly in an economy in which there is not full employment, the distribution of those dividends must be negotiated. Without unions, the negotiating table has essentially only one side.

The need for unions to maintain wages and incomes and thereby contribute to greater spending by consumers is there. This is especially true in unorganized industries where workers are saddled with inadequate and declining wages, unhealthy working conditions, and little job security. Yet, by and large, American unions do not have much experience with organizing such workers and meeting their needs for representation.

Success at organizing the unorganized requires that unions equip themselves with new organizing skills. But they must also develop forms of representation that appeal to the new worker in the service economy and not merely to the older worker in manufacturing. This will likely require an entire revamping of the traditional role of unions. They will have to become a more integral part of the planning within industry in order to help govern the introduction of new technology, new products, and new processes. Because a union cannot win high wages from an employer whose productivity is poor, unions will need to play two roles, not one. They will have to contribute part of the expertise needed to boost productivity, and then play their traditional role of obtaining as much of the dividend as possible for their members. At the present time, few trade unions are equipped to do either.

THE PUBLIC INFRASTRUCTURE

The best industrial policies in the world, the expansion of workplace democracy, and an invigoration of trade unionism will not solve all of

*On the other hand, there is cause for optimism. In our area, Boston-Cambridge, the most vital and inclusive union organizing drives in years have been occurring in the hotel, hospital, and university clerical sectors.

the domestic problems of the American economy or, by themselves, sufficiently rebuild American living standards. What is needed, in addition, is a national commitment to invest more in public facilities that foster productivity and economic revitalization in the private sector. As Pat Choate and Susan Walter have noted in their studies of *America in Ruins:*

> America's public facilities are wearing out faster than they are being replaced. The deteriorated condition of the basic public facilities that underpin the economy presents a major structural barrier to the renewal of our national economy.[20]

According to their careful analysis, more than eight thousand miles of the Interstate Highway System and 13 percent of its bridges were in use beyond the number of years they were designed to last and required rebuilding at the beginning of the 1980s. Much of the nation's rail trackbed needs replacement, municipal water systems require at least $75 billion of improvements, over $25 billion more needs to be spent to meet existing standards of water quality, and billions more have to be devoted to the development of water resources in rural areas.[21] Beyond this, the nation must set aside the funds to expand and reorganize dangerously overcrowded airports and jails, and to expand mass transit to relieve the gridlock plaguing the revitalized cities.

While these investments will—as in the past—generate well-paying jobs and thus directly boost wages and incomes, the indirect benefits they convey to the nation are even more important. Without them, productivity suffers as transportation bogs down and industry is forced to pay more exorbitant prices for such services as water and sewerage and insurance against crime.

One form of the nation's infrastructure needs special attention: education and training. While the United States has an internationally renowned system of higher education, it is increasingly clear that primary and secondary education are failing, especially but by no means exclusively in urban communities. Part of it is simply a quantitative problem, as Lester Thurow has stressed time and time again.

> Among our [international] competitors the school year and day are much longer. Foreign students work harder. In the United States the average school year is 180 days, runs five to six hours per day, and the average

student is absent twenty days per year. In contrast Japanese schools run 240 days per year and six to eight hours per day with minimal absences. Many Japanese students also go to after-school classes to better prepare themselves for the examinations necessary to get into college. The net result is almost twice as many hours in school per year in Japan as in the the United States.[22]

But part of the schooling problem is also qualitative. To comply with legislated tax cuts such as Proposition 13 in California and Proposition 2½ in Massachusetts, cities and towns were forced to reduce funds for public education. This meant layoffs and salary freezes for teachers. What was the result? Some of the best and most energetic either left the system for better rewards elsewhere or were simply fired in reverse order of seniority.

To assemble a skilled labor force that can compete internationally, it will be necessary to devote enormous additional resources to the quality of America's public schools. This is a matter to which the Reagan administration paid only lip service. The deficit the nation has created in education will come back to haunt the country every bit as much as the deficit in the federal budget and the trade deficit that we studied in the last chapter.

SOCIAL-WELFARE PROGRAMS

It will also be necessary for the nation to rebuild and restructure many of the social welfare programs that were gutted by the Reagan administration in the course of eight years. Industrial policies, democracy in the workplace, new union organizing drives, and the rebuilding of our infrastructure all will benefit those who gain the major part of their incomes from the labor market. But they will do little directly for those who, for one or another reason, cannot work or are restricted in the amount they can do. For these families, it is necessary to improve public assistance, provide more public housing, increase access to day-care for children and the elderly who can remain at home with their families, and expand family and work skills. Anything less will condemn at least the bottom fifth of the population to an ever-smaller proportion of total national income.

The rebuilding and extension of the social safety net is relevant to working people, as well—especially if they are parents. In the America of the moment, this means mainly women workers. Feminist trade-union activists are currently engaged in weaving a vision of a new social welfare system which would combine national legislation to mandate both maternal and paternal leaves of absence for rearing children; increased funding for day-care services; an increase in the minimum wage; equitable pay for women and workers of color, beginning with the federal government as a model; and a national right to adequate health care (*not* just insurance, but actual *care*) for anyone willing and able to work.[23] Many are demanding that part-time workers be legally granted the same benefits as conventionally defined full-time workers. Barbara Bergmann, Heidi Hartmann, Cathy Schoen, Karen Nussbaum, and other feminist economists and activists have called for an amendment to Title VII of the Civil Rights Act of 1964 that would make the differential provision of benefits to full and part-time workers a violation of the civil rights of part-timers.

We must keep in mind that such improvements in social welfare have more than merely a redistributive impact. They inject spendable income into the economy where it is most likely to be spent and have the largest "multiplier" effect. This can only help to spur the kind of economic growth which benefits those who pay for social-welfare programs as well as those who are its direct beneficiaries.

MANAGED INTERNATIONAL TRADE

What began the great U-turns in economic growth, wages, and family incomes was the globalization of the economy and the ensuing assault on profits. Yet the United States has still not come to grips with the trade problems that face the nation. The government continues to treat trade in the same laissez-faire manner that it would like to treat the domestic economy. Although, for better or worse, none of the countries in the rest of the world wish to—or feel they can afford to—leave trade to the unfettered marketplace, we simply continue to watch our trade balance wash away in red ink and our international debt increase each month. Something more than simply devaluing the dollar will be necessary to turn this worsening situation around. The system of free trade that developed before World War II and was codified in the General Agreement on Tariffs and Trade (GATT) needs serious restructuring. A little history helps us here.

In August of the year that the United States entered World War II, President Roosevelt and Prime Minister Churchill agreed on the principles of what would become the Atlantic Charter. On the subject of trade, the Charter pledged the United States and Britain to "endeavor, with due respect for their existing obligations, to further the enjoyment by all States, great and small, victor and vanquished, of access, on equal terms, to the trade and to the raw materials of the world which are needed for their economic prosperity."[24] After the war, in 1948, an attempt was made to incorporate these lofty principles into the GATT agreement. Since then, through seven rounds of trade negotiations, the ninety-four nations that subscribe to this international code of commercial conduct have been able to agree on policies that have resulted in a 90-percent reduction in tariffs.[25] In a period of relatively balanced trade where most trade was in basic raw materials and simple manufactured goods, GATT served the interests of global trade reasonably well.

But as trade balances deteriorated—into massive surpluses in some countries (such as Japan) and massive deficits in others (such as the United States); as the trade in such services as banking and insurance swelled to account for one-quarter of international transactions; and as foreign commerce in technically sophisticated manufactured goods, including aircraft and computers, expanded; GATT lost its effectiveness as a rule maker and monitor in trade matters. In its place, countries have increasingly resorted to bilateral trade arrangements which lie outside of the GATT's framework.

Co-production agreements, whereby two or more countries negotiate shared production of complex products, have blossomed in one industry after another. "Offset" agreements, whereby one country offers to market a trading partner's goods in return for access to its internal market, have proliferated. And "performance criteria" (also called "local content requirements") have been established whereby one country requires another to establish production facilities within its borders as a condition of marketing products to its own citizens. None of these special trading relationships involve tariffs and therefore all circumvent at least explicit GATT restrictions.

Those who support unlimited free trade argue that a renegotiated GATT must regulate these types of implicit trade barriers. But (like the domestic laissez-faire position), the ideology of full-blown free trade fails to account for the fact that unlimited competition in the world market leads to unacceptable levels of instability and risk. No matter how tightly the GATT rules are drawn, it is inevitable that individual nations will develop trade patterns intended to balance the benefits of unrestricted trade with the need for minimum levels of domestic economic security.

What does that imply about trade? Simply that global trading relationships must continue to be negotiated and planned, managed in such a way as to smooth economic transitions within and between countries.[26] One way of doing this is to produce a set of GATT regulations that acknowledges the existence of co-production, offset, and performance agreements and regulates them so that more nations can take advantage of them. Another is to recognize and regulate various forms of tariffs designed to give *temporary* protection to key industries so as to promote industrial revitalization and economic transition.

While blatant permanent protectionism should not be countenanced, GATT should consider the establishment of guidelines under which "time delimited vanishing tariffs" would be legalized, giving temporary protection to individual national industries. With such a tariff, a government would announce to its trading partners that it will begin to charge a tariff on a selected set of goods or services. These tariffs, however, would be reduced each year according to a pre-announced schedule over a span of, say, six to seven years. For example, in place of the present U.S.–imposed "voluntary" import restrictions on Japanese automobiles, the United States would set, say, a 12-percent tariff on automobiles and then reduce it by 2 percentage points a year. At the end of the sixth year, the tariff would vanish and the American auto industry would have exhausted its protection from imports.

The tariff period would have one over-riding purpose: to provide the protected industry with a temporary and limited respite from unimpeded imports so as to allow it to restructure itself into a healthy competitor—or, if unsuccessful, exit the market "gracefully." To decide which industries would receive vanishing tariff protection, the government would resort once again to the use of conditionality. Only industries agreeing to reinvest in capital and technology, to restructure their labor-management relations to permit greater involvement of their employees, and to commit themselves to maintaining production in existing locations rather than fleeing to other regions or other countries might be good candidates for tariff protection. Revenue from the temporary tariff could be used to fund assistance to displaced workers in the form of training allowances and to aid affected industries through grants for research and development.

Those who believe in free trade are fond of asserting that market forces by themselves will sooner or later bring about a "level playing field" between countries that buy from and sell to one another. They ignore the many ways that international differences in public policy— even policies that seemingly have nothing whatever to do with trade— can affect the playing surface. For example:

> . . . in most other industrialized nations a large portion of workers' health insurance is paid for by taxpayers as part of a general national health scheme. Hence this item does not appear directly in the costs of particular firms. U.S. firms, however, typically pay a much higher proportion of the costs of health insurance directly. Although the resulting coverage for the individual worker is often less than under foreign national insurance schemes, the direct cost per hour of labor to the U.S. firms is higher. This is a major "subsidy" from the taxpayers in other countries to their firms. Under the logic of an "antidumping" policy we should impose a countervailing duty to compensate our firms for their additional medical insurance costs—or institute our own national health scheme. We do neither.[27]

The important point is that to favor managed trade is not to be antitrade. Negotiated trade arrangements are simply attempts to eliminate unacceptable levels of risk in an open world economy and to provide incentives to industries within each country to restructure and revitalize themselves. Managed trade is the international analog of industrial policy at home.

Will the Pendulum Swing Back—and When?

Clearly the agenda for rebuilding the American standard of living and reversing the great U-turn in growth and inequality is no simple one. It requires a fundamental reassessment of the laissez-faire affair that government has been conducting with business since at least the late 1970s. It will not occur without a major political realignment and a renewed commitment, especially within the Democratic Party, to the principles of social security and economic justice.

For the moment, risky experimentation with planning probably still seems unnecessary to Big Business, just as it did after Ronald Reagan came to Washington in 1981 with his conservative supply-side program. But this can change. Any number of developments could tip the scales in the same way that the October 1987 stock market "meltdown" convinced many business executives of the need for stronger regulation of financial markets and greater global planning and co-ordination of individual nations' fiscal, monetary, and exchange-rate policies. A major default in the Third World could do it. A successful new wave of labor organizing in the service sector could pressure business into re-committing itself, however reluctantly, to a new social contract with its workers. Some of the new management strategies could do it. For example, many of the new production techniques enthusiastically touted by companies, such as just-in-time parts delivery systems à la Japan, depend on a steady stream of deliveries to replace the maintenance of large inventories. Such an arrangement is, in principle, very easy for disgruntled workers to sabotage. Finally, without a global growth of demand, supply-side national industrial policies paradoxically only worsen the international tendency toward excess production capacity that has been so evident since the late 1960s. This could actually bring back the profit squeeze which, in our view, triggered the restructuring experiments of the last fifteen years in the first place.

It is in the context of these long-term pressures that the historic tension between free-market competition and planning in the United States will be resolved in the years ahead. Of course, even if the most influential corporate leaders *do* decide to turn to increased planning in the future (as they have done throughout the century, sooner or later, in every previous economic crisis), it is by no means clear what *kind* of planning they will be willing to entertain. Will we move toward democratic, participatory planning? Or will we be subject to authoritarian, top-down, manipulative planning by government technocrats and corporate executives?

We are cautiously optimistic. For one thing, after every previous fling with unregulated laissez-faire, the cost of economic instability and excessive personal risk has driven individuals—corporate executives as well as blue-collar assembly workers—to demand limits to their exposure to cutthroat competition. After the late nineteenth-century heyday of the industrial revolution, the nation demanded a period of "progressive" social policy. Out of the progressive era of the early 1900s came the first state experiments with unemployment insurance, family assistance, labor law, and educational reform. After the roaring '20s, the nation demanded governmental policies to deal with the casualties of the Great Depression, which were in large measure the result of free-market excesses during the previous decade. And the Great Society programs of the 1960s constituted, at least in part, a progressive reaction to the deprivation and inequality of those still left out of the social accord created after World War II.

The second, and rather less idealistic reason we are hopeful has to do with our empirical discovery that a broader and more diverse "rainbow" of Americans—including many in the middle class—are being victimized by the stagnation and growing inequality that characterize the emerging postindustrial society. This sets up the objective conditions for the formation of a new political coalition that could begin to demand progressive change.

Peter Glotz, national secretary of the German Social Democratic Party, has published a "declaration for a New European Left" which, in its many translations, has been enormously influential throughout the continent. One of Glotz's most intriguing theoretical formulations is his notion of the emergence during the postindustrial era of what he calls the "two-thirds society." It is a social structure whose upper third contains the well-educated and prosperous technocrats who make the system run. The lowest third are the increasingly marginalized "unemployed, the odd-jobbers, the elderly of the lower classes, the migrant workers, the physically and mentally handicapped, the teenagers who cannot find their way into the job market."[28]

The key to the political stability of this polarized society, to the ability of conservative governments to be re-elected in spite of their inability to deliver steady growth in living standards, more equally shared, is the attitude of the "middle third"—insecure workers, increasingly wearing white rather than blue collars, who fall between the two poles. So long as the middle third can be mobilized to oppose the extension of the social safety net to the bottom third, so long as they can be convinced to identify themselves with the new technocrats at the top, so long can conservative laissez-faire political-economic arrangements be sustained. But only for so long.

Certainly figuratively, and in many ways literally, the United States is turning into Glotz's "two-thirds" society. Whether this will lead a significant fraction of the American middle class to continue its present endorsement of conservative party policies and governments, or prompt the beginnings of a joining with the lower tier of the American workforce in a search for more progressive social and economic arrangements, including a re-invigorated search for full employment, is probably the most important political question in the last decade of the twentieth century.

TABLE A.1

Employment and Wage Rate Components of Changes in the Wage Bill of Major Nonagricultural Private Industries, 1973 and 1986

Line Number	Industry	1 — Number of Production and Nonsupervisory Workers on Private Nonagricultural Payrolls in 1973 (in thousands)	2 — Average Hourly Earnings of Production and Nonsupervisory Workers on Private Nonagricultural Payrolls in 1973	3 — Average Hourly Earnings in 1973 Prices at 1986 Prices (1973 CPI = 100)	4 — Hourly Wage Bill in 1973 at 1986 prices Col. 1 × Col. 3	5 — Number of Production and Nonsupervisory Workers on Private Nonagricultural Payrolls in 1986 (in thousands)	6 — Average Hourly Earnings of Production and Nonsupervisory Workers on Private Nonagricultural Payrolls in 1986
	GOODS						
1	Mining	486	$4.75	$11.74	$ 5,705,640	525	$12.50
2	Construction	3,405	6.41	15.84	53,935,200	4,062	12.60
	Manufacturing						
3	Durable goods	8,728	4.35	10.75	93,826,000	7,493	10.33
4	Nondurable goods	6,107	3.70	9.15	55,879,050	5,595	9.02
	RELATED SECTORS						
	Transport, Communications,						
5	Utilities	4,034	5.02	12.41	50,061,940	4,468	11.76
6	Wholesale trade	3,547	4.08	10.09	35,789,230	4,720	9.43
	SERVICES						
	Retail trade,						
7	Finance, Insurance	11,168	2.91	7.19	80,297,920	16,383	6.05
8	Real estate	3,121	3.53	8.73	27,246,330	4,729	8.48
9	Other Services	11,606	3.47	8.58	99,579,480	20,598	8.32

TABLE A.1 (Continued)

Line Number	7 Hourly Wage Bill at 1986 Hourly Wage Rates Col. 6 × Col. 5		8 Real Change in Hourly Wage Bill from 1973 to 1986 Col. 7 − Col. 4		9 Employment Effect: Change in Hourly Wage Bill for Production Workers Since 1973 Resulting from Change in Number Employed, Holding Hourly Wage Rate Constant at 1973 Level (in 1986 prices) (Col. 5 − Col. 1) × Col. 3		10 Wage Effect: Additional Change in Hourly Wage Bill for Production Workers Since 1973, Resulting from Change in Hourly Wage Rates Col. 8 − Col. 9	
	(dollars)		(dollars)	(%)	(dollars)	(%)	(dollars)	(%)
1	$ 6,562,500		856,860	15.0	457,860	8.0	399,000	7.0
2	51,181,200		(2,754,000)	(5.1)	10,406,880	19.3	(13,160,880)	(24.4)
3	77,402,690		(16,423,310)	(17.5)	(13,276,250)	(14.1)	(3,147,060)	(3.4)
4	50,466,900		(5,412,150)	(9.7)	(4,684,800)	(8.4)	(727,350)	(1.3)
5	52,543,680		2,481,740	5.0	5,385,940	10.8	(2,904,200)	(5.8)
6	44,509,600		8,720,370	24.4	11,835,570	33.1	(3,115,200)	(8.7)
7	99,117,150		18,819,230	23.4	37,495,850	46.7	(18,676,620)	(23.3)
8	40,101,920		12,855,590	47.2	14,037,840	51.5	(1,182,250)	(1.3)
9	171,375,360		71,795,880	72.1	77,151,360	77.5	(5,355,480)	(5.4)

SOURCE U.S. Bureau of Labor Statistics, *Employment and Earnings*, January 1974 and January 1987 (negative numbers in parentheses).
Note that column 10 includes a small interaction effect.

TABLE A.2

Distribution of Employees by Wage Brackets, 1963 to 1986 Year-Round, Full-Time (YRFT) Workers

	Total Employment (in thousands)				Percentage of Total Employment				Percentage of Net Growth in Jobs[a]		
	1963	1973	1979	1986	1963	1973	1979	1986	'63–'73	'73–'79	'79–'86
ALL YRFT WORKERS											
LOW STRATUM[b]	8,243	6,875	8,091	11,898	21.4	13.1	13.8	17.2	(9.8)	19.2	36.0
MIDDLE STRATUM[c]	29,096	41,270	45,999	51,287	75.5	78.7	78.3	74.0	87.6	74.6	50.1
HIGH STRATUM[d]	1,178	4,267	4,661	6,127	3.1	8.1	7.9	8.8	22.2	6.2	13.9
TOTAL	38,516	52,412	58,751	69,312	100.0	100.0	100.0	100.0	100.0	100.0	100.0
MEN											
LOW STRATUM	3,961	2,654	3,037	4,924	14.1	7.4	8.0	11.7	(17.2)	17.9	46.9
MIDDLE STRATUM	23,014	28,932	30,409	31,454	81.8	80.9	80.3	75.0	77.8	69.1	26.0
HIGH STRATUM	1,171	4,168	4,444	5,535	4.2	11.7	11.7	13.2	39.4	12.9	27.1
TOTAL	28,146	35,754	37,890	41,913	100.0	100.0	100.0	100.0	100.0	100.0	100.0
WOMEN											
LOW STRATUM	4,282	4,222	5,054	6,974	41.3	25.3	24.2	25.5	(1.0)	19.8	29.4
MIDDLE STRATUM	6,081	12,337	15,590	19,833	58.6	74.1	74.7	72.4	99.5	77.4	64.9
HIGH STRATUM	7	99	217	592	0.1	0.6	1.0	2.2	1.5	2.8	5.7
TOTAL	10,370	16,658	20,861	27,399	100.0	100.0	100.0	100.0	100.0	100.0	100.0
WHITES											
LOW STRATUM	6,529	5,490	6,691	9,508	18.7	11.8	12.9	15.8	(8.9)	22.2	35.1
MIDDLE STRATUM	27,283	36,987	40,878	44,816	78.0	79.3	78.5	74.6	83.3	71.9	49.1
HIGH STRATUM	1,176	4,160	4,476	5,737	3.4	8.9	8.6	9.6	25.6	5.8	15.7
TOTAL	34,988	46,637	52,045	60,061	100.0	100.0	100.0	100.0	100.0	100.0	100.0

[a] The formula used was $\{[(\text{employment in stratum } i \text{ in year } t_2 - \text{employment in stratum } i \text{ in year } t_1)] / (\text{employment in all strata in year } t_2 - \text{employment in all strata in year } t_1)\} \times 100$, (negative numbers in parentheses).
[b] Low stratum = earnings of less than $11,104 a year (in 1986 dollars)
[c] Middle stratum = earnings of $11,104-$44,412 a year
[d] High stratum = earnings of $44,413 a year or more

TABLE A.2 (Continued)

	Total Employment (in thousands)				Percentage of Total Employment				Percentage of Net Growth in Jobs[a]		
	1963	1973	1979	1986	1963	1973	1979	1986	'63-'73	'73-'79	'79-'86
NONWHITES											
LOW STRATUM	1,714	1,386	1,399	2,391	48.6	24.0	20.9	25.8	(14.6)	1.4	39.0
MIDDLE STRATUM	1,813	4,281	5,122	6,470	51.4	74.1	76.4	69.9	109.9	90.3	53.0
HIGH STRATUM	2	108	185	390	0.1	1.9	2.8	4.2	4.7	8.3	8.1
TOTAL	3,529	5,775	6,706	9,251	100.0	100.0	100.0	100.0	100.0	100.0	100.0
AGE 20-34											
LOW STRATUM	2,674	2,723	3,665	6,132	22.4	13.7	14.8	21.2	0.6	19.4	57.6
MIDDLE STRATUM	9,135	16,348	20,228	21,749	76.5	82.4	81.9	75.0	91.2	80.0	35.5
HIGH STRATUM	131	780	811	1,109	1.1	3.9	3.3	3.8	8.2	0.6	7.0
TOTAL	11,940	19,851	24,704	28,989	100.0	100.0	100.0	100.0	100.0	100.0	100.0
AGE 35-54											
LOW STRATUM	3,542	2,282	2,601	3,784	18.3	10.0	10.7	12.3	(36.1)	23.4	17.9
MIDDLE STRATUM	15,039	17,874	18,746	23,090	77.6	78.1	77.3	74.9	81.3	64.0	65.7
HIGH STRATUM	806	2,718	2,889	3,974	4.2	11.9	11.9	12.9	54.8	12.6	16.4
TOTAL	19,387	22,874	24,236	30,848	100.0	100.0	100.0	100.0	100.0	100.0	100.0
LESS THAN H.S. DIPLOMA											
LOW STRATUM	4,670	2,842	2,578	3,146	30.2	21.1	24.4	34.8	—	—	—
MIDDLE STRATUM	10,656	10,263	7,721	5,771	68.9	76.3	73.1	63.9	—	—	—
HIGH STRATUM	133	347	261	120	0.9	2.6	2.5	1.3	—	—	—
TOTAL	15,459	13,452	10,560	9,037	100.0	100.0	100.0	100.0			
HIGH SCHOOL GRADUATE											
LOW STRATUM	2,626	2,908	3,787	5,762	18.4	13.3	15.4	20.7	3.7	31.8	62.0
MIDDLE STRATUM	11,338	17,840	19,878	21,001	79.6	81.7	80.8	75.6	85.7	73.7	35.2
HIGH STRATUM	274	1,079	926	1,016	1.9	4.9	3.8	3.7	10.6	(5.5)	2.8
TOTAL	14,238	21,827	24,591	27,779	100.0	100.0	100.0	100.0	100.0	100.0	100.0

TABLE A.2 (Continued)

	Total Employment (in thousands)				Percentage of Total Employment				Percentage of Net Growth in Jobs[a]		
	1963	1973	1979	1986	1963	1973	1979	1986	'63–'73	'73–'79	'79–'86
SOME COLLEGE OR MORE											
LOW STRATUM	947	1,126	1,726	2,990	10.7	6.6	7.3	9.2	2.2	9.3	14.2
MIDDLE STRATUM	7,101	13,166	18,401	24,515	80.5	76.8	78.0	75.4	72.9	80.9	68.7
HIGH STRATUM	771	2,841	3,474	4,991	8.7	16.6	14.7	15.4	24.9	9.8	17.1
TOTAL	8,819	17,133	23,601	32,496	100.0	100.0	100.0	100.0	100.0	100.0	100.0
NORTHEAST											
LOW STRATUM	1828	1242	1554	1992	16.9	9.7	11.4	13.0	(29.6)	38.5	24.7
MIDDLE STRATUM	8610	10361	10927	11835	79.6	81.0	80.3	77.0	88.4	69.9	51.3
HIGH STRATUM	379	1194	1126	1549	3.5	9.3	8.3	10.1	41.2	(8.4)	23.9
TOTAL	10817	12797	13607	15377	100.0	100.0	100.0	100.0	100.0	100.0	100.0
MIDWEST											
LOW STRATUM	1916	1713	1884	2699	17.7	11.6	12.0	16.2	(5.2)	16.5	96.0
MIDDLE STRATUM	8652	11808	12645	12604	79.7	80.2	80.2	75.9	81.4	80.8	(4.8)
HIGH STRATUM	285	1208	1236	1311	2.6	8.2	7.8	7.9	23.8	2.7	8.8
TOTAL	10853	14729	15765	16614	100.0	100.0	100.0	100.0	100.0	100.0	100.0
SOUTH											
LOW STRATUM	3676	2972	3368	4991	33.6	18.3	18.0	21.2	(13.2)	16.2	33.7
MIDDLE STRATUM	7016	12245	14106	16650	64.2	75.3	75.4	70.8	98.0	76.3	52.8
HIGH STRATUM	243	1054	1236	1888	2.2	6.5	6.6	8.0	15.2	7.5	13.5
TOTAL	10935	16271	18710	23529	100.0	100.0	100.0	100.0	100.0	100.0	100.0
WEST											
LOW STRATUM	804	948	1284	2216	13.9	11.0	12.0	16.1	5.1	16.4	29.8
MIDDLE STRATUM	4725	6856	8322	10198	81.5	79.6	78.0	73.9	75.7	71.4	60.1
HIGH STRATUM	272	812	1063	1379	4.7	9.4	10.0	10.0	19.2	12.2	10.1
TOTAL	5801	8615	10669	13793	100.0	100.0	100.0	100.0	100.0	100.0	100.0

TABLE A.2 (Continued)

	Total Employment (in thousands)				Percentage of Total Employment				Percentage of Net Growth in Jobs[a]		
	1963	1973	1979	1986	1963	1973	1979	1986	'63–'73	'73–'79	'79–'86
NEW ENGLAND											
LOW STRATUM	542	305	431	521	19.3	9.7	12.1	12.7	(70.7)	29.6	16.6
MIDDLE STRATUM	2169	2564	2848	3183	77.2	81.6	79.8	77.4	117.9	66.7	61.8
HIGH STRATUM	97	274	290	407	3.5	8.7	8.1	9.9	52.8	3.8	21.6
TOTAL	2808	3143	3569	4111	100.0	100.0	100.0	100.0	100.0	100.0	100.0
MANUFACTURING											
LOW STRATUM	1808	1523	1551	2017	14.1	9.6	9.3	12.4	(9.0)	4.1	—
MIDDLE STRATUM	10577	13163	13646	12590	82.7	82.6	82.1	77.4	81.9	71.0	—
HIGH STRATUM	397	1253	1422	1658	3.1	7.9	8.6	10.2	27.1	24.9	—
TOTAL	12782	15939	16619	16264	100.0	100.0	100.0	100.0	100.0	100.0	—
HIGH TECHNOLOGY[e]											
LOW STRATUM	—	84	105	155	—	5.8	5.3	5.5	—	3.8	6.2
MIDDLE STRATUM	—	1138	1584	2122	—	79.0	79.3	75.5	—	79.9	66.3
HIGH STRATUM	—	218	309	533	—	15.1	15.5	19.0	—	16.3	27.6
TOTAL	—	1440	1998	2810	—	100.0	100.0	100.0	—	100.0	100.0
SERVICES											
LOW STRATUM	4580	4175	5205	8061	29.4	17.3	18.2	21.7	(4.8)	23.2	33.0
MIDDLE STRATUM	10491	18058	21270	26055	67.3	75.0	74.5	70.0	88.9	72.2	55.3
HIGH STRATUM	508	1857	2061	3080	3.3	7.7	7.2	8.3	15.9	4.6	11.8
TOTAL	15579	24090	28536	37196	100.0	100.0	100.0	100.0	100.0	100.0	100.0

Source: Calculations from U.S. Department of Commerce, *March Current Population Surveys* (Washington, D.C.: Government Printing Office). (negative numbers in parentheses)

[e]Uses definition adopted by Massachusetts Division of Employment Security, which includes sixteen manufacturing and three service industries.

TABLE A.3

Changes in estimated defense output, total output, and defense share of total output, by industry, 1977–1985

[in percent]

Industry	Change in Defense Output		Change in Total Output		Defense Share of Output		
	1977–80	1980–85	1977–80	1980–85	1977	1980	1985
Shipbuilding	44	42	6	−15	45	61	93
Ammunition, large	16	96	−15	70	65	86	86
Ordnance, n.e.c.	−7	83	−28	43	61	79	86
Missiles	−6	65	−8	35	67	69	84
Aircraft and missile engines	14	69	22	−5	47	44	78
Tanks	48	110	13	105	40	68	80
Aircraft	6	80	22	2	43	37	86
Explosives	−19	22	−28	−23	36	41	86
Radio and TV communications	73	73	46	46	35	42	50
Small arms	14	110	−15	15	20	26	48
Aircraft and missile parts	42	67	73	26	36	31	41
Ammunition, small	−13	51	6	17	37	30	30
Machine tools—cutting	226	65	18	−80	3	8	34
Truck trailers	72	114	−16	−23	5	10	29
Engineering instruments	25	55	4	28	19	23	28
Electron tubes	−5	75	−15	−5	12	14	26
Mining, nonferrous, except copper	−4	63	−33	−31	8	11	26
Nonferrous forgings	11	73	86	−16	21	12	25
Transmission equipment	1	65	−56	−28	5	10	24
Optical instruments	71	189	85	51	14	13	24
Turbines	−31	55	1	−53	5	7	23
Aluminum, primary	2	67	−20	−33	7	9	22
Zinc, primary	3	68	−15	−18	9	11	22
Industrial trucks	325	54	11	−46	2	8	22
Electronic components	40	76	27	44	15	16	20
Ferrous forgings	9	74	−7	−13	8	10	19
Copper, primary	3	66	−27	−11	7	10	18
Nonferrous rolling, n.e.c.	26	70	−22	24	8	13	18
Nonmetallic mineral products	37	67	6	−15	7	9	17
Lead, primary	6	63	−4	−36	6	7	17
Castings, nonferrous	15	80	1	5	9	10	17
Copper rolling	0	275	−28	9	5	7	17

TABLE A.3 *(Continued)*

Industry	Change in Defense Output		Change in Total Output		Defense Share of Output		
	1977–80	1980–85	1977–80	1980–85	1977	1980	1985
Machine tools—forming	290	56	1	−34	2	6	15
Electrometallurgical products	5	63	−10	−34	6	6	15
Ball bearings	−15	68	−60	−27	7	7	15
General industrial machinery	47	57	33	−18	3	8	15
Carbon products	31	67	−1	−37	5	7	15
Screw machine products	12	67	7	−15	6	7	13
Hoists and cranes	52	81	33	−49	3	4	13
Plating and polishing	6	74	4	50	11	11	13
Steel mills	6	63	−13	−20	5	6	12
Boot and shoe stock	1	−35	−18	−24	11	14	12
Conveyors	103	58	10	−25	3	6	12
Copper mining	34	64	6	−14	5	6	11
Industrial controls	5	51	7	−6	5	6	11

Note: n.e.c. = not elsewhere classified
SOURCE: U.S. Department of Commerce, Office of Business Analysis.
David K. Henry and Richard P. Oliver, "The Defense Buildup, 1977–85: Effects on Production and Employment," *Monthly Labor Review,* August 1987, 6.

NOTES

Chapter 1. The Great U-Turn

1. David Halberstam, *The Reckoning* (New York: Avon Books, 1986), 366–67.

2. Family income would have plummeted even further had it not been for the growth of two-earner couples. By 1984, 70 percent of all employed husband-wife households had both spouses holding down jobs outside the home. See Lester C. Thurow, "Middle Class Lifestyles," *Boston Globe,* 26 August 1986, 44.

3. Frank Levy, *Dollars and Dreams* (New York: Russell Sage, 1987).

4. See Samuel Bowles, David Gordon, and Thomas Weisskopf, "Power and Profits: The Social Structure of Accumulation and the Profitability of the Postwar U.S. Economy," *Review of Radical Political Economics,* Vol. 18, nos. 1 & 2, Spring/Summer 1986, figure 1, p. 136. Their indicator is the average rate of return on invested capital. Other measures of profit show the same thing. The U.S. Bureau of Economic Analysis of the Department of Commerce, using a measure of profit which excludes net interest payments, has produced a profit series that declines from more than 8 percent in 1965 to less than 3 percent in 1980, as Louis Uchitelle reported in "Corporate Profitability Rising, Reversing 15-Year Downturn," *New York Times,* 30 November 1987, 1. The Organization for Economic Co-operation and Development (OECD), the foremost European statistical agency, calculates that the pre-tax rate of return on U.S. capital stock also declined by a third, from 25 percent in 1965 to an average of less than 17 percent between 1970 and 1976. See T. P. Hill, *Profits and Rates of Return* (Paris: Organization for Economic Co-operation and Development, 1979), table 6.4, p. 125). In the same period, the OECD figures suggest, the corporate rate of return fell by 37 percent in England, by 16 percent in Germany and Canada, and by 12 percent in Japan. Others reporting significant declines in corporate profitability between the 1960s and 1970s include Edward N. Wolff, "The Productivity Slowdown and the Fall in the U.S. Rate of Profit, 1947–1976," *Review of Radical Political Economics* 18, nos. 1, 2, (Spring, Summer 1986): 102; Daniel M. Holland and Stewart C. Myers, "Profitability and Capital Costs for Manufacturing Corporations," *American Economic Review* 70, no. 2 (May 1980); and Martin Feldstein and Lawrence Summers, "Is the Rate of Profit Falling?" *Brookings Papers on Economic Activity,* no. 1 (1977). For our own calculations of profit rates in individual industries, see Barry Bluestone and Bennett Harrison, *The Deindustrialization of America* (New York: Basic Books, 1982), table 6.1, 148.

5. According to the U.S. Department of Commerce, by 1986 more than 66 percent of all television and radios sets, 63 percent of all shoes, 45 percent of all machine tools, 28 percent of all automobiles, and 25 percent of all computers sold in the United States were produced elsewhere. See "Will the U.S. Stay Number One?" *U.S. News and World Report,* 2 February 1987, 18.

6. John F. Dunning, *International Production and the Multinational Enterprise* (London: Allen and Unwin, 1981).

7. On global excess capacity as a contributor to the profit squeeze, see Philip Armstrong, Andrew Glyn, and John Harrison, *Capitalism Since World War II* (London: Fontana, 1984), esp. chap. 11.

8. Charles Sabel, "The Re-emergence of Regional Economies: Changes in the Scale of Production," in Social Science Research Council, Western European Committee, "Experimenting with Scale," draft ms., August 1987, pp. 20–21.

9. However, there is a good deal of international evidence that a high "social wage," rapid

economic growth, and high corporate profits may be *positively* correlated over the long run. See Robert Kuttner, *The Economic Illusion* (Boston: Houghton and Mifflin, 1985); and Lucy Gorham, *No Longer Leading: A Comparative Study of the U.S., Germany, Sweden, and Japan* (Washington, D.C.: Economic Policy Institute, 1986).

10. Juliet Schor and Samuel Bowles, "Conflict in the Employment Relation and the Cost of Job Loss," *Review of Economics and Statistics,* forthcoming.

11. In an important book published in 1983, *Beyond the Waste Land* (New York: Anchor), Samuel Bowles, David Gordon, and Thomas Weisskopf argued that the profit squeeze resulted *mainly* from pressure by workers for higher wages and expanded social security, defined broadly to include health and safety and environmental regulation, affirmative action, and so forth. Such pressures were indeed forthcoming—although they were perhaps more important (or at any rate more successfully expressed) in Europe than in the United States. In any case, the "labor supply side" and "global competition" stories are in no way inconsistent. We choose to emphasize the latter. For more on this difference of emphasis with Bowles et al., see Bennett Harrison, "Cold Bath or Restructuring? An Expansion of the Weisskopf–Bowles–Gordon Framework," *Science and Society,* Spring 1987.

12. From 1973 through 1980, nominal hourly compensation for workers in the nonfarm business sector increased at an annual average rate of 9 percent (although, as we have seen, *real* wages had been declining steadily). Meanwhile, labor productivity was increasing at a minuscule 0.7 percent. The result was that the nominal cost of a unit of labor rose by more than 8 percent per year. See Council of Economic Advisers, *Economic Report of the President, 1987* (Washington, D.C.: Government Printing Office, 1987), table B-44, 295. Added to the obvious inflationary pressure of the two major increases in the price of oil in 1973 and 1979, the dramatic yearly boost in labor cost could be dealt with in one of two ways. Management could absorb it by accepting lower profits or it could pass it along to consumers in the form of higher prices. It did both. As a result, labor's share of total national income increased from 82.5 to 86.0 percent between 1973 and 1980 (thus squeezing profits) while inflation roared along at close to 9 percent a year. See Andrew Henley, "Labour's Shares and Profitability Crisis in the United States: Recent Experience and Post-War Trends," *Cambridge Journal of Economics,* forthcoming; and *Economic Report of the President, 1987,* table B-58, 311.

13. Cf. Thomas Kochan, Robert McKersie, and Harry Katz, *The Transformation of American Industrial Relations* (New York: Basic Books, 1986).

14. Michael J. Piore and Charles Sabel, *The Second Industrial Divide* (New York: Basic Books, 1984).

15. Sabel, "The Reemergence of Regional Economies: Changes in the Scale of Production"; Michael Storper and Susan Christopherson, "Flexible Specialization and New Forms of Labor Market Segmentation: The United States Motion Picture Industry," *Industrial and Labor Relations Review,* forthcoming; Michael Storper and Allan Scott, "The Geographic Foundations and Social Regulation of Flexible Production Complexes," in *Territory and Social Reproduction,* Jennifer Wolch and Michael Dear, eds. (London and Boston: Allen and Unwin, 1988); and Peter B. Doeringer, David G. Terkla, and Gregory C. Topakian, *Invisible Factors in Local Economic Development* (New York: Oxford University Press, 1987).

16. *The Service Economy: Portrait of a New Workforce* (Washington, D.C.: Service Employees International Union and 9 to 5, 1987).

17. A dramatic example comes from the motion picture industry. It used to take Paramount Pictures up to 36 hours to distribute film clips ("coming attractions") and print advertisements from offices in New York and Los Angeles to field agencies in thirty-two American cities. The parent conglomerate, Gulf and Western, now uses satellites to transmit the same information from a microwave relay mounted on the roof of its headquarters building in New York City. It takes roughly 30 minutes to get the job done—1 percent of the original time! Gulf and Western, *1981 Corporate Report* (New York) 34.

18. Quoted in Robert B. Reich and John D. Donahue, *New Deals: The Chrysler Revival and the American System* (New York: Penguin Books, 1986), 219. Iacocco was referring to total hourly compensation, including the value of all job benefits, not merely straight time hourly wages.

19. Susan Strange, *The Casino Society* (London: Basil Blackwell, 1984); and "Playing With Fire: Games the Casino Society Plays," *Business Week,* 16 September 1985, 78ff.

20. See "Review of the Month," *Monthly Review,* October 1986, 16.

Notes

21. "Is Deregulation Working?" *Business Week,* 22 December 1986, 50–55.

22. Mike Davis, *Prisoners of the American Dream* (London: New Left Books, 1986); and Richard Edwards and Michael Podgursky, "The Unraveling Accord: U.S. Unions in Crisis," in *Unions in Crisis and Beyond: Perspectives from Six Countries,* Richard Edwards, Paolo Garonna, and Franz Todtling, eds. (Dover, Mass.: Auburn House, 1986).

23. Thomas Ferguson and Joel Rogers, *Right Turn: The Decline of the Democrats and the Future of American Politics* (New York: Hill and Wang, 1986). The proposition that an active national government is "bad for business" is thoroughly and systematically refuted in a comparison of the recent histories of the United States, Germany, Sweden, and Japan in Gorham, *No Longer Leading.*

24. Lester Thurow, "A Surge in Inequality," *Scientific American,* May 1987.

25. Among the most prominent—and thoughtful—advocates of this view are Larry Hirschorn, *Beyond Mechanization* (Cambridge, Mass.: MIT. Press, 1984); and Piore and Sabel, *The Second Industrial Divide.*

26. Manufacturing productivity has finally begun to rebound and is now rising faster in the United States than in Western Europe. But this is at least in part a result of the massive sloughing off of older capacity—plant shutdowns and permanent layoffs of industrial workers, especially in the shell-shocked steel industry—as much as an indication that companies are finally systematically investing in a new generation of productive capacity. See "U.S. Manufacturing Productivity Leads All Industrial Countries," *UAW Research Bulletin,* August 1987, 2–4.

Moreover, new evidence strongly indicates that the Commerce Department has seriously overstated manufacturing output and productivity since the late 1970s, and that the bias is getting worse over time. U.S. Congressional Office of Technology Assessment, *Technology and The American Economic Transition* (Washington, D.C.: U.S. Government Printing Office, Summer 1988), Chapter 5; and Lawrence Mishel, *Manufacturing Numbers: How Inaccurate Statistics Conceal U.S. Industrial Decline* (Washington, D.C.: Economic Policy Institute, June 1988).

27. Computed from Council of Economic Advisers, *Economic Report of the President, 1987,* table B-72, 330; and U.S. Department of Commerce, Bureau of the Census, "Money Income and Poverty Status of Families and Persons in the United States: 1986," *Current Population Reports: Consumer Income,* Series P-60, no. 157 (Washington, D.C.: Government Printing Office, July 1987), table A, 3.

28. Anthony Bianco. "Must the Panic Get Worse to Spark Reform?" *Business Week,* 9 November 1987, 47.

Chapter 2. "Zapping Labor"

1. This advertisement covered the first three pages of *Business Week,* 4 May 1987.

2. Daniel Bell, *The Coming of Post-Industrial Society* (New York: Basic Books, 1974).

3. Lester Thurow, *The Zero-Sum Solution* (New York: Simon and Schuster, 1985), 47.

4. A recent exception proves the rule. When, in April 1986, General Motors allowed its special 9.9 percent incentive financing to expire and simultaneously hiked prices by $350 per car, Maryann N. Keller, the nation's top auto analyst declared, "It's crazy." H. Ross Perot, still a director of GM at the time, was baffled by the move. In the months ahead, both Keller and Perot's astonishment were proven warranted; GM's market share shrank. By the end of the year, Ford announced with glee that its total profit exceeded that of General Motors for the first time since the 1920s. The comments from Keller and Perot appeared in William J. Hampton, "GM's Price Hikes: Foresight or Folly!" *Business Week,* 14 April 1986, 36.

5. Based on data in Council of Economic Advisers, *Economic Report of the President, 1987* (Washington, D.C.: Government Printing Office, January 1987), table B-62, 316–17. But continuing to use steel and other metal products would not have helped, as their prices more than doubled between 1973 and 1980.

6. It is true that the power of the cartel was shored up by the quiet collaboration of the Arabian-American Oil Company and other U.S. and European refining and shipping interests. See Bennett Harrison, "Inflation by Oligopoly," *Nation,* 15 August 1975. That different fractions of the business "community" often operate at cross-purposes is nothing new in American history.

Notes

7. Council of Economic Advisers, *Economic Report of the President, 1983* (Washington, D.C.: Government Printing Office, February 1983), table B-67, 240.

8. Robert Hayes and William Abernathy, "Managing Our Way to Economic Decline," *Harvard Business Review*, July–August 1980.

9. As quantitative evidence of the shift in managerial skill, Hayes and Abernathy noted the changing professional origins of the presidents of the hundred top companies in the United States. Between the mid-1950s and mid-1970s, the number of corporate heads with a financial or legal background grew by 50 percent, while those with a marketing background declined by 20 percent and those with a technical background fell by more than 10 percent. Ibid., p. 75. Because of the enormous pecuniary rewards of majoring in finance, today's typical business school has, at best, a handful of students who specialize in production management. This is true even at the Sloan School of Management at M.I.T., the nation's pre-eminent scientific and engineering university.

10. Hayes and Abernathy, "Managing Our Way," 68.

11. Quoted in Clayton Fritchey, *New York Post*, 19 September 1974.

12. For an extension of many of the ideas stimulated by Hayes and Abernathy, see Robert Reich, *The Next American Frontier* (New York: Times Books, 1983).

13. Richard J. Barnet and Ronald E. Muller, *Global Reach* (New York: Simon and Schuster, 1974), 18.

14. For a balanced view of the opposing arguments, see Yves Doz, "International Industries: Fragmentation Versus Globalization," in *Technology and Global Industry*, Bruce Guile and Harvey Brooks, eds. (Washington, D.C.: National Academy Press, 1987).

15. Robert E. Lipsey and Irving Kravis, "The Competitiveness and Comparative Advantage of U.S. Multinationals, 1957–1983," Working Paper No. 2051, National Bureau of Economic Research, October 1986, p. 7. Between 1966 and 1983, *all* U.S. manufacturers' share of world exports declined from 17.5 to 13.9 percent, and the share of the domestically located parent companies of U.S. multinational companies declined from 11.0% to 9.1%. The growth of the exports of their affiliates, according to Lipsey and Kravis, more than offset this decline.

16. From the "International Scoreboard of U.S. Corporations," *Business Week 1985 Special Issue*, 22 March 1985, 158–94.

17. John Pearson, "Strong Dollar or No, There's Money to Be Made Abroad," *Business Week*, 22 March 1985, 155. The strong overseas performance of U.S. firms in 1983–84 occurred, according to *Business Week*, despite "sluggish economies in Europe and Canada, the after-effects of deep recessions in Latin America, and draconian currency restrictions in debt-ridden countries such as Brazil."

18. Jean-Jacques Servan-Schreiber, *The American Challenge* (New York: Atheneum, 1968); especially chap. 1.

19. These statistics are calculated from Council of Economic Advisers, *Economic Report of the President, 1987* (Washington, D.C.: Government Printing Office, January 1987), table B-10, 256, and table B-40, 290.

There is widespread debate about the interpretation of aggregate changes in the manufacturing sector. The current dollar share contributed by manufacturing to the GNP has unquestionably fallen. If *constant* dollars are used instead, one finds no trend at all [although, as the new OTA report suggests, this aggregate outcome may be mainly attributable to the particular way that the Commerce Department has chosen to deflate the computer industry time series. U.S. Congressional Office of Technology Assessment, *Technology and the American Economic Transition* (Washington, D.C.: U.S. Government Printing Office, 1988), chapter 5]. Robert Z. Lawrence, a critic of the deindustrialization thesis, advocates the constant-dollar approach. See his *Can America Compete?* (Washington, D.C.: The Brookings Institution, 1984). On the other hand, the Congressional Budget Office (CBO) has argued that the current dollar numbers are the ones that matter. The CBO believes that current dollars tell what business has to invest today, what income and value-added are being created, and determine what employment levels will be. See Norman Jonas, "The Hollow Corporation," *Business Week*, 3 March 1986, 58–59.

Nicholas S. Perna, manager of economic analysis for the General Electric Company, notes that measuring manufacturing's relative share of GNP in real terms creates serious errors in measurement, owing to the price-deflating calculations that must be made and because of serious indexing problems having to do with the base year used in adjusting for inflation. For example, using 1982 as the base year for calculations, manufacturing's share of real GNP appears to have fallen by only three-tenths of 1 percent between 1969 and 1984. Simply substituting 1972 as the base year produces a decline of 1.5 percent—five times larger! See Nicholas S. Perna, "The Shift from

Notes

Manufacturing to Services: A Concerned View," *New England Economic Review,* January–February 1987, table 7, 34.

Lawrence Mischel's calculations add substantial evidence that the Commerce Department seriously overstates the manufacturing share of GNP. See Mishel, *Manufacturing Numbers: How Inaccurate Statistics Conceal U.S. Industrial Decline* (Washington, D.C.: Economic Policy Institute, June 1988).

20. Office of Technology Assessment, *Technology and the American Economic Transition*

21. The idea of deindustrialization was first developed in the 1970s by British political economists at Cambridge University, especially Agit Singh. See Singh, "U.K. Industry and the World Economy: A Case of De-industrialization?" *Cambridge Journal of Economics* 1, no. 2, June 1977; F. Blackaby, ed., *Deindustrialization* (London: Heinemann, 1979); A. P. Thirlwall, "Deindustrialization in the U.K.," *Lloyds Bank Review,* no. 134, April 1982; and R. Martin and Robert Rowthorn, eds., *The Geography of De-industrialization* (London: Macmillan, 1986). These scholars defined the phenomenon as one in which a country is unable to export enough manufactured goods at prevailing prices to earn sufficient foreign exchange to enable it to maintain its consumption of imports at a rate consistent with full domestic employment. Deindustrialization came to imply secularly declining manufacturing employment and (perhaps also) production. In our own adaptation of the idea, we took a less formal approach, having in mind the general shift of resources out of domestic manufacturing operations, either offshore or into the service sector. See Barry Bluestone and Bennett Harrison, *The Deindustrialization of America* (New York: Basic Books, 1982).

22. Akio Morita, as quoted in Norman Jonas, "The Hollow Corporation," *Business Week,* 3 March 1987.

23. Joseph Grunwald and Kenneth Flamm, *The Global Factory: Foreign Assembly in International Trade* (Washington, D.C.: The Brookings Institution, 1985).

24. Raul A. Hinojosa-Ojeda and Rebecca Morales, "International Restructuring and Labor Market Interdependence: The Automobile Industry in Mexico and the U.S.," paper presented to the Conference on Labor Market Interdependence between the U.S. and Mexico, El Colegio de Mexico, Mexico, 25–27 September 1986.

25. These figures are reported in John J. LaFalce, "Maquiladoras Cost America Jobs," *New York Times,* 23 December 1987, F2. According to LaFalce, U.S.-based firms have invested over $2 billion in these *maquiladoras* during the last decade. At the end of 1987, there were more than 1,000 *maquiladoras* along the U.S.–Mexican border, employing some 310,000 Mexicans. See Jim Kolbe, "Made in Mexico, Good for the U.S.A.," *New York Times,* 13 December 1987, F2.

26. Grunwald and Flamm, *The Global Factory,* 17.

27. David Beers, "9 to 5 in Barbados," *In These Times,* 4–10 April 1984, 24.

28. Professor Robert Wiegand of the University of Illinois has calculated that Ireland has granted special incentives (tax abatements, training allowances, and so forth) to 70 percent of the U.S.-owned business there. South Korea, Israel, Taiwan, and Brazil have provided special arrangements for more than 40 percent of the U.S. companies they have lured. These statistics appear in Tom Ashbrook, "US Workers in Worldwide Job Scramble," *Boston Globe,* 26 September 1983, 1.

29. U.S. Department of Commerce, Office of International Sectoral Policy, *Survey of Automotive Trade Restrictions Maintained by Selected Nations* (Washington, D.C.: U.S. Government Printing Office, 1980). For a more general discussion of such "managed trade" instruments, see Barry Bluestone and Seamus O'Cleireacain, "Industrial Policy Priorities in the Trade Jungle," *World Policy Journal,* Winter 1984.

30. See data from Joel Popkin and Company as reported in Perna, "The Shift from Manufacturing to Services."

31. Folker Frobel et al., *The New International Division of Labor* (New York: Cambridge University Press, 1980).

32. David M. Gordon, "The Global Economy: New Edifice or Crumbling Foundations? *New Left Review,* forthcoming; Arthur MacEwan, "Slackers, Bankers, Marketers: Multinational Firms and the Pattern of U.S. Foreign Investment," unpublished ms., University of Massachusetts, Boston, 1982; and Andrew Sayer, "Industry and Space: A Sympathetic Critique of Radical Research," *Society and Space* 3, no. 1, 1985.

33. For an exposition of a position similar to our own on the continuing importance of arrangements among large multinational corporations in shaping international economic affairs, see Joyce Kolko, *Restructuring the World Economy* (New York: Pantheon, 1988).

34. LaFalce, " 'Maquiladoras Cost America Jobs," F2.

35. These examples are from Kenneth Dreyfack and Otis Port, "Even American Know How is Headed Abroad," *Business Week*, 3 March 1986, 60–61.

36. Quoted in Steven Prokesch, "Stopping the High-Tech Giveaway," *New York Times*, 22 March 1987, sect. 3, p. 1. See also Clyde V. Prestowitz, Jr., *Trading Places: How We Allowed Japan to take the Lead* (New York: Basic Books, 1988).

37. Roy J. Harris, Jr., and Bernard Wysocki, Jr., "Venture with Boeing Is Likely to Give Japan Big Boost in Aerospace," *Wall Street Journal*, 14 January 1986, 1.

38. Robert B. Reich, "A Faustian Bargain with the Japanese," *New York Times*, 6 April 1986, F2.

39. Quoted in Harris and Wysocki, "Venture with Boeing . . ." American firms are not alone in their use of this strategy. Since the 1970s, more and more European and Japanese companies have been copying the U.S. practice of joint venturing. Thus, Electrolux of Sweden and Thorn EMI of Britain have teamed up to produce and market consumer appliances; SGS of Italy and Thomson of France have merged their semiconductor operations; and DAF of the Netherlands and British Leyland now jointly produce trucks for the European market. See John Templeman, "Hands Across Europe: Deals that Could Redraw the Map," *Business Week*, 18 May 1987, 64. British firms have made direct investments in Matsushita, Toshiba, Hitachi, Mitsubishi, Sony, and Sanyo; French firms are involved in a joint venture with Toyoda Machine Works; Italy has forged a venture between Alfa Romeo and Nissan; and West Germany's Continental Tire is working with Toyo Rubber, one of Japan's leading producers of auto and truck tires. These examples are from the Ministry of International Trade and Industry of Japan and reported in Philip Cooke, Kevin Morgan, and David Jackson, "New Technology and Regional Development in Austerity Britain: The Case of the Semiconductor Industry," *Regional Studies* 18, no. 4, 286–87.

40. Stephen S. Cohen and John Zysman, "The Myth of a Post-Industrial Economy," *New York Times*, 17 May 1987, F2. For a more detailed discussion of this argument, see their book, *Manufacturing Matters* (New York: Basic Books, 1987).

41. Quoted in Norman Jonas, "The Hollow Corporation," 53.

42. Ronald E. Kutscher and Valerie A. Personick, "Deindustrialization and the Shift to Services," *Monthly Labor Review*, June 1986, 3. For additional evidence of this phenomenon, see Barry Bluestone, "Is Deindustrialization a Myth? Capital Mobility versus Absorptive Capacity in the U.S. Economy," *Annals of the American Academy of Political and Social Science*, 475, September 1984, 39–51.

43. Barry Bluestone, Bennett Harrison, and Alan Clayton-Matthews, "Structure vs. Cycle in U.S. Manufacturing Job Growth," *Industrial Relations* 25, no. 2, Summer 1986.

44. John Francis Welch, Jr., as quoted in Marilyn A. Harris, Russell Mitchell, and Christopher Power, "Can Jack Welch Reinvent GE?" *Business Week*, 30 June 1986, 62.

45. David E. Sanger, "G.E. Consumer Electronics Lines to Be Sold to Thomson of France," *New York Times*, 23 July 1987, 1.

46. Blanca Riemer, "Are America's Manufacturers Finally Back on the Map?" *Business Week*, 17 November 1986, 92.

47. The results of the study by the GAO and OTA were presented in William J. Gainer, "U.S. Business Closures and Permanent Layoffs during 1983 and 1984," at the OTA–GAO Workshop on Plant Closings, 20 April–1 May 1986, 3.

48. Candee S. Harris, "The Magnitude of Job Loss from Plant Closings and the Generation of Replacement Jobs: Some Recent Evidence," *Annals of the American Academy of Political and Social Science* 475, September 1984, 15, 19. These statistics do not include all the jobs lost in plant closings, for they exclude affiliates of business enterprises with less than a hundred employees. Only the larger units of multiplant firms are included in Harris's figures.

49. Richard Brandt, Aaron Bernstein, and John Hoerr, "Those Vanishing High-Tech Jobs," *Business Week*, 15 July 1985, 30–31.

50. Comments of Elaine Goldman in Susan R. Sanderson and Lawrence Schein, "Sizing Up the Down-Sizing Era," *Across the Board: The Conference Board Magazine*, 23, no. 11, November 1986, 15.

51. Cynthia Green, "Middle Managers Are Still Sitting Ducks," *Business Week*, 16 September 1985, 34. According to Eugene E. Jennings, a professor at Michigan State University quoted by

Notes

Green, 89 of the 100 largest U.S. companies have reorganized to reduce the number of management levels since 1980.

52. U.S. Department of Labor, Bureau of Labor Statistics, "Reemployment Increases among Displaced Workers," *BLS News*, USDL 86-414, 14 October 1986, table 6. Of these 782,000 displaced workers, 487,000 were from the executive, administrative, and managerial ranks. The remaining job losers had been employed in various professional specialties. One should also note that in a comparable survey of displaced workers covering an earlier period (1979–84) *not including the years of strong recovery after 1984*, the number of displaced managerial and professional workers was actually smaller: 703,000. This suggests that the pace of displacement among members of this group is increasing, despite the cyclical strength of the economy. See "BLS Reports on Displaced Workers," *BLS News*, USDL 84-492, 30 November 1984, table 5.

53. This estimate was provided to Sanderson and Schein, "Sizing Up the Down-Sizing Era," by Joe Coates, president of a Washington, D.C., management-consulting firm that serves Fortune–1,000 clients. Sanderson and Schein believe this is a conservative estimate.

54. Practically all institutionalist and radical scholars writing about the profit squeeze of the 1970s and those responses of industry and government that have to do with labor see the problem for capital as both the containment of the cost of labor *and* the re-assertion of greater control over what had been the growing power of at least the organized working class, both at the workplace and in the political realm. We could not agree more with this conception, which always lay at the core of the radical version of the labor market segmentation theory to which we ourselves have subscribed (and even made some small contribution). For ease of exposition, we have nevertheless chosen in this book to focus on the *cost* side of the dual nature of the relation between capital and labor. This choice does not make what follows incorrect so much as it inevitably makes it *incomplete*. But with friends such as Maryellen Kelley, Sam Bowles, David Gordon, Richard Edwards, Michael Reich, Juliet Schor, Thomas Weisskopf, David Noble, Gordon Clark, Michael Storper, Susan Christopherson, James Baron, Eileen Appelbaum, Ed Soja, Andrew Friedman, Michael Burawoy, Richard Walker, Heidi Hartmann, Robert Howard, Stephen Wood, Bryn Jones, and Saskia Sassen all writing these days about the problem of controlling labor during a crisis in mass production, the subject can certainly not be said to be neglected. Nevertheless, a fully integrated synthesis of the competitive and class-struggle aspects of the crisis has yet to be written. For three attempts to at least call attention to this problem, see Bennett Harrison, "Cold Bath or Restructuring? An Extension of the Gordon-Bowles-Weisskopf Framework," *Science and Society*, Spring 1987; David Harvey, "The Geographical and Geopolitical Consequences of the Transition from Fordist to Flexible Accumulation," in *America's New Economic Geography*, George Sternlieb and John Hughes, eds. (New Brunswick, N.J.: Rutgers University Press, videocassette, 1987); and Stephen Marglin, ed., *The Golden Age of Capitalism: Lessons for the 1990s*, ms. in progress, November 1987.

55. This hardly exhausts the list of cost-cutting wage experiments now under way in American industry under the heading of the search for greater flexibility. In some cases, firms substitute bonuses for part of the old base wage, thereby passing part of the short-run risk of unprofitability onto the employees. Other managers are experimenting with "pay-for-performance" wage systems, which amount to the partial restoration of the old principle of the piece rate, even when the work is being done by teams of employees. The objective is to increase work incentives and therefore productivity. For a detailed examination of these management "innovations," see Thomas Kochan, Harry Katz, and Robert McKersie, *The Transformation of American Industrial Relations* (New York: Basic Books, 1986). For critical views of these experiments, see Robert Howard, *Brave New Workplace* (New York: Simon and Schuster, 1985); and Mike Davis, *Prisoners of the American Dream* (London: Verso-New Left Books, 1986).

56. Daniel J. B. Mitchell, "Shifting Norms in Wage Determination," *Brookings Papers on Economic Activity*, no. 2, 1985, 576. Since Mitchell's data are drawn from the Bureau of Labor Statistics' *Current Wage Developments* survey, which is restricted to large firms and "major" contracts, they undoubtedly understate the incidence of concessions, even in the unionized sector alone.

57. "Who Says Concessions Are a Thing of the Past?" *Labor Notes*, June 1986, 1.

58. Jane Slaughter, "ARMCO Pact Sets Precedent: Plant by Plant Contracts," *Labor Notes*, December 1986, 16.

59. Dick Blin, "Steelworkers Give Up Jobs, Work Rules, Money, Benefits, Holidays to USX," *Labor Notes*, February 1987, 1.

60. Gregory L. Miles and Matt Rothman, "The Steel Deal that Everybody's Watching," *Business Week,* 21 April 1986, 32.

61. United Auto Workers, "Special Supplement: The Specter of Two-Tier Wages," *Research Bulletin,* October 1985, 17.

62. Mitchell, "Shifting Norms in Wage Determination," 593.

63. Davis, *Prisoners of the American Dream,* 151.

64. Jane Seabury, "The Rise of Two-Tier Wages," *Washington Post National Weekly Edition,* 22 April 1985, 22.

65. There is a huge literature on this subject. The modern classic—itself derived in important ways from the earlier research and teachings of the economists who actually erected the institutions of wage-and-price planning during World War II—is by Peter Doeringer and Michael Piore, *Internal Labor Markets and Manpower Analysis* (Lexington, Mass.: D. C. Heath, 1971). A Marxist twist, emphasizing the joint importance of management's control over its employees as well as the reproduction of skill, was later supplied by Doeringer and Piore's students. See esp. Richard Edwards, *Contested Terrain* (New York: Basic Books, 1979); and Michael Reich, David Gordon, and Richard Edwards, *Segmented Work, Divided Workers* (New York: Cambridge University Press, 1981).

66. Noyelle has been exploring this question for several years, particularly in regard to the service sector. His *Beyond Industrial Dualism* (Boulder, Colo.: Westview Press, 1987) is a marvelous book—except for its misleading title. In fact, Noyelle is writing about a *restoration* of dualism, whereby the large corporation increasingly maintains a small core of more or less "permanent," highly paid employees and a large periphery of workers of varied skills, wage levels, and degree of attachment to the company—rather on the Japanese model.

Dualism is also exacerbated by the sort of corporate rationalization that we discussed at the beginning of this chapter. In labor market segmentation theory, internal labor markets (ILMs) are said to be most commonly associated with what Piore called the "subordinate tier of the primary labor market." Deindustrialization has been displacing precisely this segment of the labor market—thereby contributing to the devolution of the ILM. For a European view of all of these issues, see John Goldthorpe, "The End of Convergence: Corporatist and Dualist Tendencies in Modern Western Societies," in *Order and Conflict in Contemporary Capitalism,* Goldthorpe, ed. (Oxford: Clarendon Press, 1984).

67. Garth Mangum, Donald Mayall, and Kristin Nelson, "The Temporary Help Industry," *Industrial and Labor Relations Review,* July 1985; and Jeffrey Pfeffer and James Baron, "Taking the Workers Back Out: Recent Trends in the Structuring of Employment," in *Research in Organizational Behavior* 10, Barry Straw and L. L. Cummings, eds. (Greenwich, Conn.: JAI Press), 1988.

68. One of the more pervasive images about the temporary help industry is that it is a hotbed of entrepreneurism, with thousands of small dynamic firms. Yet Census Bureau data indicate that the industry is in fact becoming highly concentrated. In the late 1970s, eleven firms providing "personnel supply services" billed almost four-fifths of the entire industry's receipts. Kelly Girl, now Kelly Services, is one of the largest. Similarly, among the group of "temporary help supply services," the 1 percent which employed a thousand or more people accounted for 34 percent of the total market. For more recent data, see 9 to 5, the National Association of Working Women, "Working at the Margins: Part Time and Temporary Workers in the United States," Cleveland, September 1986.

69. *Business Week,* 15 December 1986, 52.

70. Davis, *Prisoners of the American Dream,* 152.

71. "Minneapolis Nurses Strike to Save Full-Time Jobs", *Labor Notes,* 28 June 1984, 1.

72. Pfeffer and Baron, "Taking the Workers Back Out."

73. Eileen Appelbaum, "Restructuring Work: Temporary, Part-Time, and At-Home Employment," in *Computer Chips and Paper Clips: Technology and Women's Employment,* Heidi Hartmann, ed. (Washington, D.C.: National Academy Press, 1987), 271.

74. "The Disposable Employee Is becoming a Fact of Corporate Life," *Business Week,* 15 December 1986, 52.

75. Ronald Ehrenberg, Pamela Rosenberg, and Jeanne Li, "Part-Time Employment in the United States," in Robert Hart, ed., *Employment, Unemployment, and Hours of Work* (London: George Allen and Unwin, 1988).

76. Pfeffer and Baron, "Taking the Workers Out"; and Noyelle, *Beyond Industrial Dualism.*

Notes

77. Actually, the interviewer probes for the *reasons* why a person working less than 35 hours a week is doing so. Those reasons are sorted into two broad categories: "economic" (say, the plant or office shut down) and "noneconomic" (say, illness or going to school part time). Only persons employed part-time for economic reasons are considered to be *involuntary part-time* workers.

78. Full Employment Action Council, "Involuntary Part-Time Workers: Millions the Recovery Left Behind," Washington, D.C., 2 May 1986, table 4.

79. Cynthia Daniels, "There's No Place Like Home: The Politics of Home-Based Work," *Dollars and Sense,* December 1986, 18.

80. For more details, see Bluestone and Harrison, *The Deindustrialization of America,* chap. 6.

81. "The Disposable Employee Is Becoming a Fact of Corporate Life," 52.

82. Ibid., p. 56.

83. We are grateful to the Research Department of the United Auto Workers for these unpublished estimates.

84. Noyelle, *Beyond Industrial Dualism.*

85. Paul Weiler, "Promises to Keep: Securing Workers' Rights to Self-Organize Under the NLRB," *Harvard Law Review,* June 1983, 1769.

86. Richard Freeman and James Medoff, *What Do Unions Do?* (New York: Basic Books, 1984).

87. Kochan, Katz, and McKersie, *The Transformation of American Industrial Relations,* chap. 3.

88. See, for example, George H. Hildebrand, *American Unionism: An Historical and Analytical Survey* (Reading, Mass.: Addison-Wesley, 1979).

89. Philip M. Doyle, "Area Wage Surveys Shed Light on Declines in Unionization," *Monthly Labor Review,* September 1985; and Freeman and Medoff, *What Do Unions Do?*

90. Kochan, Katz, and McKersie, *The Transformation of American Industrial Relations,* 14.

Chapter 3. Restructuring and the World of High Finance

1. "Playing With Fire: Games the Casino Society Plays," *Business Week,* 16 September 1985, 78–86.

2. Ibid., p. 79.

3. John E. Parsons, "Bubble, Bubble, How Much Trouble? Financial Markets as Agents of Capitalist Development and Capitalist Crises," Sloan School of Management, M.I.T., Working Paper no. 1915–87 (November 1987).

4. Paul Sweezy and Harry Magdoff, *Stagnation and the Financial Explosion* (New York: Monthly Review Press, 1987).

5. For a brilliant disentangling of these complicated theoretical categories, see Richard Walker, "Is There a Service Economy? The Changing Capitalist Division of Labor," *Science and Society,* Spring 1985.

6. "Industry Cleans House," *Business Week,* 11 November 1985, 33.

7. See "Banking on Uncle Sam: The Government's Safety Net," *Dollars and Sense,* no. 101 (November 1984), 4.

8. Ibid., p. 86.

9. Three good primers on the subject are: Walter Adams and James Brock, *The Bigness Complex* (New York: Pantheon, 1987); John Brooks, *The Takeover Game* (New York: Dutton, 1987); and David J. Ravenscraft and Frederick M. Scherer, *Mergers, Sell-Offs, and Economic Efficiency* (Washington D.C.: Brookings Institution, 1987).

10. Judith H. Dobrzynski and Joan Berger, "For Better or for Worse?" *Business Week,* 12 January 1987, 38. The value of completed mergers tripled from $60 billion in 1983 to $180 billion in 1986.

11. This case is based on "The Raiding Game," *Dollars and Sense,* March 1987. This little article is a gem, containing a clear yet remarkably complete lexicon of terms—from "poison pills" to "golden parachutes"—and a demystifying explanation of the hostile takeover.

12. Alison Leigh Cowan, "White Knights: The Dark Side," *New York Times,* 16 July 1987, D2.

13. "Is the Financial System Shortsighted?" *Business Week,* 3 March 1986, 82–83.

14. Walter Adams and James W. Brock, "The Hidden Costs of Failed Mergers," *New York Times,* 21 June 1987, F3.

15. Cited in Steven E. Prokesch and William J. Powell, Jr., "Do Mergers Really Work?" *Business Week,* 3 June 1985, 88–91.

16. Paul O. Flaim and Ellen Sehgal, "Displaced Workers of 1979–83: How Well Have They Fared?" *Monthly Labor Review,* June 1985, 3–16.

17. Michael Podgursky and Paul Swaim of the University of Massachusetts–Amherst report that the average blue-collar worker in the government's survey "suffered a 37 percent earnings loss in the first year following displacement. The loss drops to 20 percent in the next year, where it more or less remains through the fifth year." Michael Podgursky and Paul Swaim, "Dislocated Workers and Earnings Loss: Estimates from the Displaced Worker Survey," Department of Economics, University of Massachusetts–Amherst, 18 March 1985, 24.

18. The following draws upon David Moberg, "Greyhound: Taking Workers For a Ride?" *In These Times,* 25 February–10 March 1987; Jim Woodward, "Greyhound Demands New Concessions," *Labor Notes,* November 1985, 1; Gersh Mayer, "Concessions Parade Accelerates as Greyhound Lines Gets New Owner," *Labor Notes,* February 1987, 16; and Carlton Jackson, *Hounds of the Road* (Bowling Green, Ohio: Bowling Green University Popular Press, 1984).

19. The "new" Greyhound corporation actually did not avoid the legal rules of successorship at all; it took advantage of them, according to Richard Rothstein, a California-based labor activist. "The rules of successorship have long been that, in a sale of assets (not stock), the successor employer is required to recognize and bargain with the predecessor's union only if the successor employer selects a majority of its work force from the predecessor's employees. In such cases, the successor is not required to honor the previous contract, but only to bargain in good faith. What changed is not the rules of successorship, but the willingness of employers to use this right to demand wage and benefit concessions, as well as the increase in speculation leading to more frequent asset transfers." Quoted from private correspondence from Richard Rothstein, September 1987, to the authors.

20. See Cindy Skrzycki, "Don't Call Greyhound For a Ride (or Singer For a Stitch)," *Washington Post National Weekly,* 17 August 1987, 21.

21. See Stephen Hymer, "The Multinational Corporation and the Law of Uneven Development," in *Economics and World Order,* Jagdish Bhagwati, ed. (New York: Macmillan, 1972); and "The Multinational Corporation and the International Division of Labor," in *The Multinational Corporation: A Radical Critique,* Stephen Hymer et al., eds. (Cambridge: Cambridge University Press, 1979).

22. One of the predictions of Hymer's theory which has been powerfully confirmed by all contemporary researchers is the extraordinary growth of transactions within a company of both goods and services, crossing national borders. See Joseph Grunwald and Kenneth Flamm, *The Global Factory: Foreign Assembly in International Trade* (Washington, D.C.: Brookings Institution, 1985); and Richard J. Barnet and Ronald E. Muller, *Global Reach* (New York: Simon and Schuster, 1974), 18.

23. "Agglomeration" refers to the clustering of interlinked businesses into central areas to economize on shared inputs and both formal and informal communication, to take advantage of specialized infrastructure, to facilitate informal face-to-face contact among both high-level executives and lower-level technicians and designers, and to provide labor pools large enough to assure employers a critical mass of every needed grade of skill. The classic description of agglomeration is found in Edgar M. Hoover and Raymond Vernon, *Anatomy of a Metropolis* (Cambridge: Harvard University Press, 1959). There is a prodigious literature on the subject of agglomeration as an organizing principle of the location of industrial activity in market economies.

24. For evidence that urban hotels in at least one region of the country—New England—are now substantially dedicated to providing services to other companies as well as to workers-cum-tourists, see Daniel P. Kurtz, "The Lodging Industry in New England," (Master's thesis, Department of Urban Studies and Planning, M.I.T., 1979).

25. Thierry Noyelle, *Beyond Industrial Dualism* (Boulder, Colo.: Westview Press, 1987); Noyelle and Thomas Stanback, Jr., *The Economic Transformation of American Cities* (Totowa, N.J.: Allanheld Osmun, 1983); Saskia Sassen, *The Mobility of Labor and Capital* (Cambridge: Cambridge University Press, 1987); and Sassen, *Global Cities* (Princeton: Princeton University Press, forthcoming). Another important contributor to this literature on urban restructuring was

Notes

a student of Hymer's. See Robert Cohen, "Multinational Corporations, International Finance, and the Sunbelt," in *The Rise of the Sunbelt Cities*, David Perry and Alfred Watkins, eds. (Beverly Hills: Sage, 1977).

26. Other researchers believe that this dualism also characterizes those relatively few cities where high-technology manufacturing is one of the expanding sectors. See Ed Soja, "Economic Restructuring and the Internationalization of the Los Angeles Region," in *The Capitalist City*, Michael Peter Smith and Joe R. Feagin, eds. (New York: Basil Blackwell, 1987).

27. BLS statistics cited in Robert Kuttner, "The Declining Middle," *Atlantic*, July 1963.

28. "The False Paradise of a Service Economy," *Business Week*, 3 March 1986, 82.

29. Neal Rosenthal, "The Shrinking Middle Class: Myth or Reality?" *Monthly Labor Review*, March 1985, p. 9.

30. These data are from the regular projections of the U.S. Bureau of Labor Statistics as reported in Louis Uchitelle, "Making a Living Is now a Family Enterprise," *New York Times Careers Section*, 11 October 1987, 6, 8.

31. Robert G. Sheets, Stephen Nord, and John J. Phelps, *The Impact of Service Industries on Underemployment in Metropolitan Areas* (Lexington, Mass.: Lexington Books, 1987).

32. Ibid., p. 124.

33. The data from the Boston Redevelopment Authority are cited in Women for Economic Justice, *Beyond Growth: The Underside of the Economic Miracle in Massachusetts* (Boston: Women for Economic Justice, 1987), 15.

34. Walker, "Is There a Service Economy?" The same basic idea lies at the core of the thesis presented in Stephen Cohen and John Zysman, *Manufacturing Matters* (New York: Basic Books, 1986).

35. Jeffrey Pfeffer and James Baron, "Taking the Workers Back Out: Recent Trends in the Structuring of Employment," in *Research in Organizational Behavior* 10, Barry Straw and L. L. Cummings, eds. (Greenwich, Conn.: JAI Press), 1988.

Chapter 4. The Laissez-Faire Affair

1. For this section, we draw heavily on Kim McQuaid, *Big Business and Presidential Power* (New York: Morrow, 1983); Nelson Lichtenstein, *Labor's War at Home: The CIO in World War II* (New York: Cambridge University Press, 1982); Otis L. Graham, Jr., *Toward A Planned Society: From Roosevelt to Nixon* (New York: Oxford University Press, 1976); Louis Galambos and Joseph Pratt, *The Rise of The Corporate Commonwealth* (New York: Basic Books, 1988); and Mike Davis, *Prisoners of the American Dream* (London: Verso-New Left Books, 1986).

2. The story of government planning in World War I is told in several exceptional books, including George Soule, *Planning U.S.A.* (New York: Viking, 1967), chap. 3; Edward C. Kirkland, *A History of American Economic Life* (New York: Appleton-Century-Crofts, 1969), 4th ed., chap. 18; and W. Elliot Brownlee, *Dynamics of Ascent: A History of the American Economy* (New York: Knopf, 1979), 2d ed., chap. 13.

3. For the most part, industry co-operated voluntarily with the WIB and welcomed Baruch's management as necessary to the mobilization effort. This was despite the fact that the Board, in the view of its own historian, "extended its antennae into the inner-most recesses of industry." See Kirkland, *A History of American Life*, 469. Corporations were by no means selfless in their support of the Board. Commodity prices were set high enough to assure huge profits to producers like U.S. Steel, and the Board's activities guaranteed producers a dependable supply of raw materials and transportation.

There was still another reason that industrialists favored the wartime controls. Early in 1918, the War Labor Board was established to oversee labor-management relations. During its tenure, it adjudicated some 1,500 cases; its sister agency, the Labor Policies Board, wrote policies governing hours, wages, and working conditions. In supporting the American Federation of Labor (AFL), it sought to root out the more radical unions, especially the International Workers of the World (IWW). While there were some six thousand strikes during the war, most were of extremely short duration and the AFL prospered. Between 1914 and 1920, total union membership rose by almost 2.4 million, doubling the prewar figure. These data are based on Leo Wolman, *Ebb and Flow in Trade Unionism* (New York: National Bureau of Economic Research, 1936) as reported in George H. Hildebrand, *American Unionism: An Historical and Analytical Survey* (Reading, Mass.: Addison-Wesley, 1979), 11. Unionized workers, as a percentage of the total employed, increased from 5.8 in 1910 to 11.8 in 1920. Among nonagricultural workers, the increase was from 10 to 18.9 percent. Thus, both Big Labor and Big Capital gained from the planning of the wartime economy.

4. Harry N. Scheiber, Harold G. Vatter, and Harold Underwood Faulkner, *American Economic History* (New York: Harper and Row, 1976), 9th ed., 325.

5. It also witnessed a reversal of the wartime peace between labor and management. Almost immediately after the war, as the potential long-term consequences of continued union organizing became apparent to the captains of industry and to such key agencies of government as the Office of the Attorney General, expediency turned them to active red-baiting and attacks on unions and union leaders, combined with selective experiments by a few companies in the improvement of what today we would call the "quality of work life." As a result of this "American Plan" to restrict the spread of trade unionism, union membership and power declined in the 1920s. From a peak of 5.1 million members in 1920, organized labor's ranks fell to 3.4 million in 1929. See Hildebrand, *American Unionism*, 12.

6. Data from *Historical Statistics of the United States* and *Economic Report of the President, 1976*, as reported in Douglas F. Dowd, *The Twisted Dream: Capitalist Development in the United States since 1776* (Cambridge, Mass.: Winthrop Publishers, 1977), 2d ed., 103.

7. John A. Garrity, *The Great Depression* (New York: Harcourt Brace Jovanovich, 1986), 148.

8. For a lively discussion of this period, see Edward Robb Ellis, *A Nation in Torment* (New York: Capricorn Books, 1971), chap. 14; and Garrity, *The Great Depression*, 148–51.

9. As quoted in Garrity, ibid., p. 149.

10. Eric F. Goldman, *Rendezvous with Destiny: A History of Modern American Reform* (New York: Vintage Books, 1977), 258–59. Among the converts was famed Constitutional historian Charles A. Beard, who advocated an American five-year plan consisting of a system of cartels in the basic industries controlled by a national economic council representing business, labor, and agriculture. Beard had a vision of "the imperative necessity of planning." Ellis, *A Nation in Torment*, 215.

11. Ibid., p. 211.

12. The federal government moved aggressively in other areas as well. The Tennessee Valley Authority (TVA) was established to deliver government-generated electric power to depressed Appalachia and to provide a yardstick for the cost of power throughout the nation. When Senator George Norris of Nebraska asked President Roosevelt, at a White House dinner, "What are you going to say when they ask you the political philosophy behind TVA?" he responded, "I'll tell them it's neither fish nor fowl, but whatever it is, it will taste awfully good to the people of the Tennessee Valley." Quoted in Goldman, *Rendezvous with Destiny*, 263. Such was the pragmatic approach taken by the "alphabet soup" planning agencies established during the first term of FDR's administration.

13. Ibid., p. 272.

14. See Michael D. Reagan, *Regulation: The Politics of Policy* (Boston: Little, Brown, 1987), table 3-1, p. 46.

15. Goldman, *Rendezvous with Destiny*, 299. Goldman notes that Maury Maverick, a former member of Congress and chief of the Smaller War Plants Corporation, railed against the concentration of big business in the war-production effort. In one report, Maverick noted that of $1 billion spent for scientific research in industrial laboratories, two-thirds went to the sixty-eight largest firms. Ibid., p. 300.

16. Those who held this position, including the leading Keynesian in America, Alvin Hansen, were dubbed "stagnationists." They argued, according to economist Richard Gill, that the nineteenth-century experience of the United States—during which time fairly full employment was not uncommon—was actually caused by a set of special, favorable conditions including the expansion of the country and the introduction of capital-intensive production. In the twentieth century, however, these favorable conditions no longer prevailed, according to the stagnationists. They feared a persistent tendency of the demand for investment to fall short of savings and thus a tendency toward deepening depressions or economic "stagnation." See Richard T. Gill, *Economics* (Santa Monica: Goodyear, 1978), 3d ed., 396.

17. Franklin D. Roosevelt, *1944 State of the Union Message*, reprinted for the Special Executive Seminar, Aspen Institute for Humanistic Studies (Aspen, Colo., July 1983).

18. Douglas F. Dowd, *The Twisted Dream*, p. 235.

Notes

19. The central importance of U.S. foreign policy for shaping and guarding the new international order was not lost on anyone who had been part of the wartime planning effort. Indeed, many of the same executives and economists who had managed the wartime economy in the United States went to Europe after the war to direct the Marshall Plan for the economic reconstruction of Europe. Others went to work for the new Central Intelligence Agency and the State Department's substantial economic apparatus. Among these were Averill Harriman and George Ball. Ibid., p. 234.

20. For a fascinating account of the origins and evolution of the Employment Act, the Council of Economic Advisers, and the Joint Economic Committee, see Walter Heller, "The Public Policy Experience," in *The Changing American Economy*, David Obey and Paul Sarbanes, eds. (New York: Basil Blackwell, 1986).

21. On the rise—and crisis—of Fordism in the United States, see David Gordon, Richard Edwards, and Michael Reich, *Segmented Work, Divided Workers* (New York: Cambridge University Press, 1982); Michel Aglietta, *A Theory of Capitalist Regulation: The U.S. Experience* (London: New Left Books-Verso, 1979); and Michael Piore and Charles Sabel, *The Second Industrial Divide (New York: Basic Books, 1984)*.

22. Robert Reich and John D. Donahue, *New Deals: The Chrysler Revival and the American System* (New York: Times Books, 1985).

23. For an extraordinarily detailed discussion of the *politics* of the rise and fall of "industrial policy," see Jim Shoch, "The Politics of the U.S. Industrial Policy Debate," Department of Political Science, Massachusetts Institute of Technology, Cambridge, Mass., February 1988, working paper.

While corporatist industrial policy effectively disappeared from the national scene even before the election of 1984, variations on the theme were blossoming in several major industrial states, and continued to do so throughout the 1980s. In California, for example, the Santa Clara County Manufacturing Group (SCCMG) was formed in the heart of Silicon Valley, to give local industrialists—mainly in high technology—access to government planners and vice versa. By the early 1980s, eighty-five of the region's largest employers were meeting regularly with elected county and municipal officials (but generally *not* with trade unionists) to plan for the educational, environmental, and infrastructural needs of the region. One of the SCCMG's leaders, John Young, the president of Hewlett-Packard, later became director of President Reagan's national commission on "competitiveness" in the mid-1980s. Even more significantly, in 1981 California Governor Jerry Brown crafted a statewide Commission on Industrial Innovation which was a direct outgrowth of the SCCMG. With labor representatives sitting at *this* table, the parties proposed an extraordinarily diverse range of long-run development policies for California, concerning education, job training, research and development, intra-industry cooperation, collaborative research, new experiments in employer-employee cooperation to enhance productivity, and joint business-university research. Many of these proposals have since been enacted in state law. See AnnaLee Saxenian, "In Search of Power: The Organization of Business Interests in Silicon Valley and Route 128," Department of Political Science, Massachusetts Institute of Technology, Cambridge, Mass., September 1986, working paper.

24. Samuel Bowles, David M. Gordon, and Thomas Weisskopf, *Beyond the Wasteland: A Democratic Alternative to Economic Decline* (Garden City, N.Y.: Anchor, 1983), 110. The "cold bath" refers to the deliberate use of macroeconomic policy to bring about an economic recession. The objective was to create enough unemployment to weaken workers' demands for wage increases, thus boosting profits and lessening inflation. The use of macroeconomic tools for this purpose is not new. See Raford Boddy and James Crotty, "Class Conflict and Macro-Policy: The Political Business Cycle," *Review of Radical Political Economics* 7, no. 1 (Spring 1975).

25. As the well-respected macroeconomist, Robert Eisner, has pointed out time and time again, "for deficits to matter, they must be *real* deficits. A real deficit is one which increases the real debt of the government to the public and hence increases the public's perception of its own real wealth." Robert Eisner, "The Federal Budget Crisis," in *The Changing American Economy*, Obey and Sarbanes, eds., 73–74. Inflation generates the equivalent of an "inflation tax" that eats away at the value of the public's holdings of the Treasury notes and bills that make up much of the federal debt. Similarly, rising interest rates reduce the value of outstanding federal debt instruments, also making the public poorer. As a consequence of these negative "wealth effects," the value of the federal debt as an expansionary tool is severely discounted during periods of inflation and high interest rates. For a detailed account of Eisner's research into the federal debt,

see his *How Real is the Federal Deficit?* (New York: Free Press, 1986); and Robert Eisner and Paul J. Pieper, "A New View of the Federal Debt and Budget Deficits," *American Economic Review* 74, no. 1 (March 1984).

26. Norman J. Glickman, "Emerging Urban Policies in a Slow-Growth Economy," *International Journal of Urban and Regional Research* 5, no. 4 (1981), 505n.

27. For an early description and partial assessment of Reagan's policies, see Ezra Soloman, *Beyond the Turning Point: The U.S. Economy in the 1980s* (San Francisco: Freeman, 1981), chap. 6, 127–43.

28. These estimates are from a special Congressional study analyzing the sources of federal budget deficits (1981–85). See Congressional Budget Office, *The Economic and Budget Outlook, Fiscal Years 1986–1990: A Report to the Senate and House Committees on the Budget*, part I, appendix D, "Changes in Budgetary Policies Since January 1981," (Washington, D.C.: Government Printing Office, February 1985).

29. Council of Economic Advisers, *Economic Report of the President, 1987* (Washington, D.C.: Government Printing Office, January 1987), 183.

30. Ibid.

31. In real dollars, federal spending on national defense increased by more than 55 percent during the eight years of the Reagan administration. This was nearly three times the rate of increase of the real GNP. In 1980, total federal outlays were 21.6 percent of the GNP; by 1987, despite the rhetoric of "shrinking government down to size," federal outlays had increased to 22.2 percent. See Council of Economic Advisers, *Economic Indicators* (Washington, D.C.: Government Printing Office, October 1987), 1, 32.

32. Solomon, *Beyond the Turning Point,* 128

33. Council of Economic Advisors, *Economic Indicators,* October 1987, 15.

34. Perry D. Quick, "Businesses: Reagan's Industrial Policy," in *The Reagan Record*, John L. Palmer and Isabel V. Sawhill, eds. (Cambridge, Mass.: Ballinger, 1984), 290.

35. "Study Finds Flaws in JTPA," *Jobs Impact,* Newsletter of the National Committee for Full Employment 5, no. 14 (18 October 1985), 3.

36. Research on the decimation of the nation's infrastructure through neglectful policy has been conducted most recently by David Alan Aschauer of the Federal Reserve Bank of Chicago. See David Moberg, "The Time is Right for Public Investment," *In These Times*, 25 November–8 December 1987, 2.

37. Center on Budget and Policy Priorities, *Smaller Slices of the Pie* (Washington, D.C.: CBPP, November 1985), 19.

38. David Stockman, *The Triumph of Politics* (New York: Harper and Row, 1986), 8.

39. William Greider, "The Education of David Stockman," *Atlantic* 248, no. 6 (December 1981), 34.

40. Ibid., p. 297.

41. Paraphrased by Perry Quick in "Businesses," 303.

42. The scope of deregulation since 1976 is discussed in Michael D. Reagan, *Regulation*, esp. chap. 4.

43. See "Deregulating America," *Business Week,* 28 November 1983, 80–96.

44. David M. Kotz, "Bank Deregulation Threatens Stability," *In These Times,* 22–28 October 1986, 11.

45. Reagan, *Regulation,* 75–76.

46. "Deregulating America."

47. John McLaughlin, "Going Private," *National Review,* 28 February 1986, 24.

48. Lee Smith, "Is This Any Way to Sell a Railroad?" *Fortune,* 25 May 1987, 91–98. The one bidder which never had a chance to compete was the railroad union itself, which actually made a credible case for its ability to finance the purchase.

49. Charles Hawkins and Christopher S. Eklund, "The Conrail Sale: How Much Is It Worth?" *Business Week,* 23 March 1987, 76.

50. Part of this profit came from the fact that Conrail was exempt from taxation. But even if federal taxes had been paid on these profits, the remainder would still have been $198 million. See "Arriving Soon: The Biggest Ever IPO," *Fortune,* 30 March 1987, 9.

51. Lee Smith, "Reagan's Budget: Selling Off the Government," *Fortune,* 3 March 1986, 70–71; Howard Gleckman and Seth Fayne, "Uncle Sam's Loan Sale: Low Prices, No Guarantees," *Business Week,* 26 January 1987, 41–42.

52. Ibid., 42.

Notes

53. Frances Seghers, "Computerizing Uncle Sam's Data: Oh, How the Public is Paying," *Business Week*, 15 December 1986, 102. Some government officials were even considering selling off the government's National Technical Information Service (NTIS) to a private firm. This 42-year-old agency distributes scientific and technical data to American industry and research institutions. In 1986, NTIS sold 452,000 copies of paper documents and 1.9 million documents on microfilm. Mark Crawford, "Will NTIS Go Private?" *Science* 236, no. 4798 (10 April 1987), 140.

54. David Vogel, "The 'New' Social Regulation in Historical and Comparative Perspective," in *Regulation in Perspective*, Thomas K. McCraw, ed. (Cambridge: Harvard University Press, 1981), 162.

55. Robert E. Litan and William D. Nordhaus, *Reforming Federal Regulation* (New Haven: Yale University Press, 1983), 18–27.

56. Reagan, *Regulation*, 105.

57. Gordon L. Clark, "Prospects for Labor Law Reform," Center for Labor Studies, School of Urban and Public Affairs, Carnegie-Mellon University, Pittsburgh, 24 October 1986, ms., p. 8.

58. Gordon L. Clark, "Thinking Past Full Employment: the NLRB and Economic Justice," Center for Labor Studies, School of Public and Urban Affairs, Carnegie-Mellon University, 18 November 1985, working paper, 10.

59. "Oversight Hearings on the Subject: 'Has Labor Law Failed?' " Part I, Joint Hearings before the Subcommittee on Labor-Management Relations of the Committee on Education and Labor, 98th Congress, House of Representatives (Washington D.C.: 1986), 117–27. U.S. Government Printing Office. In 1986, with the support of the White House, Sen. Orrin Hatch (R.-Utah) tried unsuccessfully to have new laws passed that would have designated such union activities as strikes as just another form of "restraint of trade" or even as criminal conspiracies. Clark, "Prospects for Labor Law Reform," 4.

60. Beatrice Freiberg and William Dickens, "The Impact of the Runaway Office on Union Certification Elections in Clerical Units," National Bureau of Economic Research, working paper no. 1693 (August 1985), i.

61. U.S. Congressional Budget Office, *Contract Out: Potential for Reducing Federal Costs* (Washington, D.C.: U.S. Government Printing Office, June 1987).

62. Davis, *Prisoners of the American Dream*, 151.

63. Robert Pear, "Temporary Hiring by U.S. Is Pushed under New Policy," *New York Times*, 2 January 1985, 1.

64. Nancy L. Ross, "Can a Man's Castle Become His Sweatshop?" *Washington Post National Weekly Edition*, 1 September 1986, 20.

65. No one has ever pulled together all of the many strands of the urban fiscal crisis into a single, coherent, and compelling whole as well as William K. Tabb. See his *The Long Default: New York City and the Urban Fiscal Crisis* (New York: Monthly Review Press, 1982).

66. John Mollenkopf, *The Contested City* (Princeton: Princeton University Press, 1983).

67. Bernard Frieden and Lynn Sagalyn, *Behind the New Downtowns: Politics, Money, and Marketplaces*, Department of Urban Studies and Planning, M.I.T., book ms., January 1988.

68. An excellent set of case studies of both successes and failed attempts in restructuring the cities to support new global headquarters is to be found in Susan Fainstein et al., *Restructuring the City* (New York and London: Longman, 1983).

69. See Richard Schaffer and Neil Smith, "The Gentrification of Harlem," *Annals of the Association of American Geographers*, 1986, 347–65.

70. Quick, "Businesses," 291, 294.

Chapter 5. The Crisis of the American Dream

1. These statistics were provided by Professor Thomas Weisskopf of the University of Michigan and are slightly revised from those that originally appeared in Samuel Bowles, David Gordon, and Thomas Weisskopf, "Power and Profits: The Social Structure of Accumulation and the Profitability of the Postwar U.S. Economy," *Review of Radical Political Economics* 18, nos. 1 and 2, Spring and Summer 1986. The revised numbers include data for 1985 and 1986 and are based on the

latest U.S. Department of Commerce statistical series on U.S. capital stock. The Bowles-Gordon-Weisskopf profit-rate series was calculated by adding adjusted corporate profits and net interest, subtracting taxes on corporate profits, and dividing the total by the sum of net capital stock and inventories. A series that shows almost precisely the same U-turn has been calculated by the Bureau of Economic Analysis of the U.S. Department of Commerce. See Louis Uchitelle, "Corporate Profitability Rising, Reversing 15-Year Downturn," *New York Times*, 30 November 1987, 1.

2. Council of Economic Advisers, *The Economic Report of the President, 1987* (Washington, D.C.: Government Printing Office, 1987), 343. These profit statistics rely on the National Income and Products Accounts measure of corporate profits, adjusted for inventory valuation and depreciation ("capital consumption"). The figures are deflated using the implicit price deflator for nonresidential fixed investment.

3. The Japanese have led the foreign move to take an equity position in U.S. securities firms. By the end of 1987, the Sumitomo Bank had purchased 12.5 percent of Goldman, Sachs; Nippon Life Insurance owned 13 percent of Shearson Lehman Brothers; Yashuda Mutual Life owned 25 percent of Paine Webber; and the Industrial Bank of Japan took complete control of Aubrey G. Lanston & Co., a $234-million dealer in primary securities. By buying into the U.S. financial services sector, the Japanese hope to improve their access to investment expertise that can presumably assist them in further capital acquisitions within the United States. See Kenneth N. Gilpin, "Japanese Buy Stake in Paine Webber," *New York Times*, 1 December 1987, D1.

4. The European statistics are based on Joyanna Moy, "Recent Trends in Unemployment and the Labor Force, 10 Countries," *Monthly Labor Review* 108, no. 8 (August 1985), p. 11; and "The OECD Member Countries, 1986 Edition," *OECD Observer*, no. 139 (March 1986). The European countries referred to are France, West Germany, the United Kingdom, Italy, the Netherlands, and Sweden. The U.S. statistics are from the *Economic Report of the President, 1987* (Washington D.C.: Government Printing Office, 1987); and Council of Economic Advisers "Economic Indicators" (Washington D.C.: Government Printing Office, 1986), May 1987. If 36 million new jobs are created in some period of time while 10 million are eliminated by plant closings, partial layoffs, bankruptcies, and so forth, the net change is 26 million. The 36 and 10 million figures are "gross" job changes; the "net" job change is the simple arithmetic difference between the two. In this chapter, we report both net and gross changes in employment.

5. Guy Standing, "Labour Flexibility: Cause or Cure for Unemployment?" Public Lecture no. 25, International Institute for Labour Studies, Geneva, 16 June 1986, 5–7.

6. The data from the March issues of *Current Population Survey (CPS)* on which these estimates are based refer to *pre-tax* wages and incomes. It is conceivable that the post-tax distribution could look more equal, but the most knowledgable experts do not think so. For example, Joseph Pechman, of the Brookings Institution, long ago concluded that the net effect of the tax system in the United States is mostly neutral with respect to the distribution of income. See his *Who Pays the Taxes? 1966–1985* (Washington, D.C.: Brookings Institution, 1985). In chapter 6, we will present new research results which suggest that the tax "reforms" of the 1980s have made the post-tax distribution of income more *unequal.*

7. There is an ongoing debate about the best measure of real living standards. It stems from the fact that the government collects data on two different measures of personal income. The one used in this book is derived from the U.S. Census Bureau's *CPS.* Using a sample consisting of approximately sixty thousand households, the *CPS* provides the basic data needed to estimate real family income each year. This measure includes wages and salaries; interest, dividends, and rent received; plus transfers of money including Social Security, unemployment insurance, and Aid to Families with Dependent Children (AFDC). A separate government agency, the Department of Commerce's Bureau of Economic Analysis (BEA), keeps track of real *per capita income* based, not on a household survey, but on Federal tax records, Social Security Administration files, and such other sources as state unemployment records.

There are significant differences between the two series. The BEA measure is calculated for individuals, not families, and is based on a broader definition of income. It includes the value of in-kind transfers (for example, food stamps, Medicare and Medicaid); the cost of fringe benefits provided by employers (for example, health insurance and pension plans); the net rental value of owner-occupied homes; wages received in kind; and the value of goods produced and consumed at home. One other important difference is that the BEA series is adjusted by the implicit price deflator for personal consumption expenditures (PCE) while the *CPS* family-income series uses the consumer price index (CPI) to adjust nominal incomes for inflation.

Notes

The two income series are highly correlated in the period before 1970, but diverge significantly thereafter. While mean family income, according to the *CPS*, reached a peak in 1973 and then stagnated, real per capita income reported by the BEA continued to rise, albeit at an annual rate between 1970 and 1984 only a little more than half the rate from 1960 to 1970.

Recent research by Paul Ryscavage suggests that half the difference in the two trends was caused by different rates of growth in the aggregate incomes as measured in each series. The higher BEA rate was due to two factors: (1) the rapid growth in nonmoney income (food stamps, Medicaid, Medicare, and certain fringe benefits), which is not included in the *CPS* measure; and (2) the large increase in the number of individuals living alone. The other important factor, accounting for more than a quarter of the difference in rates of growth, was the slower growth of the PCE. See Paul Ryscavage, "Reconciling Divergent Trends in Real Income," *Monthly Labor Review* 109, no. 7 (July 1986).

We prefer, as do most other researchers, to use the *CPS* measure of family income as the best single index of real living standards, for three reasons. The first is that most individuals live in families and share a common standard of living. We are interested in how that standard has changed over time. The second is that many of the components of BEA's measure do not directly affect disposable income. Increases in government expenditures for Medicaid and Medicare, as well as increased employer contributions to private health insurance and pension plans, generally do not boost the money available to households. Finally, if people increase the value of goods that they produce for their own consumption, again a factor included in BEA's series but ignored in *CPS*'s data, this might simply reflect how families are trying to cope with less income. An increase in this component of the BEA series might thus imply a *lower* standard of living rather than a higher one.

8. One should note that employment shifts *within* the durable-goods sector, from higher to lower-paying activities, could also have contributed to the decline in hourly wage rates.

9. Linda A. Bell and Richard B. Freeman, "The Facts About Rising Industrial Wage Dispersion in the U.S.," Industrial Relations Research Association, *Proceedings,* May 1987.

10. OECD, *OECD Employment Outlook* (Paris: OECD, September 1985), 90–91.

11. For a decycling of "wage share" data, see Barry Bluestone and Bennett Harrison, "The Growth of Low-Wage Employment 1963–1986," *Papers and Proceedings of the American Economic Association* 78, no. 2 (May 1988).

12. Another way to grasp the magnitude of the change is to simulate how many workers would have to move from the average prevailing wage bracket to the top and bottom quarters of the wage distribution to generate such an increase in inequality. Just such a computation has been made by our colleague Chris Tilly in Chris Tilly, Barry Bluestone, and Bennett Harrison, "The Reasons for Increasing Wage and Salary Inequality: 1978–1984," in a monograph published by the John W. McCormack Institute of Public Affairs at the University of Massachusetts, Boston, February 1987. According to these calculations, the increase in the inequality index experienced between 1978 and 1984 could have been produced if the wages of 15 million workers in 1978 had been shifted from the average for all workers to the wage earned by workers in the bottom quarter of the workforce and if the wages of another 15 million workers rose to the average earned by the highest-paid quarter. More precisely, the increase in wage inequality between 1978 and 1984 was equivalent to shifting the wages of 31 million workers from the mean of all workers in 1978 to the 25th and 75th percentiles of the employment distribution. See p. 19.

13. For more about this calculation, see Chris Tilly, Barry Bluestone, and Bennett Harrison, "What is Making American Wages More Unequal?" *Industrial Relations Research Association, Proceedings,* May 1987; and Tilly, Bluestone, and Harrison, "Reasons."

14. Barry Bluestone and Bennett Harrison, "The Great American Jobs Machine," U.S. Congressional Joint Economic Committee, Washington D.C., December 1986; and Bennett Harrison and Barry Bluestone, *The Dark Side of Labour Market "Flexibility"* (Geneva: International Labour Office, 1987).

15. Other researchers, including those who disagree with our particular statistical methods, have come (sometimes reluctantly) to similar conclusions about the trend of low-wage employment. Marvin Kosters and Murray Ross of the conservative-leaning American Enterprise Institute are two. Working on a Department of Labor grant, they set out to refute our original low-wage numbers. Using a different method to estimate median wages and a different inflation index to deflate the wage series, they attempted to show that the wage trends that we had discovered were mere statistical artifacts. But their own estimates corroborated the general U-turn in the low-paid proportion of YRFT workers. According to their analysis, low-paying jobs declined from 17.2

percent in 1967 to 10.1 percent in 1979 before rising to nearly 14 percent in 1985. As we did, they found the U-turn particularly acute among men, and they found strong evidence of the polarization of wages. Kosters and Ross's estimates suggest that low-wage employment nearly doubled among men between 1973 and 1985 (7.7 percent versus 14.4 percent); high-wage employment increased from 17.2 percent to 20.3 percent during this period; and thus the middle dropped by a whopping 9.8 percentage points, from 75.1 to only 65.3 percent. Marvin H. Kosters and Murray N. Ross, "The Distribution of Earnings and Employment Opportunities: A Re-Examination of the Evidence," *American Enterprise Institute (AEI) Occasional Papers*, September 1987, tables 14 and 15, 39–40. In a forthcoming article in the Department of Labor's *Monthly Labor Review*, using different wage cutoffs, economist Larry Mishel of the Economic Policy Institute shows that, between 1973 and 1985, low-wage employment accounted for 51.2 percent of net new employment, high-wage employment for 29.7 percent, and that the middle accounted for only 19 percent.

16. The year 1963 is the earliest date available in the *CPS*'s data set; 1973 and 1979 were both business-cycle peaks; and 1986 was the latest year for which these March data were available from *CPS* at the time of writing.

17. Robert Samuelson, "The American Job Machine," *Newsweek*, 23 February 1987, 57.

18. Janet L. Norwood, "The Job Machine Has Not Broken Down," *New York Times*, 22 February 1987, F3.

19. Warren T. Brookes, "Low-Pay Jobs: The Big Lie", *Wall St. Journal*, 25 March 1987. Brookes also cites the BLS as having "warned" us that the use of the CPI as a deflator to produce an inflation-adjusted data series was exaggerating the growth of low-wage employment, and that a preferable deflator would be the Personal Consumption Expenditure (PCE) from the National Income Accounts. In fact, in response to a friendly suggestion to that effect from friends in the BLS in 1986, we made an analysis using the PCE instead of the CPI and found that, while the precise estimates changed, the qualitative conclusions regarding the U-Turn did not (in other words, low-wage employment grew faster in the late 1970s and 1980s than in the prior period). As we noted earlier, Kosters and Ross subsequently found the same thing. In any case, BLS officials have long since ceased raising the choice of deflator as an issue—probably because the CPI is still used in nearly all the wage and consumption statistics published regularly by the Bureau itself.

20. Robert Z. Lawrence, "Sectoral Shifts and the Size of the Middle Class," *Brookings Review*, Fall 1984.

21. For a more rigorous discussion of our method, see Barry Bluestone and Bennett Harrison, "The Growth in Low-Wage Employment 1963–1986."

22. The variables used were deviations from (1) the trend in the GNP, (2) the trend in the natural logarithm of the GNP, (3) the trend in the unemployment rate, (4) the trend in the natural logarithm of the unemployment rate, (5) the trend in the index of capacity utilization by all business enterprises, and (6) the trend in the natural logarithm of the capacity utilization rate. Ibid.

23. The poverty line for a family of four in 1986 was $11,203, approximately the same as our low-wage cutoff. One should note at the outset, however, that investigating the low-wage work force is *not* equivalent to studying the "working poor"—those who are working, yet fail to pull themselves or their families above the poverty line. Whether a worker's wage will be sufficient to keep a family out of poverty depends on the size of the family, whether other members of the family or household work, how much unearned income the family receives, and so on. Path-breaking research on the structure of *family* incomes is under way at the Institute for Research on Poverty at the University of Wisconsin, under the direction of Professor Sheldon Danziger. Also, an excellent handbook produced under the direction of Paul Flaim at the BLS uses the March issues of *CPS* to link the situation of individual workers to the economic conditions of their families. See U.S. Department of Labor, Bureau of Labor Statistics, "Linking Employment Problems to Economic Status," Bulletin 2270 (Washington D.C.: U.S. Government Printing Office, September 1986).

24. In fact, by 1984, 70 percent of all husband-wife households with wages had both spouses holding down jobs outside the home. See Lester C. Thurow, "Middle Class Lifestyles," *Boston Globe*, 26 August 1986, 44.

25. Council of Economic Advisers, *Economic Report of the President, 1987* (Washington, D.C.: Government Printing Office, January 1987), 337–38.

26. These data are from the official National Income and Product Accounts and appear in Jeff

Notes

Faux, "Reducing the Deficits: Send the Bill to Those Who Went to the Party," *Economic Policy Institute Briefing Paper*, November 1987, p. 17, table D.

27. Congressional Budget Office, *The Changing Distribution of Federal Taxes: 1975–1990* (Washington D.C.: Government Printing Office, October 1987), table A-3, 66.

28. Indeed, the decline in the median would have been much steeper if it were not for the increased participation of spouses in the work force. If two-parent families had not had increased earnings from working wives, their incomes would have fallen by 10.7 percent from 1973 to 1984, far more than the 3.1 percent loss actually experienced by this group. See Sheldon Danziger and Peter Gottshalk, "Families with Children Have Fared Worst," *Challenge* 29, no. 1, March–April 1986. Our figures are computed from table 6, p. 46.

29. For example, see Richard S. Belous, Linda H. LeGrande, and Brian W. Cashell, "Middle Class Erosion and Growing Income Inequality: Fact or Fiction?" U.S. Congressional Research Service, Library of Congress, Washington, D.C., Report no. 85-203E, 28 November 1985; McKinley L. Blackburn and David E. Bloom, "Family Income Inequality in the United States: 1967–1984," Industrial Relations Research Association, *Proceedings*, May 1987; Kenneth Cahill, "The Distribution of Income among Families with Children, 1968–1984," Congressional Research Service, Report no. 85-1017EPW (October 23, 1985); Peter Gottschalk and Sheldon Danziger, "A Framework for Evaluating the Effects of Economic Growth and Transfers on Poverty," *American Economic Review*, March 1985; "Survey of Consumer Finances, 1983," *Federal Reserve Bulletin*, September 1984; Lester C. Thurow, "A Surge In Inequality," *Scientific American*, May 1987; and Kitty Gilman and Joy Dunkerley, "Is The Middle Class Shrinking?" U.S. Congressional Office of Technology Assessment (Washington D.C., October 1987).

30. The Gini coefficient or index ranges from zero, perfect equality (that is, every family receives an equal share of the total national family income) to one, perfect inequality, defined as the condition where one family receives everything and all other families receive nothing.

31. Statistics on the distribution of family income are hard to come by for any years before 1947. However, there are some data on the distribution of personal income, by quintiles, going back to 1935–36. According to this information, World War II marked an important turning point in the degree of inequality in the United States. In 1935–36, the poorest fifth of all persons in the nation had 4.2 percent of all personal income, while the richest fifth had 51.5 percent. After the war, in 1947, the share of the poorest fifth had increased to 6.2 percent, and that of the highest fifth had dropped to 44.4 percent of the total. See George Garvy, "Changing Patterns of Income Distribution," *Analysts Journal*, November 1954, table 4, p. 7.

32. These figures were calculated by applying the income distribution shares for 1968 and 1986 to total family income in 1986. The total number of families reported by the Census Bureau in 1986 was 64.5 million. Multiplying this number by reported average income in that year ($34,924) yields total family income: $2.253 trillion. In 1986, the poorest fifth of families received 4.6 percent of total family income—$103.6 billion. Hence, the average income of this group of families was $8,003. In 1968, the poorest fifth of all families received 5.6 percent of total family income. This percentage of $2.253 trillion yields $126.2 billion, or $9,779 per family, for the 12.9 million poorest families. The richest fifth of all families received average incomes in 1986 and 1968 of $76,310 and $70,722, respectively. The basic data for this analysis is found in U.S. Department of Commerce, Bureau of the Census, "Money Income of Households, Families, and Persons in the United States: 1984," *Consumer Income Series* P-60, no. 151 (Washington, D.C.: Government Printing Office, April 1986), table 12, p. 37. The data for 1986 were supplied by the Bureau of the Census to the authors.

33. The "middle class," as used here, is a segment of the population defined by its income level alone. While we shall adhere to this definition for the purpose at hand, we believe that class has to do with the *source* of a person's income, not its level, and especially with whether or not that income is derived principally from work for wages. While the size of the middle class, defined in terms of income alone, has declined, surely the proportion of Americans who depend *mainly* on working for other people to pay their rent and raise their families has not declined since the early 1970s. Nor is there any reason to suspect that it will decline in the foreseeable future.

34. Robert Kuttner, "The Declining Middle," *Atlantic*, July 1963.

35. Peter Behr, "Wage Study Doesn't Find a Two-Tier Society," *Washington Post*, 1 April 1984, F2; Belous, Le Grande, and Cashell, "Middle Class Erosion"; *op. cit.*; James Fallows, "America's Changing Economic Landscape," *Atlantic*, March 1985; Sar A. Levitan and Peter E. Carlson, "Middle Class Shrinkage?" *Across the Board* (journal of the Conference Board),

October 1984; James Medoff, "The Structure of Hourly Earnings among U.S. Private Sector Employees: 1973–1984," Cambridge, Mass., National Bureau of Economic Research, December 1984; Neal H. Rosenthal, "The Shrinking Middle Class: Myth or Reality?" *Monthly Labor Review*, March 1985; Robert J. Samuelson, "Middle Class Media Myth," *National Journal*, 31 December 1983; and Victor Zonana, "Is the U.S. Middle Class Shrinking Alarmingly? Economists are Split," *Wall Street Journal*, 20 June 1984, 1.

36. McKinley Blackburn and David Bloom, "What is Happening to the Middle Class?" *Demography*, January 1985; Thomas Edsell, "More Than Ever, the Electorate is Polarized on Economic Lines," *Washington Post National Weekly Edition*, 6 January 1986, 23; Thierry Noyelle and Thomas Stanback, *The Economic Transformation of American Cities* (Totowa, N.J.: Rowman and Allanheld, 1984); Stephen J. Rose, *Social Stratification in the U.S.* (Baltimore: Social Graphics Co., 1983); Saskia Sassen, "The New Labor Demand in Global Cities," in *Cities in Transformation*, Michael Peter Smith, ed. (Beverly Hills, Calif.: Sage, 1984); Lester B. Thurow, "The Disappearance of the Middle Class: It's Not Just Demographics," *New York Times*, 5 February 1984, F3.

37. Katherine L. Bradbury, "The Shrinking Middle Class," *New England Economic Review*, September–October 1986.

38. Gilman and Dunkerley, "Is the Middle Class Shrinking?"

39. Bradbury, "The Shrinking Middle Class,"

40. Frank S. Levy and Richard C. Michel, "An Economic Bust for the Baby Boom," *Challenge* 29, no. 1 (March–April 1986), fig. 3, 35.

41. Frank Levy, *Dollars and Dreams* (New York: Russell Sage, 1987).

42. Gottschalk and Danziger, "A Framework for Evaluating the Effects of Economic Growth and Transfers on Poverty."

43. "Survey of Consumer Finances, 1983," 682.

44. Levy and Michel, "An Economic Bust for the Baby Boom," table 1, p. 37.

45. "Survey of Consumer Finances, 1983," 685.

46. Ibid., 689.

47. Considered as evidence of trends, these 1983 statistics could be biased upward because of the lingering cyclical effects of the 1982 recession, forcing a disproportionate number of lower-income people to draw down their savings. Unfortunately, no data on the distribution of wealth are available for later in the recovery period (we may expect to see some new data soon, from the Census Bureau's monthly household Survey of Income and Program Participation. Unfortunately, the two series are unlikely to be strictly comparable). On the other hand, Robert Pollin, an economist at the University of California who has studied the 1983 computer tapes closely, concludes that the Fed staff has quite drastically *understated* the concentration of wealth as a consequence of its treatment of "outliers," its procedure for imputing values to households reporting zero wealth, and other technical matters. For a popular version of Pollin's criticism, see "Scandal at the FED? Doctoring the Numbers on Wealth Concentration," *Dollars and Sense*, April 1987.

Chapter 6. The Illusion of Solid Growth

1. David A. Stockman, *The Triumph of Politics* (New York: Harper and Row, 1986), 11.

2. Ronald Reagan, *America's New Beginning: A Program for Economic Recovery* (Washington, D.C.: Government Printing Office, February 1981), 1.

3. Ronald Reagan, "Economic Report of the President to the Congress of the United States" in the *Economic Report of the President, 1987* (Washington, D.C.: Government Printing Office, January 1987), 3–4.

4. Ted Koppel's interview with Robert Prechter on ABC's "Nightline," 23 January 1987.

5. For a fascinating déjà vu account of the stock market, see John Kenneth Galbraith, "The 1929 Parallel," *Atlantic* 259, no. 1 (January 1987), 62–66.

6. The statistical journey on which we are about ready to embark draws exclusively on the Reagan administration's own statistics as compiled in appendix B of the Council of Economic Advisers' Report for 1987. See *Economic Report of the President, 1987*, 244–368.

7. Ibid., table B-25, p. 274.

Notes

8. Ibid., table B-16, p. 263. Also see Council of Economic Advisers, *Economic Indicators* (Washington, D.C.: U.S. Government Printing Office, October 1987), 10.

9. Ibid.

10. Benjamin M. Friedman, "The Vaunted Investment 'Boom' Is a Bust," *New York Times*, 7 July 1985, B3.

11. Barry Bosworth, "Taxes and the Investment Recovery," *Brookings Papers on Economic Activity*, January 1985, 4.

12. These figures refer to output per hour of all persons employed in the nonfarm business sector. If one includes the agricultural sector, the decline in productivity is even steeper. See *Economic Indicators*, 16. To be sure, productivity began to rebound in the manufacturing sector as a result of the sharp cutbacks in manpower and rationalization of production, but the continued decline in productivity outside of manufacturing was more than sufficient to offset this improvement.

13. Kenneth Bacon, "Productivity Growth Lags Normal Pace," *Wall Street Journal*, 15 June 1985, 1.

14. *Economic Indicators*, 17. This re-emergence of chronic excess capacity is showing up even in the service sector, especially in the form of rising vacancy rates in those expensive new downtown office buildings whose construction provided a refurbished home to the global corporations and their suppliers. For two ideologically opposing views of the same fact—the emerging glut of office space in the late 1980s—see Joe Feagin, "Irrationality in Real Estate Investment: The Case of Houston," *Monthly Review*, March 1987; and William Wheaton and Raymond Torto, "The National Office Market: History and Future Prospects," Center for Real Estate Development, Massachusetts Institute of Technology, February 1985.

15. Judith H. Dobrzynski, "Why Nothing Seems to Make a Dent in Dealmaking," *Business Week*, 20 July 1987, 75. In 1987, the most intense merger-and-acquisition activity occurred in deregulated industries such as banking and communications and in older lines of business such as textiles and machinery.

16. *Economic Indicators*, 33.

17. Office of Management and Budget, *Historical Tables, Budget of the U.S. Government FY 1986*, Department of Defense, DOD Deflator Tables, 23 January 1985, as reported in Gordon Adams et al., "The FY 1986 Defense Budget: The Weapons Buildup Continues" (Washington, D.C.: Defense Budget Project-Center on Budget and Policy Priorities, April 1985), table 1, 42.

18. David K. Henry and Richard P. Oliver, "The Defense Buildup, 1977–85: Effects on Production and Employment," *Monthly Labor Review*, August, 1987, p. 6. An independent study of this matter, conducted by Data Resources, Inc., resulted in lower estimates, but the direction of change is the same in both reports. See George F. Brown, Jr., and Ralph M. Doggett, "Defense Contributions to Industry and Employment Growth," *Data Resources U.S. Review*, December 1986, 19–24.

19. Charles L. Schultze, "Economic Effects of the Defense Budget," *Brookings Bulletin* 18, no. 2 (Fall 1981), 4.

20. In his classic argument against the "deindustrialization" hypothesis, Robert Z. Lawrence notes that the share of the GNP originating in the manufacturing sector did not change appreciably between 1960 and 1982. Nevertheless, he notes that the rise in defense procurement after 1979 played a not insignificant role in propping up U.S. manufacturing. See Robert Z. Lawrence, *Can America Compete?* (Washington, D.C.: Brookings Institution, 1984), 8.

21. Fred Kaplan, "For Arms Contractors, 'Gravy Days' May Be Over," *Boston Globe*, 6 October 1986, 3.

22. David K. Henry and Richard P. Oliver, "The Defense Buildup, 1977–85: Effects on Production and Employment," 7.

23. During the first quarter of 1987, the proportion of all families (including those with only one parent in the home) having two or more wage earners reached a record 50.5 percent. U.S. Bureau of Labor Statistics, "Employment and Earnings Characteristics of Families: First Quarter 1987," *BLS News*, 21 April 1987, table 2. In 1985, an average of 5.4 percent of all employed workers held two or more jobs at the same time. This was up from 4.9 percent in the previous peak business year of 1979 (and had in fact been declining slowly for years, until the early 1980s). See John Stinson, Jr., "Moonlighting by Women Jumped to Record Heights," *Monthly Labor Review*, November 1986, 23. We are grateful to Paul Flaim, chief of user services at the BLS, for bringing this material to our attention.

24. Avery F. Gordon, Paul G. Schervish, and Barry Bluestone, *The Unemployment and Reem-*

ployment Experiences of Michigan Auto Workers, Social Welfare Research Institute, Boston College, August 1985, 70.

25. Economic Report of the President, 1987, table B-72, p. 330.

26. The following table contains Shilling's calculations:

	Ratio of New Consumer Debt to Net Change in Disposable Income:
Current Recovery (Roman numerals refer to quarters):	
1983:I to 1986:I	0.44
Previous Recoveries:	
1975: II to 1978: II	0.26
1971: I to 1973:IV	0.24
1961: II to 1964: II	0.28
1954:III to 1957: II	0.29

From A. Gary Shilling, The World Has Definitely Changed (New York: Lakeview Press, 1986), fig. 6, p. 15.

27. Ibid., p. 15.

28. "The Mounting Debt Burden," New York Times, 7 July 1985.

29. Economic Indicators, 32.

30. In late 1986, 80 percent of all outstanding consumer credit was in the form of installment credit. Such loans are defined by the Federal Reserve Board as "short and intermediate-term credit extended to individuals through regular business channels, usually to finance the purchase of consumer goods and services or to refinance debts incurred for such purposes, and scheduled to be repaid in two or more installments." See Economic Report of the President, 1987, table B-72, 330. About one-third (33 percent) of the total outstanding in late 1986 was in the form of automobile loans. Another 19 percent was noninstallment credit, scheduled to be repaid in a lump sum. This includes single-payment loans, regular nonfinance charge accounts, and charges for credit services. Revolving credit accounted for another 17 percent, and the remainder was in miscellaneous installment forms, such as short-term home improvement loans. The typical loan period is therefore quite short, usually three years or less, in which time the consumer must repay both principal and interest.

In early 1987, the interest rate for conventional auto loans was 9 to 10 percent for a three-year term. Interest on revolving credit was 15–18 percent. Thus, 12 percent seems a reasonable estimate of the average interest charged consumers on outstanding debt for purchases made on credit.

31. The calculation of the mean monthly household income for 1986 is based on the mean annual after-tax monthly income in 1983 ($20,001) multiplied by a a growth rate of 5 percent per year and divided by twelve. The 1983 after-tax figure is taken from U.S. Department of Commerce, Bureau of the Census, Statistical Abstract of the United States, 1986 (Washington, D.C.: Government Printing Office, December 1985), table 747, p. 448.

32. Ibid., table 888, "Bankruptcy Petitions Filed, by Type of Bankruptcy and Chapter of the Bankruptcy Code: 1975 to 1984," 522. A "Chapter 13 bankruptcy" is one in which individuals with regular income petition for an adjustment of their debts.

33. Robert Pear, "U.S. Expanding Use of Private Groups to Collect Debts," New York Times, 26 March 1987, 1.

34. Quoted by Paul Sweezy and Harry Magdoff, "Four More Years—Of What?" Monthly Review, January 1985, 9.

35. These data are drawn from Michael Moffitt, The World's Money: International Banking from Bretton Woods to the Brink of Insolvency (New York: Touchstone Books, 1983).

36. Economic Indicators, 36.

37. It should therefore not be too surprising to learn that the trade balance in recent years has

Notes

had a strong negative impact on domestic employment—outside as well as within manufacturing. According to a Commerce Department study incorporating a detailed input-output analysis: "For the 1972–77 period, the combined effect of changes in exports and imports was somewhat negative on the overall level of output but very positive on employment, indicating that increases in exports were relatively more labor-intensive than increases in imports over this period. [F]or the more recent 1977–84 period, however, the deterioration of the trade balance had pervasive negative effects on most parts of the economy. The only private sectors that appeared to gain from the more recent changes in international trade were: mining; wholesale and retail trade; construction; and finance, insurance, and real estate. *Within manufacturing, the only industry that showed gains of output and employment (and each of these by less than one percent) over the more recent period was ordnance.* " [Emphasis added.] Kan Young, Ann Lawson, and Jennifer Duncan, "Trade Ripples Across U.S. Industries: The Effects of International Trade on Industry Output and Employment," Office of Business Analysis, Office of the Undersecretary for Economic Affairs, U.S. Department of Commerce, 14 January 1986, p. iii.

38. *Economic Report of the President, 1987,* table B-103, p. 363.

47. William Glaberson, "Misery on the Meatpacking Line," *New York Times,* 14 June 1987, F8.

48. Ibid.

49. Ibid.

50. "Has the FCC Gone Too Far?" *Business Week,* 5 August 1985, 49.

51. "Complaints on Flights Increasing," *New York Times,* 16 July 1987, A16.

52. Quoted in "Is Deregulation Working? Prices Have Fallen, but the Top Players May Stifle Competition," *Business Week,* 22 December 1986, 52. On the reappearance of barriers to entry in airlines and on the wave of mergers and acquisitions which has greatly reduced the independence of the smaller carriers, see Peter Capelli, "Settling Inexorably Into an Oligopoly," *New York Times,* 7 September 1986, F2; and "Airlines in Flux: And Then There Were Five?" *Business Week,* 10 March 1986, 107.

53. Paul Starr, *The Limits of Privatization* (Washington, D.C.: Economic Policy Institute, 1987).

54. See Robert Fare, Samuel Grosskopf, and James Logan, "The Relative Performance of Publicly-Owned and Privately-Owned Electric Utilities," *Journal of Public Economics* 26, (1985), 89–106.

55. William G. Blair, "Workers' Resignations Threaten Quality of Private Social Services," *New York Times,* 20 December 1987, 44.

56. John L. Palmer and Isabel V. Sawhill, "Perspectives on the Reagan Experiment," in *The Reagan Experiment: An Examination of Economic and Social Policies under the Reagan Administration,* John L. Palmer and Isabel V. Sawhill, eds. (Washington, D.C.: Urban Institute Press, 1982), 19.

57. The details of this study can be found in John Havens et al., "The Microeconomic Impacts of Macroeconomic Fiscal Policy 1981–1985," *MRPIS Project,* Social Welfare Research Institute, Boston College, November 1985. See also Barry Bluestone and John Havens, "How to Cut the Deficit and Rebuild America," *Challenge* 29, no. 2, May–June, 1986; and Barry Bluestone and John Havens, "The Microeconomic Impacts of Macroeconomic Fiscal Policy, 1981–1985," *Journal of Post-Keynesian Economics* 8, no. 4 (Summer 1986).

58. Congressional Budget Office, *The Economic and Budget Outlook, Fiscal Years 1986–1990: A Report to the Senate and House Committees on the Budget,* Part I, appendix D, "Changes in Budgetary Policies since January 1981" (Washington, D.C.: Government Printing Office, February 1985).

59. The key entitlement changes included a reduction in Social Security benefits of $9.1 billion, cuts of $4.2 billion in supports of farm prices, reductions in food-stamp and child-nutrition programs amounting to $3.3 billion, and cuts in welfare assistance payment of $1 billion. The largest reductions in nondefense procurement affected hospital services, education, construction, and social services. "The Microeconomic Impacts of Macroeconomic Fiscal Policy 1981–1985," 6–7.

60. Stockman, *The Triumph of Politics,* 11.

61. Edward Denison, *Trends in American Economic Growth, 1929–1982* (Washington, D.C.: Brookings Institution, 1985), xvi.

62. Michael Podgursky, "Sources of Secular Increases in the Unemployment Rate, 1969–82," *Monthly Labor Review* 107, no. 7 (July 1984), 19–25. The "marginality index" was computed

by the staff of the U.S. Congressional Joint Economic Committee from data in U.S. Department of Labor, Bureau of Labor Statistics, *Handbook of Labor Statistics* (Washington, D.C.: U.S. Government Printing Office, 1985).

63. "Business Failures: What Does the Epidemic Mean?" *Business Week,* 28 April 1986, 17.

64. Alan S. Blinder, "A Handicapper's Guide to Reagonomics," Business Week, 9 February 1987, 18.

65. For one of the most admired treatments of this issue, see Arthur Okun, *Equality and Efficiency: The Big Tradeoff* (Washington, D.C.: Brookings Institution, 1975).

66. Robert Kuttner, *The Economic Illusion: False Choices between Prosperity and Social Justice* (Boston: Houghton Mifflin, 1984).

Chapter 7. Swings of the Pendulum

1. Milton Friedman, *Capitalism and Freedom* (Chicago: University of Chicago Press, 1962), 36.

2. Charles E. Lindblom, *Politics and Markets: The World's Political-Economic Systems* (New York: Basic Books, 1977), 82, 84.

3. A good example is the rapidly building public outcry against the unexpected consequences of airline deregulation. Instead of cheaper and better service (including greater safety and on-time arrivals and departures), deregulation has brought us exactly the opposite. In the words of *Washington Post* columnist Hobart Rowen: "We know that near-collisions occur nearly every day; but even more occur than are reported because pilots and other airline personnel don't want to get 'involved' if they can help it". Moreover, Rowen observed, "deregulation was supposed to promote healthy competition in the airline industry. In fact, it has done just the reverse: A few big carriers dominate the country's major airports and routes and control the availability of airport terminal gates." And finally, "what the public deserves—and doesn't now get—is safe air transportation." The title of Rowen's column says it all: "Bring Back Regulation," *Washington Post National Weekly Edition,* 31 August 1987, 5. Similarly, one hears more and more frequent calls—even from some Republican legislators—for the imposition of some kind of regulatory control over totally irresponsible corporate mergers and acquisitions.

4. See Lucy Gorham, *No Longer Leading: A Scorecard on U.S. Economic Performance and the Role of the Public Sector Compared with Japan, West Germany, and Sweden* (Washington, D.C.: Economic Policy Institute, 1987).

5. The following discussion draws heavily on a brilliant paper by Jay Stowsky, "Beating Our Plowshares Into Double-Edged Swords: The Impact of Pentagon Policies on the Commercialization of Advanced Technologies," Berkeley Roundtable on the International Economy, Working Paper no. 17, April 1986.

6. A good survey of the issues may be found in John Tirman, "The Defense-Economy Debate," in *The Militarization of High Technology,* John Tirman, ed. (Cambridge, Mass.: Ballinger, 1984).

7. Stowsky, 60.

8. Ibid., p. 61.

9. Kan Young, Ann Lawson, and Jennifer Duncan, "Trade Ripples across U.S. Industries," in U.S. Department of Commerce, *Implications of Internationalization of the U.S. Economy: Proceedings of a Workshop on Structural Change* (Washington, D.C.: Government Printing Office, January 1986), 55.

10. *Economic Report of the President, 1987,* table B-108, p. 368.

11. The Europeans and Japanese are justly concerned about the potential impact of reducing their interest rates while those in the United States drift upward. A growing differential in interest rates leads to massive capital exports from other countries as foreigners attempt to take advantage of greater earnings in interest-bearing investments denominated in dollars rather than marks, francs, or yen. The only way to circumvent this problem is to develop an international agreement by the central banks to co-ordinate monetary policy or to legislate currency restrictions which limit overseas investment. While the central bankers from the key developed nations have been able to agree on concerted action to re-align exchange rates through monetary action, the next step in the process—co-ordination of interest rates—seems to have stalled. Every nation is loath, for political reasons, to impose currency restrictions on its own investors.

Notes

12. Daniel Cantor and Juliet Schor, *Tunnel Vision: Labor, the World Economy, and Central America* (Boston: South End Press, 1987). Salutory (and quite brave) demands for better wages and working conditions are now being articulated by labor movements across the Third World, on every continent, from South Korea to South Africa to Central America. Another important development is the emergence of networks of workers (typically shop stewards) from the international plants within a particular industry (sometimes even within the same company). Representatives from these different plants meet periodically in one another's countries to compare wages, working conditions, and the investment and technological policies of the managers for whom they work. It is only a matter of time before these networks begin to plan coordinated bargaining and mutual support for strikes. Sponsored by church groups, or by such internationalist European-based organizations as the Transnational Information Exchange, these networks of workers now exist within such multinational corporations as General Motors, IBM (which is not even unionized now), and Philips (the Dutch conglomerate). For journalistic treatments of two such meetings, see Mike Parker, "Conference Brings Together Auto Workers from 16 Countries," *Labor Notes,* May 1987, 1; and Lee Conrad, "IBM Workers From Three Continents Hold Solidarity Meeting, Confront Stockholders," *Labor Notes,* June 1987, 6.

13. Clyde H. Farnsworth, "Trade Benefit for Chile is Withdrawn by U.S.," *New York Times,* 25 December 1987, D1. The other four countries that have had their duty-free access suspended for violations of rights are Nicaragua, Paraguay, and Rumania. A total of 135 other developing countries maintain their trade rights under the General System of Preferences, a program begun in 1976 to aid the economies of the Third World by stimulating trade.

14. Charles Schultze, "Industrial Policy: A Dissent," *Brookings Review* 2, no. 1 (Fall 1983).

15. *Global Competition: The New Reality,* The Report of the President's Commission on Industrial Competitiveness (Washington, D.C.: Government Printing Office, January 1985).

16. See Lester Thurow, *The Zero-Sum Solution* (New York: Simon and Schuster, 1985), esp. 263–65.

17. In thinking about possible union approaches to industrial planning that are least likely to compromise the principle of labor solidarity, Mike Parker offers a useful distinction: "When a union challenges management on product quality, service to the public, the company's role in the community, its environmental impact, or the way it treats its workers, it is dealing with issues which are consistent with the union's basic goals. But when the issue becomes 'mismanagement has reduced profitability,' a union's attempt to develop an alternative draws it into whipsawing, concessions, and enterprise unionism." It is undeniable that, in a market economy, the workers' livelihoods depend ultimately on the profitability of their employers. Yet to organize their demands around profitability per se (rather than, for example, around turning out a better product or service) makes workers vulnerable to precisely the antilabor strategies that business has deployed so successfully since the mid-1970s. See Mike Parker, "Is Mismanagement the Union's Business?" *Labor Notes,* July 1987, 11.

18. For further information on democracy in the workplace, see Jerome M. Rosow, ed., *Teamwork: Joint Labor-Management Programs in American* (New York: Pergamon Press, 1986); and Martin Carnoy and Derek Shearer, *Economic Democracy: The Challenge of the 1980s* (White Plains, N.Y.: M. E. Sharp, 1980). On the recent European experience of the exchange of job or income security for the introduction of team work and flexible assignments, see Werner Sengenberger, "Revising the Legal and Institutional Framework for Employment Security: An International Comparative Perspective," paper presented to the International Symposium on Employment Security and Labor Market Flexibility, Yokohama National University, Japan, December 1986.

19. *Economic Indicators,* 16.

20. Pat Choate and Susan Walter, *America in Ruins: Beyond the Public Works Pork Barrel* (Washington, D.C.: The Council of State Planning Agencies, 1981), 1.

21. Ibid., pp. 1–4.

22. Lester Thurow, *The Zero-Sum Solution,* 192–93.

23. This is the program being advanced by the Service Employees International Union and 9 to 5. In this connection, comparisons between the United States and other countries are scandalous. For example, all of Europe and Japan already have leave policies that provide from twelve to twenty-six weeks of paid leave for one or the other or both parents for rearing children, with full job security. *The Service Economy: Portrait of a New Workforce* (Washington, D.C.: Service Employees International Union and 9 to 5, 1987).

24. As quoted in Susan F. Rasky, "Groping for a New Order on Trade," *New York Times*, 30 August 1987, F1.

25. Ibid.

26. For more on managed trade, see Robert Kuttner, *The Economic Illusion: False Choices between Prosperity and Social Justice* (Boston: Houghton Mifflin, 1984), esp. chap. 3.

27. Committee on Energy and Commerce, U.S. House of Representatives, *The United States in a Changing World Economy: The Case for an Integrated Domestic and International Commercial Policy* (Washington D.C.: U.S. Government Printing Office, 1983), 23.

28. We are grateful to Jim Schoch of the Democratic Socialists of America for acquainting us with Glotz's manifesto. For one version, see Peter Glotz, "Forward to Europe," *Dissent* 33, no. 3 (Summer 1986), 327–39.

INDEX

AAA (Agricultural Adjustment Act), 82

ABC (American Broadcasting Company), 142

Abernathy, William, 24–25, 58, 61–62, 208n9

Abu Dhabi, 23

Adams, Walter, 62

Aerospace industry, 33, 34, 43, 98

Agreements, collective-bargaining, 40, 101, 116

Agricultural sector, 78, 80, 165

Agriculture, U.S. Department of, 98

Aircraft industry, 34, 178–79

Airline industry: deregulation of the, 14–15, 64, 87, 90, 95–97, 160–61, 228n3; two-tiered wage systems in the, 43

Air-traffic controllers, 15, 102, 174

Altman, Roger, 61–62

American Airlines (company), 31, 42, 96

American Brands (company), 27

American Family Products (company), 27

American Motors (company), 22

Anti-trust laws, 97

Apparel industry, 9, 54

Appelbaum, Eileen, 45, 46

Argentina, 31

ARMCO (company), 40

AT&T (American Telephone and Telegraph Co.), 38, 95

Atlantic Charter, the, 191

Atlantic Monthly, The, 93

ATU (Amalgamated Transit Union), 64, 65

Automation, 114

Automobile industry, 9, 30, 54, 107, 192; "annual improvement factor" in the, 84–85; and changing consumer tastes, 24; cost of raw materials in the, 23; the Japanese, vs. the American, 25; layoffs in the, 149; outsourcing in the, 48; during the recession of 1980, 87

Baby-boom generation, 119, 120, 166; and home ownership, 136; and the trend towards lower wages, 124, 125, 134

Banking: deregulation of, 95, 96–97, 158; foreign trade in, 191; investment, 36, 56. *See also* Banks

Bankruptcies, 50, 86, 91, 104; among banks, 36, 56, 58, 97, 159; increase in, 152

Banks, 105; bankruptcies among, 36, 56, 58, 97, 159; "problem," the FDIC's list of, 167; savings-and-loan associations, 58, 96; U.S., and Third World debt, 180. *See also* Banking

Baron, James, 46, 75

Baruch, Bernard, 80, 82

Bell, Daniel, 22

Bell, Linda, 117, 119

Benefits, 4, 19, 31

Benetton (company), 25

Bergmann, Barbara, 190

Blinder, Alan, 167

BLS (Bureau of Labor Statistics), 36, 38, 45, 49, 124; *Current Population Survey (CPS)*, 117, 118; Occupational Outlook Division, 71; statistics on injury in the workplace, 160; statistics on job

Index

tees of, 162; health and safety laws passed by, 99; hearings on labor law, 101–2; and military spending, in the 1980s, 90, 147; Reagan's economic report to (1987), 141–42; Reagan's first address to (February, 1981), 140

Congressional Budget Office, 162–63

Conrail (Consolidated Rail Corporation), 15, 97–98

Conservative ideology, 3, 171–75, 175–81. See also Reaganomics

Conservative Party of Britain, 97

Constitution, the, 84, 150

Construction industry, 43, 87, 116

Consulting industry, 33

Consumer electronics, 25

Consumer Product Safety Commission, 99, 100

Consumer spending, 11, 19, 38–39, 187

Continental Airlines (company), 50

Continental Illinois Bank, 58, 97, 184

Contingent labor, 39, 43–47, 78, 107, 161; government promotion of the use of, 102–6; and the low-wage work force, 127

Coolidge, Calvin, 81

Corporate restructuring. See Restructuring, corporate

Corporatism, 81

Cost-benefit analysis, 90

Council of Economic Advisors, 84, 90, 152, 178

Council on Economic Quality, 99

Credit, revolving installment, 149–50

Crown Zellerbach (company), 55

Currey, Fred, 65

Danziger, Sheldon, 134–35

Day care. See Child care

Debt: consumer, 149–50; -to-equity ratios, of nonfinancial corporations, 150; and Reaganomics, viii, 146–51; and the weakness of the U.S. economy, 3. See also Budget deficit; Trade deficit

Decentralization, of production. See Globalization

Defense, U.S. Department of, 147–48, 177–78

Defense contractors, 149

Defense spending. See Military spending

Deflation, 15

Deindustrialization, 35, 36, 182, 186–87, 209n21; and the middle class, 133, 137; and the polarization of the job market, 120, 125, 127. See also Manufacturing sector, the

Democracy, workplace, 181, 184–85

Democratic Party, the, 159, 170–71, 176, 194

Denison, Edward, 166

Denver, real-estate values in, 67

Depository Institutions Deregulation and Monetary Control Act of 1980, 96

Depression, the. See Great Depression of the 1930s, the

Deregulation, 14, 15, 78, 99–102, 143; of the airline industry, 14–15, 64, 87, 90, 95–96, 160–61, 228n3; of banking, 95, 96–97, 158; of the communications industry, 160; financial, 157–59; and interest rates, 157–58; and the Reagan administration, 89, 90, 94–102, 140, 157–62; of the trucking industry, 14–15, 87, 90, 95

Devaluation, 155

Dioxins, 90

Disintermediation, 57

Dollar, the, 32, 37, 142, 153. See also Exchange rates

Dow Chemical (company), 27

Dow Jones Industrial Average, 111, 142

Doyle, Philip, 49, 149

Drexel-Burnham (company), 56, 59

Drobnick, Richard, 34–35

Duty-free goods, 30

Eastman Kodak (company), 33

Economic: growth, 139–68, 169–96; planning, 79–108, 169–71, 181–82; recovery, 139–68, 169–96; regulation, "Fordist" system of, 85

Economic Bill of Rights, 83, 84

Index

GAO (U.S. General Accounting Office), 37

Garn-St. Germain Depository Institutions Act, 96

GATT (General Agreement on Tariffs and Trade), 191–92

General Electric (company), 33, 36–37, 66, 81

General Motors (company), 22, 33, 48, 104, 207n4; *maquiladoras* of, 30; Packard Electric Division, 42; two-tiered wage system at, 42

Genetic engineering, 33

Gentrification, *vii*, 106

German Social Democratic Party, 195

Germany, West, 9, 30, 153

Gibbon, Edward, 43

Gini index, 118n, 129–31, 164–65, 223n30

Glickman, Norman, 87

Global economic competition. *See* Competition, global economic

Globalization, 26–30, 51, 67; and the decline of domestic employment, 37; and the growth of the consulting industry, 33; as an indicator of domestic weakness, 28; and labor costs, 31

Glotz, Peter, 195–96

GNP (gross national product), the, 17, 53, 92, 139, 158, 166; the components of, 176; the EEC's, growth rate of, 179; the federal government's share of, in 1988, 15; during the Great Depression, 81; growth of, during the 1980s, 140, 141, 142, 143, 147, 151, 168; the ratio of nonresidential fixed investment to, 144; during the recession of 1981–82, 91; and the trade deficit, 179

Goldman Sachs (company), 59

Goldsmith, James, 61

Goldwater, Barry, 15

Goodyear Tire and Rubber Company, 60–61

Gordon, David M., 87, 110

Gottschalk, Peter, 134–35

Government, American: control over the domestic economy, 18; and corporate restructuring, 12, 76–79, 86–108, 137; and labor disputes, 81, 102; promotion of the use of contingent labor, 102–6; and the recessions of 1980 and 1981–82, *viii*, 77–78; regulation, 11, 14, 15, 88–89; subsidies for urban revitalization, 104

Grain, world price of, 165

Great Depression of the 1930s, the, 8, 17, 53, 79, 80–83, 114, 169; the Gini index since, 130; and the need for government policies, 195

Great Society programs, 130, 195

Greece, 31

Greenspan, Alan, 159–60

Greider, William, 93

Greyhound (company), 64–66, 78, 214n19

"Growth coalitions," 104

Grunwald, Joseph, 29–30

GTE (company), 21

Haiti, 30

Halberstam, David, 4

Harding, Warren, 81

Harris, Candee, 37

Hartmann, Heidi, 190

Harvard Business Review, 24

Hayes, Robert, 24–25, 58, 61–62, 208n9

Health: care professionals, 45, 69; care services, 45, 87, 161, 177, 190; insurance, 18, 19, 40, 46

Heritage Foundation, 124

Hewlett-Packard Company, 183–84

Homeless, the, 92

Hong Kong, 30, 31, 32

Hoover (company), 27

Hoover, Herbert, 77, 80, 81

Housing, 14

Houston, real-estate values in, 67

Hymer, Stephen, 67–68, 72, 214n22

Hyundai (company), 48

Iacocca, Lee, 13

Imports, foreign, 106, 142, 153; appear-

Index

Index

143–45; the restoration of, 170–71, 176–82. *See also* Manufacturing sector, the

Profits: emphasis on short-term, 29, 56, 58, 62, 145; during the 1980s, 110, 138. *See also* Profit Squeeze, the

Profit squeeze, the, 7–11, 12, 21, 77–79, 137; and the airline industry, 96; and "big government," 15; and corporate restructuring, 109, 114, 137, 194; and labor-management relations, 50–52; and the middle class, 109; after the recession of 1981–82, 145

Proposition 13 (California), 189

Proposition 2½ (Massachusetts), 189

Protectionism, 192

Railroad industry, 78, 80

Raw materials, 23

RCA (Radio Corporation of America), 36, 37, 81

Reagan, Ronald (Reagan Administration), 7, 14, 15, 42, 79, 91–104; address to Congress (February, 1981), 140; and the budget deficit, 150, 157–58; and the domestic budget, 158; economic report to Congress (1987), 141–42; election of, in 1980, 76, 77, 78, 86, 169; fiscal and monetary policy under, 91–97; and U.S.-Soviet relations, 90

Reaganomics, 15, 88–108, 132; assessments of, 139–68, 171–75; and military spending, 146–49, 163, 166. *See also* Conservative ideology; Deregulation; Laissez-faire policy

Real assets, rate of return on, during the 1980s, 110

Real estate, 54, 131. 136; foreign investment in, 106; urban, 52, 67, 104–6. *See also* Urban Revitalization

Recession, 107, 155

Recession of 1980, the, 27, 36, 168; and the federal government, *viii*, 77–78

Recession of 1981–82, the, 27, 75, 91–94, 106, 168; and the federal government, *viii*, 77–78; increase in the level of

profits during, 110, 186; and low-wage employment, 124; macroeconomic trends since, 147; profit rebound after, 145; wage concessions during, 39–40

Recession of 1954, the, 130

Recession of 1961, the, 130

Recession of 1975, the, 123

Reflation, global, 20, 176, 179–80

Regulation: in the financial sector, 18, 159, 194; social, 99–102

Regulation Q, 57

Reich, Robert, 25, 34

Republican Party, the, 141

Research and development, 183; civilian, 17, 18, 177; military, 90, 177–78

Restructuring, corporate, 12–13, 53–75, 109–38; and corporate profits, 109; and deregulation, 14–15, 107. *See also* Deregulation; and the devolution of internal labor markets, 44–47; and globalization. *See* Globalization; and the growth of the service sector, 73–75; and the leaders of the European Common market, 111–12; middle management as a casualty of, 38; and "paper entrepreneurialism," 25; and the poor, 134–35; and the Reagan administration, 94–104; and "union avoidance," 15, 39, 48–52, 64

Retail trade sector, 116, 117

Revitalization. *See* Urban revitalization

Roach, Stephen S., 142

Roberts, Paul Craig, 88

Robotics, 62

Roosevelt, Franklin Delano, 80, 82, 83, 86, 171, 191. *See also* New Deal, the

Rosenthal, Neal, 71

Rural Housing Administration, the, 98

Sabel, Charles, 10

Safeway Stores (company), 61

Sagalyn, Lynn, 105

Salomon Brothers (company), 59

Samuelson, Robert J., 124

Sassen, Saskia, 69

Saudi Arabia, 23

Index